The Portuguese African Paper Money of the Banco Nacional Ultramarino

The Portuguese African Paper Money of the Banco Nacional Ultramarino

LAURENCE POPE WITH
PARCÍDIO CAMPOS E MATOS
AND ANDREW PATTISON

This meticulously researched and fully illustrated catalogue details all of the paper money of the Banco Nacional Ultramarino used in the five Portuguese African colonies of Angola, Cape Verde, Mozambique, Portuguese Guinea and Saint Thomas & Prince, between 1865 and 1975.

Drawing on previously unpublished material from the authors' collections, the archives of several banknote printers and The Banco Nacional Ultramarino itself, clarification is brought to some of the most complex signature combinations and serial number runs in the whole of world paper money.

Lavishly illustrated to include images of unique and ultra-rare notes obtained from museums and major private collections, it contains up-to-date pricing in three grades of condition and fills a major gap in the numismatic literature relating to this fascinating field of collecting.

SPINK

First published in 2021 by Spink and Son Ltd

A CIP catalogue record for this book is available from the British Library.

ISBN 978-1-912667-60-4

Typeset by Russell Whittle

Printed and bound in Malta by Gutenberg Press Ltd

Spink and Son Ltd
69 Southampton Row
London WC1B 4ET

www.spinkbooks.com

CONTENTS

Cape Verde

Mozambique

Portuguese Guinea

St Thomas and Prince

Signature Tables

AUTHOR'S PREFACE 1

I had been collecting and studying the paper money of the Banco Nacional Ultramarino (BNU) for many years, but never had I even thought about collating my research with a view to creating a catalogue. All that was to change when one morning in the autumn of 2015, Thomasina Smith, then working for Spink, received a telephone call from Parcídio Campos e Matos, a longstanding collector of these issues, living in Lisbon. At the time, he was researching and writing a paper on the Cedula Issues of the BNU with a view to publishing an article in the IBNS Journal. He suspected that a missing archival specimen (see Cape Verde CV20bs) was likely to resolve a discrepancy in his research and this was the reason for his call to Thomasina on that autumn morning. Not knowing the whereabouts of the missing note, Thomasina suggested Parcídio might contact me and thus began my friendship and collaboration with a Portuguese expert on the BNU and her paper money. Although looking for this missing note was rather like searching for a needle in a haystack, I was astounded to find it already in my collection. Having now resolved the conundrum, Parcídio published his article, which appeared in Volume 55, Numbers 1 and 2 of the 2016 IBNS Journal.

Soon afterwards I began corresponding with Parcídio, who expressed an interest in collaborating with me on a new catalogue. Initially we considered covering both the Portuguese Asian and African colonies, but realising that specialist works were already available for Goa and Macau, we later decided to concentrate solely on the five Portuguese African colonies. So in November 2016, I made a week-long trip to Portugal. Staying in Lisbon and Porto, Parcídio and I first of all spent time researching the BNU archives in Lisbon, followed by an important visit to see Alberto Correia de Almeida, the curator of the Cupertino de Miranda Museum in Porto. This superb purpose-built museum, set in beautiful gardens, houses one of the world's finest collections of the paper money of Portugal and her colonies. The curator expressed an interest in our project and kindly supplied us with numerous scans of the banknotes in the museum's collection.

It is, of course one thing to have an idea for a new catalogue, but quite another matter to actually find a publisher. At this time Andrew Pattison was working with Thomasina at Spink and he became increasingly interested in the research I was doing with Parcídio. He therefore approached Emma Howard, Head of Books at Spink, and the project was born. Andrew was a particularly important addition to the team, with extensive international contacts in the banknote world and excellent computing skills. So I was introduced to the rarefied world of Google Sheets and Google Docs and for the first time in my life was caught up in a Google Cloud! Once I had completed the text, Andrew stepped in to organise all the written material and the scans. He then reviewed all the prices with me and liaised with dealers, collectors and the graphic designer to bring the longstanding project to fruition.

Unfortunately, this project has been affected by the Covid-19 pandemic, which began to sweep through the world from the latter part of 2019. It has meant that a further trip to Portugal, Andrew and I had planned, has had to be abandoned and much of our collaboration during lockdown has had to be conducted during frequent long telephone calls. It has also meant that further research, particularly on the pre 1908 issues, has not been possible and educated guesses have had to be made in some cases as to the existence or otherwise of certain early notes and also to complete tables of signatures. Where this has been necessary, the relevant statistics have been marked with an asterisk and we invite readers to contact us with any information to corroborate or correct the asterisked information. Finally it has not been possible to upgrade the quality of several scans, resulting in some of the illustrations being of a lesser quality than we would have liked. We could have delayed publication to try and resolve such matters, but in the end decided it was preferable to proceed on the basis that further information could be left for a possible subsequent edition.

Laurence Pope

AUTHOR'S PREFACE 2

Although my association with numismatics started very early in adolescence, with influence from my father, my discovery of notaphily is more recent, corresponding with a time when a winding down of my professional activities allowed me more free time to concentrate on this aspect of the hobby.

In my youth, I lived in Mozambique for two years and this probably influenced my attraction to Portuguese colonial issues and the paper money of the Banco Nacional Ultramarino (BNU). However, I very soon discovered there was a paucity of literature on the subject and initially began to research the BNU Historical Archive in order to clarify doubts and discrepancies relating to the first issues of Macau.

The answer to one particular question gave rise to several others and from that investigation of Macau, I moved on to a detailed study of the identification and systemisation of the signatures on the BNU's notes. My study of the archive also led to a more detailed research into the so-called London or Cedula Issue pub ished in 2016 in the International Bank Note Society Journal Volume 55, Numbers 1 and 2.

As others became aware of the knowledge I had acquired through many hundreds of hours of study in ledgers and old papers in the archive, I was encouraged to pool my research for the benefit of this project. The opportunity to join Laurence and Andrew and combine our knowledge and experience will, I am sure, serve as a solid base for others in the future to deepen and develop our understanding of these complex and fascinating issues.

Parcídio Campos e Matos

AUTHOR'S PREFACE 3

In the English speaking world, the Portuguese efforts at empire building are rarely acknowledged or discussed. When I was learning about European imperialism in school I was obviously very aware of the British Empire and also peripherally aware of the Spanish, French and even German imperial aspirations. Portugal was discussed as a nation of explorers, but it was never mentioned that the Portuguese once controlled important swathes of Africa and Asia. When I started working with banknotes, I therefore recall being surprised and struck by the beauty and quality of the notes issued all over Portuguese Africa in 1909. This series, featuring Vasco da Gama, with its wonderful print quality, striking imagery and bright colours, is one of the most spectacular bank note designs ever produced.

When Laurence asked me about collaborating to produce this catalogue I have to admit I had no idea of the quantity of work that would be involved. Initially the work was done almost entirely by Laurence, and of course drawing on Parcídio's decades of experience and knowledge. However, over the last two years Laurence and I have had to do a huge amount of the serious production and editing, and most of this was done remotely. I have spent countless hours on the phone to both Laurence and Russ, the supremely dedicated and talented designer of the book, going through spreadsheets, images, auction records and drafts in an attempt to get the catalogue ready for publication. It has been a challenging but immensely rewarding experience and one that I can honestly say was accomplished with very few real frustrations and never a cross word.

I have learned an enormous amount while producing this catalogue. Mainly, it must be acknowledged, from Laurence, whose enthusiasm has been infectious throughout. In return, I have given him a crash course in modern computer technology, including cloud drives, screen shares, and vast amounts of PDF commenting. I must also thank him for bearing with me during the entire process. The amount of time I have had available to put into the project has varied depending on work and life commitments and he has been both understanding and supportive throughout.

I have now been producing banknote auctions for a decade and in the course of that work have used a multitude of books and catalogues almost every day. I therefore have a good idea of what works and what doesn't work when it comes to layout and usability. My primary focus when producing this catalogue was on how to make it as usable as possible for the reader, and it is my fervent hope that this catalogue will be an accurate, accessible and definitive resource for collectors of this fascinating field.

Andrew Pattison

ACKNOWLEDGEMENTS

Alberto Correia de Almeida, Administrator of the António Cupertino de Miranda Foundation, Porto, Portugal

Ana Monteiro, Arquivo Histórico, CGD, Lisbon, Portugal

Barnaby Faull, Director of Banknotes, Spink

Caixa Geral de Depositos S.A. Lisbon, Portugal

Carlos Pinto

Dennis Lutz

Elaine Fung, Specialist, Spink

Emma Howard, Head of Books, Spink

Hussam Chaban

Ian Marshall

Jaime Sainz

Ludek Vostal

Martin Burger

Nuno Fernandes Carvalho, Arquivo Histórico, CGD, Lisbon, Portugal

Owen Linzmayer

Russell Whittle

Sally Goodsir

Thomasina Smith, Head of Numismatics, Dix Noonan Webb

SOURCES

Ana Bela Nunes, Carlos Bastien, Nuno Valério, Rita Martins da Sousa, Sandra Domingos Costa. *Banking in the Portuguese Colonial Empire (1864-1975),* Instituto Superior de Economia e Gestão Universidade de Lisboa, Lisbon, Portugal.

António Trigueiros. *Papel Moeda Ultramarino, Revista MOEDA*, Lisboa 1975

BNU Documentation, Archive and Library Services. *Emissões de Papel Moeda do Banco Nacional Ultramarino para Mocambique 1877 – 1973,* Lisbon, Portugal 1978.

Fernando Alberto Pereira de Sousa. *A Fundação Dr. António Cupertino de Miranda,* Porto, Portugal, 2004.

Fórum de Numismatíca (www.forum-numismatica.com).

Javier Salgado. *O Papel Moeda das antigas Colónias Portuguesas, Edição da Fundação António Cupertino de Miranda*, Porto 1997

Luis Manuel Rebelo de Sousa. *O Papel-Moeda em Angola, Luanda,* Angola, 1969.

Parcidio Campos e Matos. *Fractional Notes Issued By The "Banco Nacional Ultramarino" (BNU) For Portuguese Colonies,* IBNS Journal Volume 55, Number 1, p20 and Volume 55, Number 2, p8.

Tracy L. Schmidt. *Standard Catalogue of World Paper Money, General Issues 1368-1960,* 16th Edn. 2016, Krause Publications, Iola, WI, USA.

USE OF THIS CATALOGUE

Asterisks (*)

Where a serial number or any figure or signature has been marked with an asterisk (*), this indicates that the figure or signature is subject to confirmation and collectors are invited to submit supporting evidence for such information to the authors.

Grading

The grades used in this catalogue are Good (G), Very Good (VG), Fine (F), Very Fine (VF), Extremely Fine (EF), About Uncirculated (AU) and Uncirculated (Unc). Pricing information for each type of note is given in three different grades, depending on the age and rarity of the particular note. An earlier or rarer type may be listed in Good, Very Good and Fine, whereas a modern or common note may be listed in Very Fine, Extremely Fine and Uncirculated. In certain cases where a note is only available at best in one particular grade (e.g. printer's archival specimens in Extremely Fine or About Uncirculated), only that particular grade is given.

The grading system used for this catalogue is the International Bank Note Society (IBNS) scale. Any readers who prefer to use the 70 point "Sheldon" scale, favoured by many third party grading companies, may need to adjust by between half and a whole grade up in accordance with the differences in those scales. Furthermore, when considering prices, it has been assumed that the notes are in their original condition and not pressed or treated in any way. Any notes which have been repaired, reconstructed or doctored may need to be priced downwards depending on the severity of the treatment.

Pricing

The currency used is the U.S. dollar based on an exchange rate of $1 = €0.90 or £0.80. Market prices are changing all the time, but every effort has been made by consulting auction realisations, dealer price lists and eBay sales (as opposed to eBay listings) to adhere to the most recent pricing trends. The prices given are merely advisory and most importantly represent the relative rarity of certain types, signatures, print runs and colonies.

Rarity: The use of the term "Rare" in this catalogue

In this catalogue either a note is priced or it is stated to be "Rare". A note, or a note above a certain grade, is either obtainable, and will accordingly have some sale records, or is so rare that no information is available.

Bearing this in mind, the authors of this catalogue were faced with the challenge that a significant percentage of the notes listed are extremely rare. Furthermore, many of the notes that are relatively common in lower grades are prohibitively difficult to find in better condition and obtaining information on pricing for such notes is often impossible.

This is certainly not a phenomenon unique to the paper money of Portuguese Africa and many banknote catalogues simply use a dash or blank space in such circumstances. However, this is not a satisfactory solution to the problem, because the catalogue user can have no idea precisely why the dashes or blanks are being used. For example they can indicate any one of the following:-

- Inability to find any recent or relevant prices.
- No knowledge of the price and no effort to make an educated guess.
- Extreme rarity deeming it unnecessary to include a price, because the note is regarded as unobtainable or with the only known examples being in museums.

- The note was never actually printed, or was destroyed after printing, leaving none available to the collector.
- The note was fully redeemed (see MZ73), leaving none available for the collector.
- There is no confirmation the note ever existed (see MZ2).

There are a small number of exceptions to this rule in the catalogue, where a dash has been used, but in all cases the reason for this has been given below the relevant listing (for example MZ80k-t).

GLOSSARY OF TERMS AND EXPLANATORY NOTES

Various abbreviations and terms are used throughout the text and these are listed in this section with appropriate explanatory notes as follows:-

Archival photographs

Many of these are included in the listings with the designation **ph**. Owing to lack of space in the Bradbury Wilkinson and De La Rue archives, much artwork and many composite essays of banknotes were destroyed. However, prior to destruction, sepia and later black and white photographs were taken and affixed to pages bound together in large albums. These too were later jettisoned, but many were saved from destruction, removed from the pages, and sold to dealers and collectors between 2014-15. Most, but not all, were authenticated by Andrew Pattison, who worked for Spink at the time, and these bear a sticker on the reverse, dated November 2014, recording the fact. All archival photographs are rare, many are unique, and those which record lost or unissued designs make particularly desirable additions to any collection. The rarest of all these photographs are those which depict hand-drawn portraits or vignettes sketched in pencil. Very few of these survived to be photographed and all are of the utmost rarity. Examples have been listed under Portuguese Guinea (see PG55ph1 and PG55ph2) and Saint Thomas and Prince (see ST53ph1 and ST53ph2). None of the photographs that appear in the listings have been priced, because their rarity and the present volatile state of the market for them, makes this impossible.

Artwork

Items in the listings marked **aw** are either complete pieces of artwork, or more commonly composite essays, where the artist/designer painted part of the design (usually the portrait) and then affixed partly printed strips and pieces to complete the whole. These are always unique, but are difficult to price and are therefore just marked "Unique" in the pricing column.

BNU

Throughout the catalogue the Banco Nacional Ultramarino is referred to as the BNU. This is also the official reference for this catalogue, which has been approved by the grading company PMG for use on its holders. For example the note on the front cover of the catalogue, the Cape Verde 100 escudo colour trial of 1921, would be referenced as BNU CV45ct.

Caixa Geral de Depositos Image Logos

Throughout the text this bank is referred to as CGD. Many illustrations of notes in this catalogue, which are held by the CGD archive in Lisbon, bear their black stamp in the lower left hand corner. The stamps are electronic and do not feature on the original notes.

Colour trials

Many of these appear in the listings and with increasing frequency after World War II. Some of the colour trials for earlier notes, particularly from the omnibus Vasco da Gama, Cedula and Chamiço issues are very rare and seldom appear on the market. They are designated **ct** in the listings and other unlisted examples of the earlier issues probably exist.

Decreto Nos.
The issuance of all the series of notes circulated by the BNU was authorised by individual laws identified by Decreto numbers. These numbers first appear in the top left corners of the notes issued under Decreto No. 17154 of 26 July 1929. All notes issued thereafter include the relevant Decreto No. at the time. An example of a proof note prepared to add the Decreto No. to the 100$00 1921 note of Cape Verde from 1929, but never issued, can be seen in the listings (CV45p).

Die proofs
Die proofs, which are always uniface, are individually printed directly from the dies. They show only the intaglio portion of the design, and never include any elements from the lithographed underprint. These are known in black and white, issued colours and alternative colours. It has not been possible to provide an exhaustive list, but where we have come across them they have been included with the designation **dp**. Where a particular die proof has not been listed, it may be possible to assess its value from prices given for other examples in the same series. Die proofs in alternative colours to the issued note tend to command a small premium. Very few examples of each of the different listed notes have actually survived and all are of considerable rarity. However they form a specialist field and prices tend not to be commensurate with their limited availability.

Escudo
The monetary unit of Portugal and its colonies introduced in 1911, after the overthrow of the monarchy, to replace the real. The word "escudo" is derived from the scutum shield, used by Italic peoples in antiquity, and later adopted by the Romans. It is subdivided into 100 centavos. The Vasco da Gama omnibus issues which circulated between 1909-21 were the last series of notes to use the real. Thereafter until independence all the African colonies used the escudo. The symbol for the currency is the $, but it is used in a different way from the U.S. currency with the $ sign placed after the numeral, thus 0$50, 1$00, 2$50 etc.

Order Dates
Order dates are taken primarily from printer's archival specimens originally held in the De La Rue archive in Basingstoke, U.K. However, where such information has not been available from that source, in some cases order dates have been taken from documentation held by the CGD archive in Lisbon. Discrepancies of up to a fortnight can occur between the dates recorded in Basingstoke and those recorded in Lisbon because of postal and shipping delays.

Printer's Archival Specimens
The printer Bradbury Wilkinson & Co developed a unique system of recording serial number and signature runs in their archive. Groups of specimen notes were numbered with the serial number runs corresponding to the various signatures used. Each specimen featured two different serial numbers denoting the start and end of a print run, the first number appearing on the left of the note or its counterfoil and the second number appearing on the right. The governor's signature remained the same, but the BNU employed many administrators (administradores) in an assistant capacity and all those in office at the time of the printing of the notes took turns to sign with the governor. However, there was never any fixed order as to how these signatures were used, with the result that the signature varieties on the BNU note issues are some of the most complicated in the history of world paper money. Generally only two copies of each specimen, with its serial number run and associated signature combination, were retained in the archive and these were usually affixed to large

sheets of thick paper. There is no record of any additional copies of these extraordinary specimens being retained and accordingly a maximum of two copies of each printer's archival specimen exist. All of these are therefore of the greatest rarity and, so far as research to date has allowed, have been included in the listings. They provide a unique resource for researchers, enabling them to allocate precisely which numbered notes in any particular series were signed by a particular administrador. In addition, they frequently bear manuscript annotations of the relevant order number and its date, enabling researchers to gain some idea of the note circulation at any particular time. Many have come on to the market in the last few years, as the De La Rue archive was put under the hammer and sold to the public. This has meant pricing of these issues has been particularly difficult, but it is quite clear that as very few remain in the De La Rue archive their value has risen substantially and continues to do so. Furthermore many of the earlier issued notes are either only available in low grade or are completely unobtainable, meaning these specimens are frequently the only way collectors can obtain examples of some of the rarest notes. All of these notes having been stuck to sheets, they are usually only available in AU grade with glue residue and ink annotations. However, in some cases all known examples have been folded or damaged and, where this is known, a lower grade than AU has been specified in the pricing column.

Proofs

A large number of both progressive and complete proofs were found in the Bradbury Wilkinson and De La Rue archives, but it has only been possible to list a few of these. Generally progressive proofs, where parts of the design appear in stages as part of the printing process, have not been included. They are all very rare, but there is at the time of writing a somewhat limited demand for them. However many are very attractive and enable underprints, portraits and other parts of the design to be viewed and studied in a way that is not always possible where the whole completed note is concerned. It is the authors' belief that such items are underpriced in today's market and always add something special to any collection.

Real (plural Reis)

The currency of Portugal (and later her colonies) from around 1380 until 1911 was the real, meaning "royal". A decimal system for the currency was adopted in 1837, with the first decimal banknotes of the Banco de Portugal being issued in 1847. Portugal adopted a gold standard of 1000 reis = 1.62585 grams of fine gold and this was maintained until 1891. Large sums were often expressed as mil-reis or milreis and such sums are to be found on the earlier note issues of Portugal's colonies. On 22 May 1911, the real was replaced by the escudo at a rate of 1000 reis = 1 escudo. One million reis (1000$000) was known as a "conto de reis". After the introduction of the escudo, the term "conto" survived and came to mean 1000 escudos. It even survived the introduction of the euro in 2002, after which it came to mean 5 euros.

Specimens

A large variety of specimens exist and it has not been possible to record them all. Most in the Portuguese colonial series have zero serial numbers, with or without a serial letter. Some are perforated or overprinted SPECIMEN, some are perforated CANCELLED and many are overprinted ESPÉCIME, being the Portuguese for specimen. Bradbury Wilkinson sometimes used a special seal incorporating its name, whilst De La Rue often used two ovals containing its name. These are listed and priced separately from the generally much rarer printer's archival specimens.

Steamship Seals. The BNU used seals on the Vasco da Gama and Cedula omnibus series. These were of three distinct types as follows:-

Steamship Seal Type 1, which was used on the first issue of the Vasco da Gama notes issued between 1908 and 1919. Each of the five colonies had its own designation at the base of the seal, LOANDA for Angola, S. THIAGO for Cape Verde, LOURENÇO MARQUES for Mozambique, BOLAMA for Portuguese Guinea and S. THOMÉ for St. Thomas and Prince.

Steamship Seal Type 1
Angola

Steamship Seal Type 1
Cape Verde

Steamship Seal Type 1
Mozambique

Steamship Seal Type 1
Portuguese Guinea

Steamship Seal Type 1
St Thomas and Prince

Steamship Seal Type 2, which was used on the earlier omnibus Cedula issues of 1914. It came in three distinct colours, green for the 10 centavos, red for the 20 centavos and blue for the 50 centavos.

Steamship Seals Type 2

Steamship Seal Type 3, which was used on the second issue of the Vasco da Gama notes issued between 1919 and 1921 and the second issue of the Cedula omnibus issues. Once again, for the Cedula issues only, it came in the same three colours as Steamship Seal Type 2.

Steamship Seal Type 3

A SUMMARY OF THE MAIN BANKNOTE ISSUES OF THE BANCO NACIONAL ULTRAMARINO

Afonso V Issues

King Afonso V (1432-81) funded the voyages of João de Santarém and Pedro Escobar, who discovered the islands of St Thomas and Prince in 1471. His portrait appears on the notes of Mozambique from 1972-75 (see MZ117) and St Thomas and Prince from 1946-75 (see ST42-ST44 and ST49-ST52).

Chamiço Issues

Francisco de Oliveira Chamiço (1819-88) was the first governor of the BNU from its founding in 1864 until his death. An omnibus issue for all five of the African colonies featuring a portrait of Chamiço was dated 1 January 1921. There were seven denominations, 1$00, 2$50, 5$00, 10$00, 20$00, 50$00 and 100$00. Mozambique only, issued a 500$00 note dated 25 August 1932. Later issues with the same design included 50$00 and 100$00 notes dated 1 August 1941 for Cape Verde, 1$00, 2$50, 5$00 and 10$00 notes dated 1 September 1941 for Mozambique and 5$00, 10$00, and 20$00 notes dated 26 June 1935 and 20$00, 50$00 and 100$00 notes dated 21 March 1944 for Saint Thomas and Prince. The 500$00 note of Mozambique and the 1935 series for Saint Thomas and Prince were the only notes in the whole series to use the shortened form of the signature of the President of the Administrative Council, Antonio dos Santos Viegas. See the Signature Table (PC8a) for an illustration of this shortened signature.

Cedula Issues

Also known as fractionals and in Portugal as the London Issue, these were emergency notes issued during World War I as a substitute for metal coinage in short supply. They were all dated 5 November 1914 and issued in denominations of 4 centavos and 5 centavos (Cape Verde only) and for all five African colonies in denominations of 10 centavos, 20 centavos and 50 centavos. Each colony had its own overprint – Loanda for Angola, S. Tiago for Cape Verde, Lourenço Marques for Mozambique, Bolama for Portuguese Guinea and S. Tomé or S. Thomé for Saint Thomas and Prince. For detailed research on these issues see the article by Parcídio Campos e Matos in IBNS Journal Volume 55, Numbers 1 and 2.

Dias Issues

Bartolomeu Dias (1450-1500) was the first Portuguese navigator to sail round the Cape of Good Hope, thus opening up the sea route to Mozambique and India. His portrait appears on the notes of Cape Verde from 1945-58 (see CV55-CV60).

Ennes Issues

António José Ennes (1848-1901) was a Portuguese politician and writer, who was the governor of Mozambique from 1891-96. In that capacity he oversaw the conduct of a victorious war against the Empire of Gaza, in the southern part of the colony. His portrait appears on the banknotes of Mozambique from 1937-47 (see MZ77-MZ82 and MZ88-MZ106).

Pinto (Serpa) Issues

Alexandre de Serpa Pinto (1846-1900) was a Portuguese explorer of southern Africa and a Portuguese colonial administrator. He travelled to Mozambique in 1864 and to the area around the Zambezi River in 1869. Eight years later he led an expedition to Benguela in Angola, explored the Congo and traversed southern Africa as far as Pretoria. In later life he was appointed governor of Cape Verde from 1894-98 and his portrait appears on the banknotes of Cape Verde from 1958 until independence in 1975 (see CV61-CV64 and CV66-CV67).

Pinto (Teixeira) Issues

João Teixeira da Rocha Pinto (1876-1917) was a Portuguese military officer, who spent most of his career in the Portuguese colonial administration. He saw service first of all in Angola between 1902-11 and then transferred to Portuguese Guinea, where between 1912-16 he brought peace to the Oio region. He won a name for himself putting down a rebellion in Mozambique during World War I, but was killed during an attack on German forces in northern Mozambique. His portrait appears on a series of notes issued by Portuguese Guinea between 1937-64 (see PG31-PG54).

Vasco da Gama Issues

Vasco da Gama (1460/69-1524) was a Portuguese nobleman and explorer, who was the first European to reach India by sea. This discovery led to Portugal establishing a global empire in Africa and Asia and brought vast wealth to the Portuguese crown. His extraordinary achievements were celebrated throughout Portuguese Africa in an omnibus series of notes bearing his portrait, which circulated in the five African colonies between 1908-21. The series included denominations of 2$50, 5$00, 10$00, 20$00 and 50$00 with a low denomination 1$00 note which did not feature his portrait. The three lower values bearing his portrait had a vignette of Vasco da Gama's passage around the Cape of Good Hope, whilst the two higher values had a vignette depicting his embarkation from Lisbon in 1497.

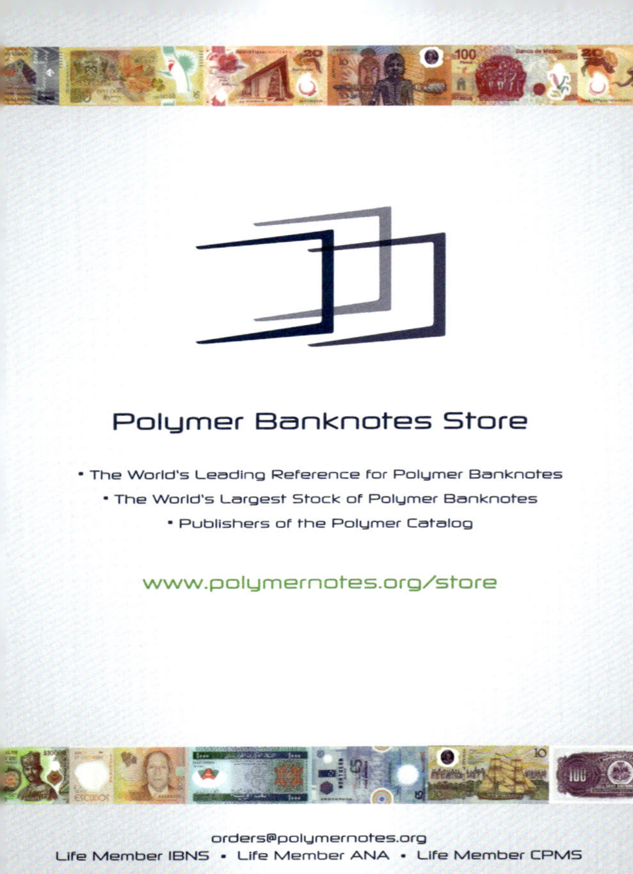
Polymer Banknotes Store
• The World's Leading Reference for Polymer Banknotes
• The World's Largest Stock of Polymer Banknotes
• Publishers of the Polymer Catalog
www.polymernotes.org/store
orders@polymernotes.org
Life Member IBNS • Life Member ANA • Life Member CPMS

BUYING OLD BANKNOTES:
PORTUGUESE AFRICA
INDIA
MACAU
(1865-1930)
BANCO NACIONAL ULTRAMARINO
DEZ RUPIAS
notas.excolonias@gmail.com

CONSIGN NOW
THE GLOBAL COLLECTABLES
AUCTION HOUSE
LONDON | NEW YORK | HONG KONG | SINGAPORE | SWITZERLAND
SPINK
WHERE HISTORY IS VALUED
WWW.SPINK.COM
#SPINK_AUCTIONS

A BRIEF HISTORY OF THE RISE OF THE PORTUGUESE EMPIRE

The Portuguese Empire can trace its influence and extent to the position of the country on the extreme western littoral of the Eurasian landmass. Whereas landlocked countries lying to the east looked to the eastern Silk Road for development of their trade, Portugal, bordered by the waters of the Atlantic Ocean, looked rather to the south and west.

Since the collapse of the Roman Empire, there had been no empire with a European base, which extended outside the continent. All this was to change in the 15th century with Portugal, and then Spain, taking advantage of a favourable political climate in the Iberian Peninsula to turn their attention to exploration on a grand scale. In their great voyages during the 15th century, Portugal's so-called "Illustrious Generation" sailed ever further south and west. This started with a Portuguese fleet which set sail on July 25th 1415, significantly for this intensely Catholic country, the feast day of the apostle St James. King João I himself, accompanied by his three sons Prince Duarte, Prince Henry ("The Navigator") and Prince Afonso along with Supreme Constable Nuno Alvares Pereira, began an exploration of the North African coast leading to the conquest the following month of the trading ports of Tangier and Ceuta. With the fall of Ceuta, knowledge of the gold trade with west and central Africa across the Sahara came into the hands of the Portuguese. Since Portugal suffered a gold shortage from the 1380s, this was in due course to act as a stimulus for further exploration along the west coast of Africa. This thirst for trade was also to be combined with a geographical curiosity and a religious crusade against the Berbers and Moors, creating an extraordinary incentive for maritime exploration.

Whether or not Prince Henry the Navigator ever founded a sailing school at Sagres, near Cape St Vincent, in the south west of the country, a subject hotly contested by Portuguese historians, it cannot be denied that maritime skills were rapidly developed during this period. In his *Atlas of Columbus and the Great Discoveries* published in 1990, Kenneth Nebenzahl claims that by 1420 Prince Henry had founded a renowned school for mathematicians, astronomers, navigators, cartographers and instrument makers at Sagres. In any event, Prince Henry organised further sailing expeditions from Lagos near Sagres and the islands of Porto Santo and Madeira were discovered in 1419 and 1420 respectively, the Azores archipelago following in 1427. A portrait of Prince Henry the Navigator is featured on the 500 escudo note of Cape Verde, which circulated between 1971 and 1976 (see Cape Verde CV65).

In 1434, Gil Eanes, under the direction of Prince Henry, rounded Cape Bojador, the most westerly point of the African continent, which at latitude 27 degrees north was at that time the furthest extent of European knowledge of the West African coastline. With the extreme difficulties experienced sailing back to Portugal against the prevailing north-east trade winds and their associated ocean currents, the Portuguese in the second quarter of the 15th century, developed the practice of "high sea sailing". This involved the use of an adapted fishing vessel, the caravel, with a shallow draught and a tonnage between 60 and 150 tons, whereby they could return by a course far away from the coastline and thus save a great deal of time and money. A caravel features in the iconic vignette of a group of ships observed by a maiden on the reverse of so many of the paper money issues of the BNU, and there are splendid examples on the reverse of Portugal's last banknotes, the 2,000 and 10,000 Escudos issued between 1995 and 2000.

Vignette of an allegorical young woman looking out at ships from various eras

A caravel featured on the reverse of the 10,000 escudo note issued by the Bank of Portugal in 1995

In 1441, Prince Henry commissioned one of his most trusted sea captains, Nuno Tristão, to undertake further exploration of the African coast. Sailing in one of two caravels, the other captained by Antão Gonçalves, the two ships rendezvoused at the Rio do Ouro in Western Sahara. By this time, Muslim slave traders were active in this part of the continent and after a skirmish at a market, ten slaves were taken prisoner and Gonçalves then returned with them to Portugal. This is one of the earliest recorded instances of the importation of enslaved Africans.

Nuno Tristão then sailed on alone for more than 300 miles down the African coast to latitude 20 degrees north, reaching Cape Blanc. The tip of this peninsula, which was named by Tristão after its intense white sand, is today jointly administered by Mauritania and Western Sahara. Arguin Island was occupied in 1443 and the mouths of the Senegal and Gambia Rivers were discovered in 1444 and 1446. There is some dispute over whether Tristão ever reached what became known as Portuguese Guinea. However, his portrait is featured on the 50 and 100 escudo notes of Portuguese Guinea, which circulated between 1971-75 (see Portuguese Guinea PG56 and PG57).

The first of Portugal's African overseas possessions to be colonised was the archipelago of Cape Verde. Some of these islands were discovered in 1456 by Alvise Cadamosto (1432-88) and Antoniotto Usodimare (1416-62), Venetian and Genoese captains respectively in the service of Prince Henry the Navigator. Further islands, including Santiago Island, were soon afterwards discovered by Diogo Gomes (1420-1500). In the same year the Geba River, which rises in Guinea, passes through Senegal and enters the Atlantic in Guinea-Bissau, was also discovered by Diogo Gomes leading to the colonisation of a second African territory, Portuguese Guinea. By 1460, Pedro da Sintra (died 1484) had arrived off the coast of Sierra Leone and over 1,500 miles of the West African coastline had been explored and navigated in a period of only 26 years. The political and economic reverberations from these discoveries were immense, with enormous wealth derived from an ever increasing flow of gold, spices and enslaved people. In particular the discovery of African red pepper led to the first major challenge to the Venetian monopoly of the spice trade with the east. Furthermore, the beginnings of the African slave trade, which attained increasing importance from 1442, led to a plentiful supply of cheap labour. The overall increase in supply of gold from Africa resulted in the minting of gold coins being resumed by Portugal in 1457.

Prince Henry died in 1460 and as a result there was a brief hiatus in the exploration programme. However, in 1470 João de Santarém accompanied by Pedro Escobar set out from Lisbon and sailed into the Gulf of Guinea, making landfall at Sassandra in the Ivory Coast and exploring the coastline from Ghana up to the Niger delta. From there he discovered the island which he named São Tomé, because he landed on the feast day of St Thomas, 21 December 1471. Discovery of the island of Princípe followed in January 1472. These islands, though uninhabited at the time, were colonised as St. Thomas and Prince. They became the third Portuguese African territory, and later one of the five Portuguese African colonies to have their paper money issued by the BNU. Significantly, Santarém's portrait appears on the 1000 escudo note of the colony, which circulated between 1964 and 1975 (see St Thomas and Prince ST53).

Resumption of the quest to find a sea route to India began in the reign of King João II, when in 1482 he sent Diogo Cão (1450-86) to explore the African coast south of the equator. Cão discovered the Congo River in August of that year and Angola in 1483. He set up a "padrão" or stone pillar at Shark Point on the Congo River and another at Cape Saint Mary in present day Angola. These tall limestone pillars surmounted by crosses, were used by the Portuguese to stake their claims to sovereignty and act as guideposts for future explorers. The stone pillar originally set up at Cape Saint Mary still survives in the Museum of the Lisbon Geographical Society and appears in a variety of depictions on several issues of the Banco de Angola. Illustrated below is the reverse of the 50 centavos issued by the Republica Portuguesa in 1923.

Diogo Cão supervising the setting up of a padrão at Cape Saint Mary, Angola in 1483

Cão returned to Lisbon in April 1484. Between 1484-86, Cão undertook a second voyage, revisited the Congo and sailed along it as far as Matadi. There he erected two more padrãoes, one at Cabo Negro in Angola, and the other at Cape Cross, in present day Namibia, thought to be the southernmost point of his voyage. All four padrãoes were later discovered in situ, replaced with replicas and the originals are now held by museums in Lisbon and Berlin. Despite these landings, colonisation of Angola, Portugal's fourth African possession, did not begin until 1575.

In 1486, King João II appointed Bartholomew Dias (1450-1500) to head an expedition to attempt discovery of a sea route to India. Following in the wake of Diogo Cão, Dias set out from Lisbon in August 1487 with three ships. Included in his cargo were more of the padrãoes, which he would use to stake further claims to sovereignty in the name of the Portuguese crown. By the end of January 1488 his ships arrived off the southernmost point of the African continent, which he named Cabo das Aghulas (Cape of Needles). Several days later he entered the Indian Ocean, making landfall about 300 miles east of the first cape along this coastline, which he named Cabo das Tormentas (Cape of Storms), subsequently renamed by King João II as Cabo da Boa Esperança, the present day Cape of Good Hope.

In 1493, Pope Alexander VI issued a papal bull, "Inter Caetera" in which he authorised Portugal and Spain to colonise the Americas and its native peoples as subjects. It gave rights to colonise, convert and enslave and was used as a precedent to justify the enslavement of Africans. Following the return of Christopher Columbus (1451-1506) from his discoveries in the New World in 1492, negotiations took place between King João II and King Ferdinand and Queen Isabella. This led to the signing of the Treaty of Tordesillas on 7 June 1494, authenticated subsequently at Setubal in Portugal. Its effect was to divide the newly discovered lands outside Europe between the Portuguese Empire and the Crown of Castile along a line 370 leagues (equivalent to 1184 nautical miles) west of the Cape Verde Islands. The other side of the world would be decided in 1529 by the Treaty of Zaragoza, which specified the antemeridian to the demarcation line.

In July 1497, Vasco da Gama (1460/69-1524) set sail from Lisbon in his flagship the St. Gabriel with three other ships, rounding the Cape of Good Hope in November. Arriving along the eastern seaboard of South Africa on Christmas Day, he aptly named it Natal and reached Mozambique by March 1498. In accordance with established tradition, he set up yet more padrãoes in every new territory claimed for his king. His dramatic rounding of the Cape of Good Hope is depicted on the BNU's omnibus series of banknotes depicting Vasco da Gama and used in all five of Portugal's African colonies from 1909 until 1921. Mozambique was colonised by the Portuguese from 1544 and became Portugal's fifth African possession.

Vasco da Gama then sailed north up the east African coast as far as Malindi in Kenya. Here he found a pilot well acquainted with the sea route across the Indian Ocean as far as Calicut, an important trading post in southern India. After 23 days at sea, he arrived at Calicut, set up yet another stone pillar and received the welcome of the local Hindu ruler. Having spent three months here, he returned to Africa and finally arrived back in Lisbon in September 1499 to a tumultuous welcome arranged by the grateful King Manuel I (1469-1521). Although he did not manage to sign a trade treaty with Calicut, crucially it had been proved that trade between Portugal and India was possible by sea.

Six months later, King Manuel I sent Pedro Cabral on a similar journey to India. Driven off course by unfavourable winds, he made landfall in Brazil, but then continued to Calicut in India, where those he left behind to run a warehouse were murdered. To avenge this, Vasco da Gama returned there in 1502, bombarded the town with mortars, and as a result concluded a trade treaty with the local inhabitants. These events both in the west and the east provided the basis for the establishment of Portugal's empire in Brazil, Africa and Asia.

The profitable spice trade now conducted by the Portuguese through their maritime links with India had the effect in the 16th century of undercutting Venice, which had had a virtual monopoly in this area for several centuries. The new route was further secured by Afonso de Albuquerque (1453-1515), who was created Viceroy of India in 1508. Like many of Portugal's great explorers, he appears on the paper money of Portugal, with his portrait also featured on two series of banknotes issued by the BNU for Portuguese India between 1945 and 1961.

Portrait of Afonso de Albuquerque featured on a 10 escudo note of Portugal issued in 1919

The expeditions to India had also left Portugal with bases in Zanzibar and the Persian Gulf and later Goa was added in 1510, Malacca in 1511, the island of Bombay in 1534 and Macau in 1557. The Portuguese were also the first Europeans to settle in Timor in the year 1515, exporting sandalwood in such vast quantities that the tree nearly became extinct. However, the Dutch came to occupy the western half of the island in the 17th century and Portugal only occupied the eastern half until independence. So in the extraordinarily brief period between 1415 and 1557, all eight of the Portuguese colonies, for which the BNU was to become the note issuer, were added to the ever-expanding Portuguese empire.

A BRIEF HISTORY OF THE BANCO NACIONAL ULTRAMARINO

On 16 May 1864, King Luis I of Portugal (1838-89), known as the "Numismatic King", signed the decree that would create the BNU. His enthusiasm for numismatics led to his collaboration with Teixeira de Aragão (1823-1903), considered the father of Portuguese numismatics, to build a collection that is still one of the very finest in Portugal today. The BNU would in time become the issuer of all paper money for Portugal's eight overseas colonies in Africa and Asia. It also had as its objective the assistance of the colonies' economic development, utilising its long experience to contribute to the success of businesses and projects relating to international trade, transport, construction, manufacturing, public utilities and real estate. Through its provision of short and long-term finance, it furthered such aims by the advance of working capital to both companies and individuals throughout the colonies.

Bas-relief at the BNU Lisbon of the coats of arms of the Portuguese Empire and various colonies

The first governor of the BNU was Francisco Oliveira de Chamiço (1819-88), who was granted the position for life, and served in the role for a total of 24 years. Chamiço combined great intellectual gifts with energy and stamina and rose to head his father's business in Porto by the early age of twenty. Later he supervised the construction of roads and utilities in northern Portugal and was elected a deputy in the city of Porto in 1854, until resigning his post ten years later and founding the BNU in the same year. The rest of his life was largely spent dedicated to the development and well-being of the Portuguese Colonies. His highly prized signature appears as governor of the BNU on several of the very earliest issues of Angola, Mozambique and Saint Thomas and Prince and is regarded as the Holy Grail by collectors of Portuguese colonial paper money. For examples of his signature see the illustrations for AN2, AN5, MZ24, MZ26, ST1 and ST2. His portrait also appeared on an omnibus series of notes for all five of the African colonies issued between 1921-44. These are known as the Chamiço Issues and were printed in denominations of 1$00, 2$50, 5$00, 10$00, 20$00, 50$00 and 100$00. In addition a 500$00 note was issued for Mozambique in 1932, but only specimens are available for collectors, as all of the issued notes were redeemed.

Although the BNU was based in Portugal, establishing its head office in Lisbon, it greatly expanded its influence during the first fifty years of its existence. Branches were opened in Angola and Cape Verde in 1865 and in St Thomas, Goa and Mozambique in 1868. In 1901, the BNU lost its banking monopoly, but continued to be the sole note issuer for the eight colonies in which it operated. Further branches were opened in Macau and Guinea-Bissau in 1902 and Timor in 1912. Representative offices were set up in Kinshasa and Mumbai in 1919 and 1920 respectively and subsidiary offices opened in London and Paris in 1929.

The Portuguese Banking Crisis of 1925-26, brought about by the infamous fraud perpetrated by Alves Reis (1896-1955), was to have significant repercussions for the Portuguese economy, the BNU and particularly the colony of Angola. It involved the forgery of a contract with the Bank of Portugal authorising Reis to print banknotes in return for an alleged loan to aid development in Angola. At the same time Alves Reis created his own bank, the Banco Angola e Metropole as a vehicle to perpetuate his fraudulent activity. It should however be noted that this bank had nothing whatsoever to do with the Banco de Angola.

The printer drawn into the fraud was Waterlow & Sons of London and the banknote printed in large quantities was the 500$00 note of 1922. 200,000 of these with a face value of 100 million escudos, amounting to nearly 1% of Portugal's GDP at the time, entered circulation in February 1925, with the result that there were nearly as many false notes in circulation as legitimate ones. Reis used part of his proceeds from the fraud to try and acquire a controlling interest in the Bank of Portugal so that all traces of his fraud could be covered up. Eventually an investigation of all 500$00 notes dated 17 November 1922 was ordered by the Bank of Portugal. Numerous notes with duplicate serial numbers were discovered and Reis's elaborate fraud was uncovered. The ensuing 1932 court case of *Banco de Portugal v Waterlow & Sons Limited*, was appealed from the High Court to the House of Lords, and was one of the most complex ever held. It resulted in a final victory for the Banco de Portugal and was a decisive factor in the eventual demise of Waterlow & Sons, which never recovered from the financial and reputational damage of its involvement. The security printing arm was acquired by Thomas De La Rue & Sons Ltd. in 1961 and the remainder of the firm wound up in 2009.

The repercussions of the Alves Reis fraud and the general loss of confidence in the BNU meant that in 1926 it lost its note issuing monopoly in Angola to the newly formed Banco de Angola. This bank was created with its capital being 50% owned by the Portuguese state and the remaining 50% owned by the BNU. In the same year, a revolution in Portugal gave rise to a dictatorial political regime with a more hands-on view of colonial politics. In 1929 the BNU share in the Banco de Angola decreased, but the BNU was nevertheless able to defend its interests. Accordingly in the same year it signed a new contract with the government on very favourable terms. This was regulated by Decreto No. 17,154, which from this time began to be printed on all of the BNU's paper money (see Cape Verde CV45p). However, very soon after the signing of the new contract, the effects of the severe global banking crisis began seriously to impact the country's finances and, in particular, the banking sector. This led to intervention in 1931 by the government to save the BNU from insolvency by controlling its management through a "Conselho Administrativo" appointed by the government. As a result all of the BNU's paper money issued between 1932 and 1951 was signed by the President or Vice President of the Conselho Administrativo rather than the Governor or Vice Governor (see Signature Table for Governadores – PCA8, PCA8a and VPCA9).

In 1951, the BNU was released from governmental restraint and in 1953 a new contract was signed under the terms of Decreto No. 39,221, extending its privileges for another 30 years. This new Decreto No. appears on the paper money from that date (see for example Mozambique MZ109). After 1950, the BNU further expanded its activities in international financial markets and by the end of the 1960s had the largest branch network of any bank in Portugal. In 1965, it was involved with the establishment of the Bank of Lisbon and South Africa Limited and its headquarters in Sandown, Johannesburg, acquiring a major stake in it by 1995. In the 1970s, the BNU also acquired a stake in the Banque Interatlantique, based in Luxembourg.

After India gained independence from Britain in 1947, Portugal lost effective control of her three Indian enclaves, Dadra and Nagar Haveli in 1954, with Goa falling to Indian military action in 1961. In 1974, the Portuguese government nationalised the BNU after what is known as the Carnation Revolution. This was a peaceful military coup which overthrew the authoritarian dictatorship called the Estado Novo, returned democracy to Portugal after four decades and ended the unpopular Colonial War. Its aftermath led to the dissolution of the Portuguese Empire with all the colonies of Sub-Saharan Africa being granted immediate independence. East Timor was also offered independence, before being invaded by Indonesia on 7 December 1975.

In 1988, CGD became the majority shareholder in the BNU, the minority shareholder being the Republic of Portugal. Branches were subsequently opened in London, China, East Timor, Mumbai and Goa. In the meantime agreement was reached with the Chinese authorities for the BNU to remain the note issuer for Macau until 2010 and an agent of the Treasury. A formal merger of the BNU with CGD was announced in March 2001 and the Macau branch became incorporated in the Macau Special Administrative Region, retaining the name BNU SA. Meanwhile in 1950, the Banco da China had established a subsidiary in Macau and on 16 October 1995 became the second bank with authority to issue notes in the Special Administrative Region. Since then the paper money of both banks has circulated together.

ANGOLA

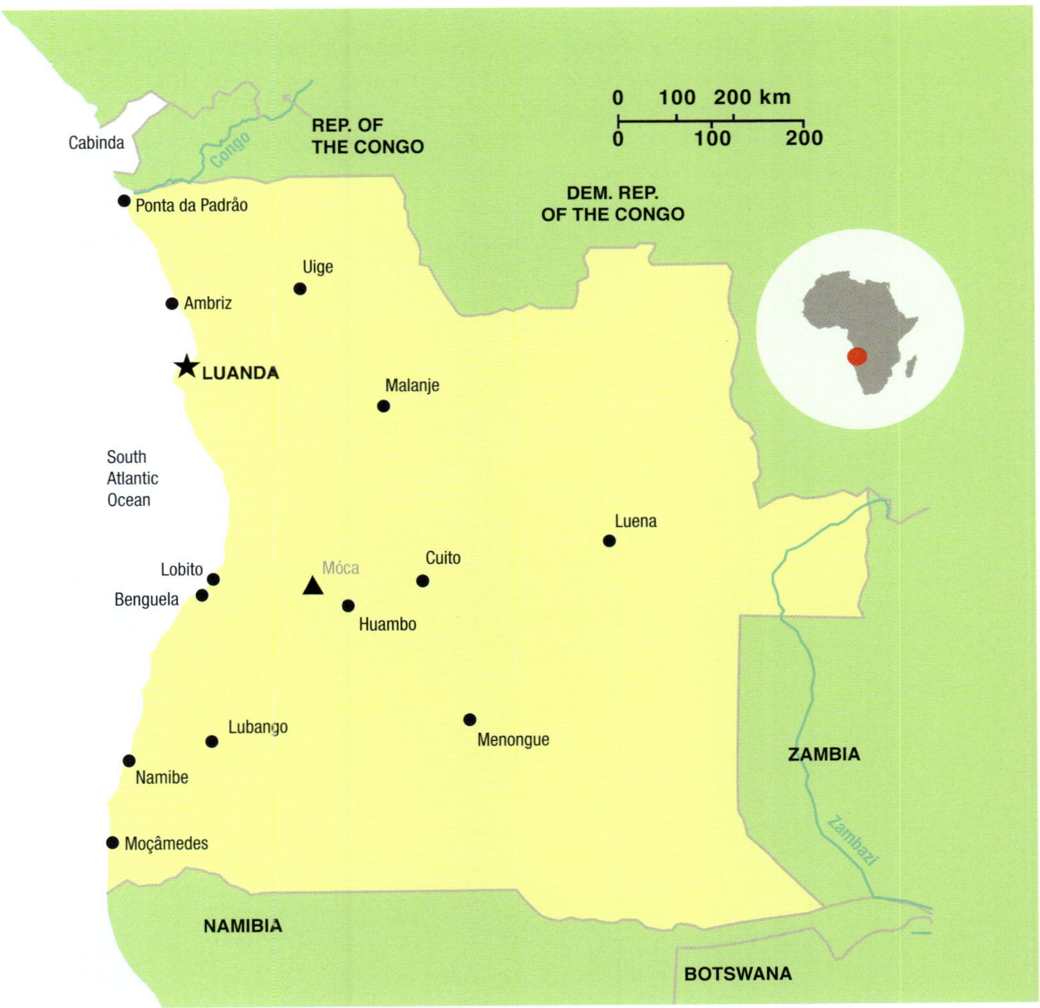
Cabinda
Congo
REP. OF
THE CONGO
0 100 200 km
0 100 200
DEM. REP.
OF THE CONGO
Ponta da Padrâo
Uige
Ambriz
LUANDA
Malanje
South
Atlantic
Ocean
Luena
Lobito
Móca
Cuito
Benguela
Huambo
Lubango
Menongue
ZAMBIA
Namibe
Zambazi
Moçâmedes
NAMIBIA
BOTSWANA

INTRODUCTION

The Portuguese arrived along the west coast of Africa south of the equator, towards the end of the 15th century and Diogo Cão (1450-86) discovered the Kongo Kingdom and the mouth of the Congo River in 1482. In accordance with the normal practice of the Portuguese explorers, he erected a stone pillar (padrão), bearing the coat of arms of Portugal, at the mouth of the Congo, being the north-western boundary of present-day Angola. To this day the settlement established there is known as Ponta da Padrão. Although examples of these stone pillars do not appear on the paper money of the BNU, a vignette of the erection of the pillar at the mouth of the Congo River is featured on the reverse of the Republica Portuguesa 50ct note of 1923 (see SCWPM 63, and illustration in "A Brief History of the Rise of the Portuguese Empire" on page 14). The name Angola is derived from *Ngola*, meaning king in the Kimbundu language.

Padrão in situ near Ponta da Padrão

Reaching the Angolan coast in 1484, Cão entered into a trading relationship with King Nzinga-a-Nkuwu and other rulers of the Kongo Kingdom, establishing a formal embassy in 1491. Christian missionaries followed in his wake, the king being baptised and his kingdom accepting Catholicism. By 1520, Christianity had been nominally accepted as the national religion, and subsequently a Portuguese colony was founded when Paulo Dias de Novais (1510-89), the grandson of Bartholemeu Dias, arrived in 1575 with a hundred colonist families and four hundred soldiers. They settled at Luanda, which was granted city status in 1605. In the meantime, Pope Clement VIII had established the episcopal see of the Kongo in 1595.

Between 1580-1640 Portugal and her colonies were under the control of the Spanish Habsburg monarchy. During the latter part of this period, when Spanish control was loosening, forces from the Spanish Netherlands made inroads in Portugal's ovserseas possessions. They captured Luanda in 1641 with the assistance of local states, who aligned with them. This occupation interfered with the trade in enslaved peoples from Angola to Brazil, which was vital for the development of the Brazilian economy. With the Portuguese Restoration War (1640-63) and the ending of the Portuguese union with Spain, Portugal now concentrated on regaining overseas territories lost to other European powers during its period of weakness and indecision. In 1648 a large force, under the leadership of Salvador Correia de Sá (1602-88) attacked the Dutch and recaptured Luanda and the surrounding area for the Portuguese crown, completely subduing the area by 1671.

Trade was mostly with the Portuguese colony of Brazil, trade and education being influenced by an influx of Brazilian Jesuit priests. The economy centred on agriculture and the export of raw materials such as rubber and ivory and this, combined with extensive taxation of the colonial population, brought vast wealth to the Portuguese crown.

The slave trade was not abolished until 1836 and in 1844 Angola's ports were opened to foreign shipping. This facilitated the continuation of slave smuggling to the United States and Brazil. By 1850, Luanda was one of the largest Portuguese colonial cities. Along with Benguela, it exported, coffee, cocoa, rubber, beeswax, palm and peanut oil, copal, timber, ivory and cotton, almost all being the product of plantations employing local enslaved people.

Portugal never attempted to colonise the interior, but came under pressure to do so by the Berlin Conference of 1884-5. However the complete occupation of the colony only came about after the First World War. Notwithstanding, Portugal failed to invest substantially in the colony with the result that political organisations began to orchestrate demands for reform, leading to the growth of an armed independence movement in the 1950s and 1960s. The so-called Colonial War raged from 1961 until the Portuguese Carnation Revolution led to the grant of independence on 11 November 1975. Civil war then broke out between three rival factions, displacing one third of the population of twelve million people, rendering hundreds of thousands homeless and resulting in the loss of up to a million lives. This state of affairs continued until peace was achieved in 2002.

The BNU established a branch in Luanda in August 1865 and three years later, opened two more in Benguela and Moçâmedes. Although it was intended to act as a commercial bank, its development was hindered in Angola and the other Portuguese African colonies, because it was often forced to undertake what in fact amounted to the full range of operations of a colonial company: transport activities, trade in colonial commodities, mortgage lending, and even farming, as a consequence of the defaults in the payments of plantation owners.

The principal office of the BNU in Luanda. Address:
Praça do Bressane, corner of Rua da Alfandega. Building nº. 267.

The first paper money was issued by the BNU in 1865 and all subsequent issues up until 1914 were denominated in reis (singular real), being the currency unit of Portugal, until replaced by the escudo in 1911. Thereafter the Portuguese escudo was used until 1925. The earlier omnibus Vasco da Gama and Cedula issues were overprinted "LOANDA". However as a result of the scandal involving Alves Reis and the Portuguese Banking Crisis of 1925, the BNU ceased to issue paper money for the colony with the establishment of a new monetary authority, the Banco de Angola in 1926. Furthermore a new currency, the angolar, was introduced in 1928 at an exchange rate of 1 angolar = 1.25 escudos. These issues are not the subject of this catalogue.

1865-75 ISSUE

AN1	**5000 reis**	1 January 1868 (Other dates may exist)	SCWPM 10
	Printer	Chambers & Sons, London	
	Total Printed	Unknown	
	Circulation	Withdrawn 15. 12. 1899	
	Colour	Black	
	Obverse Design	Sailing ship at upper centre, value in numerals in oval at upper right, and in words in panel at lower left. Succursal (branch) am Loanda	
	Reverse Design	Uniface	
	Watermark	BANCO NACIONAL / ULTRAMARINO	
	Size	178 x 111 mm	
	Signatures	Facsimile signature of G1 and manuscript signatures of two managers	

AN1	Start of Print Run	End of Print Run	VG	Fine	VF
a	Unknown	Unknown	Rare	Rare	Rare

N.B. For an illustration of this note overprinted for use in St Thomas and Prince see ST1

AN2	**10000 reis**	7 July 1865 (Other dates may exist)	SCWPM 11
	Printer	Chambers & Sons, London	
	Total Printed	Unknown	
	Circulation	Withdrawn 15. 12. 1899	
	Colour	Black	
	Obverse Design	Sailing ship at upper centre, value in numerals in oval at upper right, and in words in panel at lower left. Succursal (branch) am Loanda	
	Reverse Design	Uniface	
	Watermark	BANCO NACIONAL / ULTRAMARINO	
	Size	178 x 111 mm	
	Signatures	Facsimile signature of G1 and manuscript signatures of two managers	

AN2a

AN2	Start of Print Run	End of Print Run	VG	Fine	VF
a	Unknown	Unknown	Rare	Rare	Rare

AN3	**20000 reis**	9 January 1870 (Other dates may exist)	SCWPM 12
	Printer	Chambers & Sons, London	
	Total Printed	Unknown	
	Circulation	Withdrawn 15. 12. 1899	
	Colour	Black	
	Obverse Design	Sailing ship at upper centre, value in numerals in oval at upper right, and in words in panel at lower left. Succursal (branch) am Loanda	
	Reverse Design	Uniface	
	Watermark	BANCO NACIONAL / ULTRAMARINO	
	Size	178 x 111 mm	
	Signatures	Facsimile signature of G1 and manuscript signatures of two managers	

AN3	Start of Print Run	End of Print Run	VG	Fine	VF
a	Unknown	Unknown	Rare	Rare	Rare

N.B. For an illustration of this note overprinted for use in St Thomas and Prince see ST2

1876-77 ISSUE

AN4	**1000 reis**	1876-77	SCWPM 13
	Printer	Nissen & Arnold, London	
	Total Printed	Unknown	
	Circulation	Withdrawn 16. 4. 1909	
	Colour	Green	
	Obverse Design	Sailing ship at upper centre, value in figures at left and right and in words at lower centre	
	Reverse Design	Decorated rectangular panel with value in micro-lettering	
	Watermark	SUCCURSAL DO / 1$00 / BANCO NACIONAL / ULTRAMARINO	
	Size	173 x 120 mm	
	Signatures	Facsimile signature of G1 and manuscript signatures of two managers	

AN4	Start of Print Run	End of Print Run	VG	Fine	VF
a	Unknown	Unknown	Rare	Rare	Rare

AN5	**2000 reis**	1 June 1877 (Other dates may exist)	SCWPM 14
	Printer	Nissen & Arnold, London	
	Total Printed	Unknown	
	Circulation	Withdrawn 16. 4. 1909	
	Colour	Blue-green	
	Obverse Design	Sailing ship at upper centre, value in figures at left and right and in words at lower centre	
	Reverse Design	Decorated rectangular panel with value in micro-lettering	
	Watermark	SUCCURSAL DO / 2$00 / BANCO NACIONAL / ULTRAMARINO	
	Size	173 x 120 mm	
	Signatures	Facsimile signature of G1 and manuscript signatures of two managers	

AN5a

AN5a

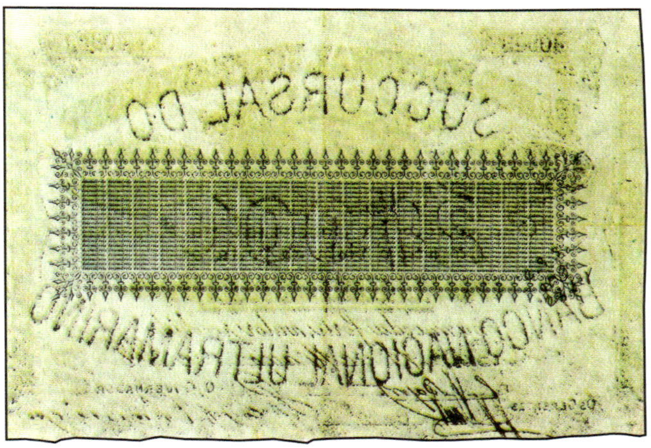

AN5	Start of Print Run	End of Print Run	VG	Fine	VF
a	Unknown	Unknown	Rare	Rare	Rare

N.B. It is believed only three copies are known, two of which are in museums

AN6 **2500 reis** 1876-77 SCWPM 15

Printer Nissen & Arnold, London
Total Printed Unknown
Circulation Withdrawn 16. 4. 1909
Colour Purple
Obverse Design Sailing ship at upper centre, value in figures at left and right and in words at lower centre
Reverse Design Decorated rectangular panel with value in micro-lettering
Watermark SUCCURSAL DO / 2$50 / BANCO NACIONAL / ULTRAMARINO
Size 173 x 120 mm
Signatures Facsimile signature of G1 and manuscript signatures of two managers

AN6	Start of Print Run	End of Print Run	VG	Fine	VF
a	Unknown	Unknown	Rare	Rare	Rare

1880 ISSUE

AN7 **5000 reis** 30 June 1880 (Other dates may exist) SCWPM 18a

Printer Chambers & Sons, London
Total Printed Unknown
Circulation Withdrawn 16. 4. 1909
Colour Black
Obverse Design Sailing ship at upper centre, value in numerals in oval at upper right, and in words in panel at lower left
Reverse Design Uniface
Watermark BANCO NACIONAL / ULTRAMARINO
Size 178 x 111 mm
Signatures Facsimile signature of G1 and manuscript signatures of two managers

AN7	Start of Print Run	End of Print Run	VG	Fine	VF
a	Unknown	Unknown	Rare	Rare	Rare

AN8 **10000 reis** 30 June 1880 (Other dates may exist) SCWPM 19

Printer Chambers & Sons, London
Total Printed Unknown
Circulation Withdrawn 16. 4. 1909
Colour Unknown
Obverse Design Sailing ship at upper centre, value in numerals in oval at upper right, and in words in panel at lower left, and in words at lower centre
Reverse Design Uniface
Watermark BANCO NACIONAL / ULTRAMARINO
Size 178 x 111 mm
Signatures Facsimile signature of G1 and manuscript signatures of two managers

AN8	Start of Print Run	End of Print Run	VG	Fine	VF
a	Unknown	Unknown	Rare	Rare	Rare

1890 ISSUE

AN9	**1000 reis**	28 January 1890	SCWPM 16
	Printer	Nissen & Arnold, London	
	Total Printed	Unknown	
	Circulation	Withdrawn 16. 4. 1909	
	Colour	Reddish-brown	
	Obverse Design	Sailing ship at upper centre, value in numerals in oval at upper right, and in words in panel at lower centre	
	Reverse Design	Decorated rectangular panel with micro-lettering	
	Watermark	SUCCURSAL DO / 1$00 / BANCO NACIONAL / ULTRAMARINO	
	Size	173 x 120 mm	
	Signatures	Facsimile signature of G1 and manuscript signatures of two managers	

AN9	Start of Print Run	End of Print Run	VG	Fine	VF
a	Unknown	Unknown	Rare	Rare	Rare

AN9a

AN10	**2000 reis**	28 January 1890	SCWPM 17
	Printer	Nissen & Arnold, London	
	Total Printed	Unknown	
	Circulation	Withdrawn 16. 4. 1909	
	Colour	Blue-green	
	Obverse Design	Sailing ship at upper centre, value in numerals in oval at upper right, and in words in panel at lower centre	
	Reverse Design	Decorated rectangular panel with micro-lettering	
	Watermark	SUCCURSAL DO / 2$00 / BANCO NACIONAL / ULTRAMARINO	
	Size	173 x 120 mm	
	Signatures	Facsimile signature of G1 and manuscript signatures of two managers	

AN10	Start of Print Run	End of Print Run	VG	Fine	VF
a	Unknown	Unknown	Rare	Rare	Rare

AN11	**20000 reis**	28 January 1890	SCWPM 20
	Printer	Nissen & Arnold, London	
	Total Printed	Unknown	
	Circulation	Withdrawn 16. 4. 1909	
	Colour	Black	
	Obverse Design	Sailing ship at upper centre, value in figures at left and right and in words at lower centre	
	Reverse Design	Decorated rectangular panel with micro-lettering	
	Watermark	SUCCURSAL DO / 20$00 / BANCO NACIONAL / ULTRAMARINO	
	Size	173 x 120 mm	
	Signatures	Facsimile signatures of G2 and VG4 and manuscript signatures of two managers	

AN11a

AN11a

AN11	Start of Print Run	End of Print Run	VG	Fine	VF
a	Unknown	Unknown	Rare	Rare	Rare

1896 PROVISIONAL ISSUE

AN12 **5000 reis** 30 June 1880 SCWPM 18b

Printer Chambers & Sons, London

Overprint "COBRE 1896" in two purple ovals on AN7a (SCWPM 18a)

Total Overprinted Unknown

Colour Black

Obverse Design Sailing ship at upper centre, value in numerals in oval at upper right, and in words in panel at lower left

Reverse Design Uniface

Watermark BANCO NACIONAL / ULTRAMARINO

Size 178 x 111 mm

Signatures Facsimile signature of G1 and manuscript signatures of two managers

AN12a

AN12	Start of Print Run	End of Print Run	VG	Fine	VF
a	Unknown	Unknown	Rare	Rare	Rare

N.B. Only one copy of this note is known and it is in the António Cupertino de Miranda Museum in Porto, Portugal.

1897-1906 ISSUES

AN13 **1000 reis** a. 2 January 1897; b. 20 February 1906 SCWPM 21

Printer Casa de Moeda, Lisbon

Total Printed Unknown

Circulation Withdrawn 12. 2. 1912

Colour Purple. Reverse olive-green

Obverse Design Sailing ship at upper centre, value in numerals in oval at upper right, and in words in panel at lower left

Reverse Design Value at upper and lower centre, bank legend

Watermark BANCO NACIONAL / ULTRAMARINO

Size 178 x 111 mm

Signatures G3, VG6 or VG8 and manuscript signatures of two managers

AN13a

AN13a

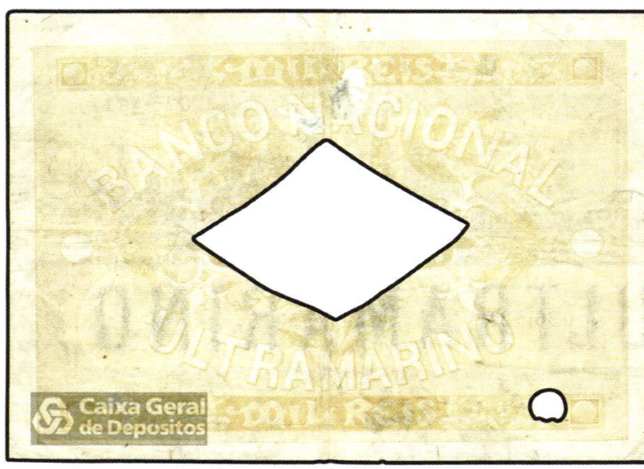

AN13b

AN13	Start of Print Run	End of Print Run	VG	Fine	VF
a 1897	Unknown	Unknown	$10,000	Rare	Rare
b 1906	Unknown	Unknown	$9,000	Rare	Rare

AN14	**2500 reis**	a. 2 January 1897 b. 20 February 1905	SCWPM 22
	Printer	Casa da Moeda, Lisbon	
	Total Printed	Unknown	
	Circulation	Withdrawn 17. 02. 1912	
	Colour	Grey. Reverse carmine-pink	
	Obverse Design	Sailing ship at upper centre, value in numerals in oval at upper right, and in words in panel at lower left	
	Reverse Design	Large winged vessel, waves, seadogs and seaweed	
	Watermark	Unknown	
	Size	178 x 111 mm	
	Signatures	G3, VG6 or VG8 and manuscript signatures of two managers	

AN14a

AN14a

AN14b

AN14	Start of Print Run	End of Print Run	VG	Fine	VF
a 1897	Unknown	Unknown	Rare	Rare	Rare
b 1905	Unknown	Unknown	Rare	Rare	Rare

AN15	**5000 reis**	a. 2 January 1897; b. 20 February 1905	SCWPM 23
	Printer	Casa de Moeda, Lisbon	
	Total Printed	Unknown	
	Circulation	Withdrawn 12. 2. 1912	
	Colour	Purple. Reverse bistre	
	Obverse Design	Bush set in columns at left, seated woman holding caduceus, steamship and flora at right	
	Reverse Design	Bank name and value in floral surround	
	Watermark	Unknown	
	Size	170 x 125 mm	
	Signatures	G3, VG6 or VG8 and manuscript signatures of two managers	

AN15p

AN15p

AN15	Start of Print Run	End of Print Run	VG	Fine	VF
a 1897	Unknown	Unknown	Rare	Rare	Rare
b 1905	Unknown	Unknown	Rare	Rare	Rare
p	Obverse and reverse proof with counterfoil in issued colours				AU - Rare

AN16 **10000 reis** a. 2 January 1897 b. 20 February 1905 SCWPM 24

Printer Casa de Moeda, Lisbon

Total Printed Unknown

Circulation Withdrawn 12. 2. 1912

Colour Lilac

Obverse Design Woman representing agriculture seated at left, sailing ship at centre, Mercury at right

Reverse Design Bank legend and value in foliate surround

Watermark Unknown

Size 170 x 125 mm

Signatures G3, VG6 or VG8 and manuscript signatures of two managers

AN16b

AN16	Start of Print Run	End of Print Run	VG	Fine	VF
a 1897	Unknown	Unknown	Rare	Rare	Rare
b 1905	Unknown	Unknown	Rare	Rare	Rare

1907 DESIGNS FOR AN UNISSUED SERIES

ANA1	**2500 reis**	1907 (no date)
	Format	Obverse and reverse sepia archival photographs mounted on card, 1907 (no date), of an unissued design, 000000 serial number
	Obverse Design	Maiden with globe, symbolising geography, at left,arms at upper centre, value in figures at right and in each corner, steamship at lower right
	Reverse Design	Mercury at centre, bank legend at upper and lower centre, value set in guilloches at left and right
	Signatures	VG8 as Acting Governor, VG6, with VG9 and VG10 as Gerentes — One Pair Known

ANA1

ANA1

ANA2	**5 mil reis**	1907 (no date)
	Format	Obverse and reverse sepia archival photographs mounted on card, dated 10. 9. 07, of an unissued design, 000000 serial number
	Obverse Design	Maiden with globe, symbolising geography, at left, arms at upper centre, value in figures at right and in each corner, steamship at lower right, indication of orange and blue colours in ink manuscript on card
	Reverse Design	Mercury at centre, bank legend at upper and lower centre, value set in guilloches at left and right, indication of orange and blue colours in ink manuscript on card
	Signatures	VG8 as Acting Governor, VG6, with VG9 and VG10 as Gerentes One Pair Known

ANA2

ANA2

ANA3 **10 mil reis** 1907 (no date)

Format Obverse and reverse sepia archival photographs mounted on card, dated 10. 9. 07, of an unissued design, 000000 serial number

Obverse Design Neptune with trident riding biga at right, arms at lower right, value in words at left and in figures in each corner, steamship at lower left, indication of blue and light orange colours in ink manuscript on card

Reverse Design Mercury at centre, bank legend at upper and lower centre, value set in guilloches at left and right, indication of orange and purple colours in ink manuscript on card

Signatures VG8 as Acting Governor, VG6, with VG9 and VG10 as Gerentes One Pair Known

ANA3

ANA3

ANA4	**20 mil reis**	1907 (no date)
	Format	Obverse and reverse sepia archival photographs mounted on card, dated 10. 9. 07, of an unissued design, 000000 serial number
	Obverse Design	Neptune with trident riding biga at right, arms at lower right, value in words at left and in figures in each corner, steamship at lower left, indication of orange, red and blue colours in ink manuscript on card
	Reverse Design	Mercury at centre, bank legend at upper and lower centre, value set in guilloches at left and right, indication of blue and brown colours in ink manuscript on card
	Signatures	VG8 as Acting Governor, VG6, with VG9 and VG10 as Gerentes — One Pair Known

ANA4

ANA4

ANA5	**50 mil reis**	1907 (no date)
	Format	Obverse and reverse sepia archival photographs mounted on card, dated 10. 9. 07, of an unissued design, 000000 serial number
	Obverse Design	Neptune with trident riding biga at right, arms at lower right, value in words at left and in figures in each corner, steamship at lower left, indication of red and green colours in ink manuscript on card
	Reverse Design	Mercury at centre, bank legend at upper and lower centre, value set in guilloches at left and right, indication of green and purple colours in ink manuscript on card
	Signatures	VG8 as Acting Governor, VG6, with VG9 and VG10 as Gerentes — One Pair Known

ANA5

ANA5

1909 VASCO DA GAMA ISSUE

By the Law of 27 April 1901, a new legal framework for banking activity in the Portuguese Colonial Empire was established. The new legislation divided banking operations into two groups; the issuance of paper money and the grant of loans secured by real estate. Although the banknote issue was open to competitive tendering, each colony could only have one bank and the BNU was the only bidder for Angola and the other four African colonies. Under this new contract, the BNU prepared a new issue of notes, which were known as the Vasco da Gama Issue.

In the meantime, before the notes of the new issue had been released, the BNU was authorised to leave in circulation for some time the previous issues and increase the amount in circulation. These repeated the designs of 1897, which circulated during the interval with the date 20 February 1905 and 1906.

The notes issued under the new contract for Angola were all dated 1 March 1909 with denominations of 1$000, 2$500, 5$000, 10$000, 20$000 and 50$000 reis, all being signed by the Governor Antonio Teixeira de Sousa (G4) and various Vice Governors (VG6, VG9, VG10 and VG11) and with a manuscript or facsimile signature of a manager. Two different types of steamship seal were used: the earlier issues used Type 1 and the later issues used Type 3.

See also "A Summary of the Main Banknote Issues of the Banco Nacional Ultramarino" on page 7 and "A Brief History of the Rise of the Portuguese Empire" on page 11 for further information on Vasco da Gama.

Steamship seal Type 1

Steamship seal Type 3

Reverses of the Vasco da Gama Issue

AN17 and AN18

AN19 and AN20

AN21 and AN22

AN23 and AN24

AN25 and AN26

AN27 and AN28

AN17	**1000 reis**	1 March 1909	SCWPM 27
	Printer	Bradbury Wilkinson & Co. Ltd.	
	Total Printed	1198000	
	Circulation	Withdrawn 27. 07. 1922	
	Colour	Black on green and yellow underprint	
	Obverse Design	Value in guilloches, crowned arms at upper right, overprint LOANDA	
	Reverse Design	Allegorical maiden looking at ships	
	Size	138 x 80 mm	
	Ship Seal	Type 1	

AN17i

					Issued Notes			Archival Specimens
AN17	Start of Print Run	End of Print Run	Order Date (If Known)	Signatures	Fine	VF	EF	AU
a	00001	20000*		G4, VG9*	$450	$750	$1,200	$800
b	20001*	50000		G4, VG6*	$400	$700	$1,100	$700
c	50001	79333	Oct 1913	G4, VG9	$450	$750	$1,200	$800
d	79334	108666		G4, VG6	$400	$700	$1,100	$700
e	108667	138000		G4, VG10*				
f	138001	168000	15.11.17	G4, VG6*				
g	168001	198000	15.11.17	G4, VG10				
h	198001	698000	16.6.19	G4, VG6				
i	698001	1198000	16.6.19	G4, VG10				

AN18	**1000 reis**	1 March 1909	SCWPM 28
	Printer	Bradbury Wilkinson & Co. Ltd.	
	Total Printed	752000	
	Circulation	Withdrawn 27. 07. 1922	
	Colour	Black on green and yellow underprint	
	Obverse Design	Value in guilloches, crowned arms at upper right, overprint LOANDA	
	Reverse Design	Allegorical maiden looking at ships	
	Size	138 x 80 mm	
	Ship Seal	Type 3	

AN18as

					Issued Notes			Archival Specimens
AN18	Start of Print Run	End of Print Run	Order Date (If Known)	Signatures	Fine	VF	EF	EF
a	1198001	1595000 (1698000 deleted)	9.11.21	G4, VG6	Rare	Rare	Rare	$1000
b	1698001	1950000 (2198000 deleted)		G4, VG10				

N.B. Even though this note was the subject of two orders in 1921, it is unclear whether it was ever issued, since an order for the 1$00 Chamiço note had already been made in 1920. No issued notes of AN18 have been traced, so it remains unconfirmed

AN19	**2500 reis**	1 March 1909	SCWPM 29
	Printer	Bradbury Wilkinson & Co. Ltd.	
	Total Printed	550000	
	Circulation	Withdrawn 27. 07. 1922	
	Colour	Black on green and yellow underprint. Reverse blue	
	Obverse Design	Vasco da Gama and his passage round The Cape, overprint LOANDA	
	Reverse Design	Allegorical maiden looking at ships	
	Size	148 x 94 mm	
	Ship Seal	Type 1	

AN19a

AN19	Start of Print Run	End of Print Run	Order Date (If Known)	Signatures	Issued Notes VG	Issued Notes Fine	Issued Notes VF	Archival Specimens AU
a	000001	130000		G4, VG11	$500	$850	$1,200	$1,000
b	130001	390000		G4, VG6				
c	390001	520000		G4, VG10				
d	520001	535000	15.11.17	G4, VG6	$300	$500	$750	$750
e	535001	550000	15.11.17	G4, VG10				
ph	Obverse and reverse sepia photographs mounted on card, dated 19--, serial number 0000, VG8 as Acting Governor, VG6 with VG9 and VG10 as Gerentes							One Pair Known

AN19ph

AN20	**2500 reis**	1 March 1909	SCWPM 30
	Printer	Bradbury Wilkinson & Co. Ltd.	
	Total Printed	200000	
	Circulation	Withdrawn 27. 07. 1922	
	Colour	Black on green and yellow underprint. Reverse blue	
	Obverse Design	Vasco da Gama and his passage round The Cape, overprint LOANDA	
	Reverse Design	Allegorical maiden looking at ships	
	Size	148 x 94 mm	
	Ship Seal	Type 3	

AN20b

					Issued Notes			Archival Specimens
AN20	Start of Print Run	End of Print Run	Order Date (If Known)	Signatures	VG	Fine	VF	AU
a	550001	650000		G4, VG6	$350	$550	$950	$850
b	650001	750000	20.7.21	G4, VG10				

AN21 **5 mil reis** 1 March 1909 SCWPM 31

Printer	Bradbury Wilkinson & Co. Ltd.
Total Printed	220000
Circulation	Withdrawn 27. 07. 1922
Colour	Black on blue and multicoloured underprint. Reverse green
Obverse Design	Vasco da Gama and his passage round The Cape, overprint LOANDA
Reverse Design	Allegorical maiden looking at ships
Size	160 x 100 mm
Ship Seal	Type 1

AN21a

AN21	Start of Print Run	End of Print Run	Order Date (If Known)	Signatures	Issued Notes VG	Issued Notes Fine	Issued Notes VF	Archival Specimens AU
a	000001	066667*		G4, VG9	$500	$950	$2,000	$1,250
b	066668*	133334		G4, VG6				
c	133335	200000		G4, VG10				
d	200001	207500		G4, VG6				
e	207501	215000	15.11.17	G4, VG10	$300	$700	$1,500	$1,000
f	215001	217500	18.2.18	G4, VG6				
g	217501	220000	18.2.18	G4, VG10				
ph	Obverse sepia photograph mounted on card, dated 19--, serial number 0000, VG8 as Acting Governor, VG6 with VG9 and VG10 as Gerentes							One Copy Known

AN21ph

AN22	**5 mil reis**	1 March 1909	SCWPM 32
	Printer	Bradbury Wilkinson & Co. Ltd.	
	Total Printed	250000	
	Circulation	Withdrawn 27. 07. 1922	
	Colour	Black on blue and multicoloured underprint. Reverse green	
	Obverse Design	Vasco da Gama and his passage round The Cape, overprint LOANDA	
	Reverse Design	Allegorical maiden looking at ships	
	Size	160 x 100 mm	
	Ship Seal	Type 3	

AN22bs

AN22	Start of Print Run	End of Print Run	Order Date (If Known)	Signatures	Issued Notes VG	Issued Notes Fine	Issued Notes VF	Archival Specimens AU
a	220001	240000	7.11.19	G4, VG6	$400	$900	$1,750	$1,000
b	240001	260000	7.11.19	G4, VG10				
c	260001	265000		G4, VG6				
d	265001	270000		G4, VG10				
e	270001	370000	11.10.21	G4, VG6				
f	370001	470000	11.10.21	G4, VG10				

AN23	**10 mil reis**	1 March 1909	SCWPM 33
	Printer	Bradbury Wilkinson & Co. Ltd.	
	Total Printed	120000	
	Circulation	Withdrawn 27. 07. 1922	
	Colour	Black on yellow and multicoloured underprint. Reverse brown	
	Obverse Design	Vasco da Gama and his passage round The Cape, overprint LOANDA	
	Reverse Design	Allegorical maiden looking at ships	
	Size	175 x 105 mm	
	Ship Seal	Type 1	

AN23c

<table>
<tr><th></th><th></th><th></th><th></th><th></th><th colspan="3">Issued Notes</th><th>Archival Specimens</th></tr>
<tr><th>AN23</th><th>Start of Print Run</th><th>End of Print Run</th><th>Order Date (If Known)</th><th>Signatures</th><th>VG</th><th>Fine</th><th>VF</th><th>AU</th></tr>
<tr><td>a</td><td>00001</td><td>23334*</td><td></td><td>G4, VG9</td><td>$1,400</td><td>$2,500</td><td>$3,750</td><td>$1,250</td></tr>
<tr><td>b</td><td>23335</td><td>46667</td><td></td><td>G4, VG6</td><td rowspan="2">$1,100</td><td rowspan="2">$2,000</td><td rowspan="2">$3,250</td><td rowspan="2">$1,100</td></tr>
<tr><td>c</td><td>46668</td><td>70000</td><td></td><td>G4, VG10</td></tr>
<tr><td>d</td><td>70001</td><td>76666</td><td></td><td>G4, VG9</td><td>$1,400</td><td>$2,500</td><td>$3,750</td><td>$1,250</td></tr>
<tr><td>e</td><td>76667</td><td>83333</td><td></td><td>G4, VG6</td><td rowspan="6">$1,100</td><td rowspan="6">$2,000</td><td rowspan="6">$3,250</td><td rowspan="6">$1,100</td></tr>
<tr><td>f</td><td>83334</td><td>90000</td><td></td><td>G4, VG10</td></tr>
<tr><td>g</td><td>90001*</td><td>95000*</td><td></td><td>G4, VG6*</td></tr>
<tr><td>h</td><td>95001</td><td>100000</td><td></td><td>G4, VG10</td></tr>
<tr><td>i</td><td>100001</td><td>110000</td><td></td><td>G4, VG6</td></tr>
<tr><td>j</td><td>110001</td><td>120000</td><td></td><td>G4, VG10</td></tr>
<tr><td>ph</td><td colspan="7">Obverse and reverse sepia photographs mounted on card, dated 19--, serial number 0000, VG8 as Acting Governor, VG6 with VG9 and VG10 as Gerentes</td><td>One Pair Known</td></tr>
</table>

AN23ph

AN24	**10 mil reis**	1 March 1909 — SCWPM 34
	Printer	Bradbury Wilkinson & Co. Ltd.
	Total Printed	250000
	Circulation	Withdrawn 27. 07. 1922
	Colour	Black on yellow and multicoloured underprint. Reverse brown
	Obverse Design	Vasco da Gama and his passage round The Cape, overprint LOANDA
	Reverse Design	Allegorical maiden looking at ships
	Size	175 x 105 mm
	Ship Seal	Type 3

AN24f

AN24	Start of Print Run	End of Print Run	Order Date (If Known)	Signatures	Issued Notes VG	Issued Notes Fine	Issued Notes VF	Archival Specimens AU
a	120001	140000	7.11.19	G4, VG6	$1,100	$2,000	$3,250	$1,100
b	140001	160000	7.11.19	G4, VG10				
c	160001	165000		G4, VG6				
d	165001	170000		G4, VG10				
e	170001	270000	11.10.21	G4, VG6				
f	270001	370000	11.10.21	G4, VG10				

AN25	**20 mil reis**	1 March 1909	SCWPM 35
	Printer	Bradbury Wilkinson & Co. Ltd.	
	Total Printed	85000	
	Circulation	Withdrawn 27. 07. 1922	
	Colour	Black on blue and yellow underprint. Reverse brown-red and orange	
	Obverse Design	Vasco de Gama and his embarkation, overprint LOANDA	
	Reverse Design	Allegorical maiden looking at ships	
	Size	180 x 112 mm	
	Ship Seal	Type 1	

AN25a

AN25	Start of Print Run	End of Print Run	Order Date (If Known)	Signatures	Issued Notes VG	Issued Notes Fine	Issued Notes VF	Archival Specimens AU
a	00001	20000*		G4, VG9	$1,800	$3,250	$5,000	$1,250
b	20001*	35000		G4, VG6*	$1,500	$2,750	$4,500	$1,100
c	35001	45000	24.6.15	G4, VG9	$1,800	$3,250	$5,000	$1,250
d	45001	55000		G4, VG6				
e	55001	65000		G4, VG10				
f	65001	70000	15.11.17	G4, VG6	$1,500	2,750	$4,500	$1,100
g	70001	75000	15.11.17	G4, VG10				
h	75001	80000	18.2.18	G4, VG6				
i	80001	85000	18.2.18	G4, VG10				
ph	Obverse sepia photograph mounted on card, dated 19--, serial number 0000, VG8 as Acting Governor, VG6 with VG9 and VG10 as Gerentes							One Copy Known

AN25ph

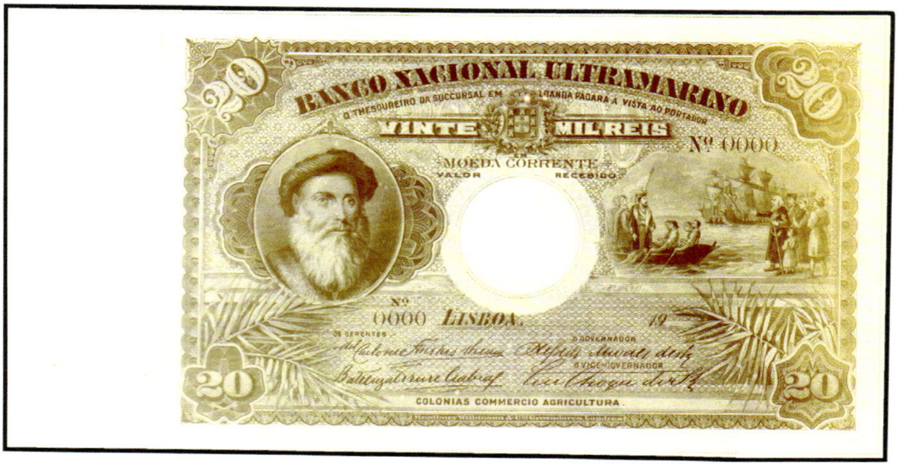

AN26	**20 mil reis**	1 March 1909	SCWPM 36
	Printer	Bradbury Wilkinson & Co. Ltd.	
	Total Printed	185000	
	Circulation	Withdrawn 27. 07. 1922	
	Colour	Black on blue and yellow underprint. Reverse brown-red and orange	
	Obverse Design	Vasco de Gama and his embarkation, overprint LOANDA	
	Reverse Design	Allegorical maiden looking at ships	
	Size	180 x 112 mm	
	Ship Seal	Type 3	

AN26a

					Issued Notes			Archival Specimens
AN26	Start of Print Run	End of Print Run	Order Date (If Known)	Signatures	VG	Fine	VF	AU
a	85001	105000		G4, VG6				
b	105001	125000		G4, VG6				
c	125001*	150000*		G4, VG10*	$1,500	$2,750	$4,500	$1,100
d	150001*	200000		G4, VG6				
e	200001	270000 (275000 deleted)	9.11.21	G4, VG10*				

AN27 **50 mil reis** 1 March 1909 SCWPM 37

Printer Bradbury Wilkinson & Co. Ltd.

Total Printed 17000

Circulation Withdrawn 27. 07. 1922

Colour Black on yellow, green and multicoloured underprint. Reverse green, blue, yellow and pink

Obverse Design Vasco de Gama and his embarkation, overprint LOANDA

Reverse Design Allegorical maiden looking at ships

Size 198 x 120 mm

Ship Seal Type 1

AN27i

AN27	Start of Print Run	End of Print Run	Order Date (If Known)	Signatures	Issued Notes VG	Fine	VF	Archival Specimens AU
a	0001	2000		G4, VG9	Rare	Rare	Rare	$2,000
b	2001*	3333*		G4, VG6*	Rare	Rare	Rare	$1,500
c	3334*	4666*		G4, VG9*	Rare	Rare	Rare	$2,000
d	4667*	6000*		G4, VG6*	Rare	Rare	Rare	$1,500
e	6001*	7333		G4, VG10*				
f	7334	8666	24.6.15*	G4, VG6				
g	8667	10000		G4, VG10				
h	10001	13500	15.11.17	G4, VG6				
i	13501	17000	15.11.17	G4, VG10				
ph	Obverse sepia photograph mounted on card, dated 19--, serial number 0000, VG8 as Acting Governor, VG6 with VG9 and VG10 as Gerentes							One Copy Known

AN27ph

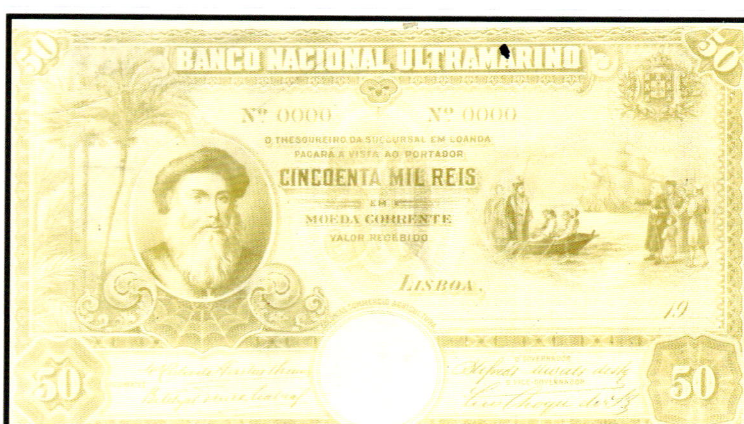

AN28	**50 mil reis**	1 March 1909	SCWPM 38
	Printer	Bradbury Wilkinson & Co. Ltd.	
	Total Printed	65000	
	Circulation	Withdrawn 27. 07. 1922	
	Colour	Black on yellow, green and multicoloured underprint. Reverse green, blue, yellow and pink	
	Obverse Design	Vasco de Gama and his embarkation, overprint LOANDA	
	Reverse Design	Allegorical maiden looking at ships	
	Size	198 x 120 mm	
	Ship Seal	Type 3	

AN28as

					Issued Notes			Archival Specimens
AN28	Start of Print Run	End of Print Run	Order Date (If Known)	Signatures	VG	Fine	VF	AU
a	17001	27000	7.11.19	G4, VG6				
b	27001	37000	7.11.19	G4, VG10				
c	37001	62000	11.10.21	G4, VG6	Rare	Rare	Rare	$1,750
d	62001	82000 (87000 deleted)	11.10.21	G4, VG10				

1914 CEDULA ISSUES

The fractional notes issued by the BNU for the Portuguese African colonies, all dated 5 November 1914, are known as the Cedula Issues and in Portugal as "the London Issue". They were emergency notes printed in London during World War I as a substitute for metal coinage in short supply. They were issued in denominations of 10cts, 20cts and 50cts for all five of the African colonies. Each colony had its own overprint, with Loanda used for Angola.

It is important to recognise that the issue of these notes, like metallic coins, was a privilege of the state, which was never transferred to the BNU. Accordingly, to be legal tender every issue had to be the subject of specific legislation proposed by the Minister of Colonies and approved by the Council of Ministers and Parliament in Lisbon. Furthermore, the fulfilment of the orders for the notes experienced all the constraints of a world at war. Among the difficulties encountered, which led to serious delays, were the lack of proper materials (appropriate paper and ink), the absence of skilled workers and the disruption of regular maritime transport. Shortages in the supply of the 50cts denomination led to notes of Saint Thomas and Prince being overprinted for use in Angola.

Two types of steamship seal were used for these issues: the earlier issues used Type 2 and the later issues Type 3. The seals were green for the 10cts, red for the 20cts and blue for the 50cts.

Steamship seal Type 2

Steamship seal Type 3

Reverses of the 1914 Cedula Issues

AN29 to AN32

AN 33 to AN36

AN37 to AN40

AN29	**10 Centavos**	5 November 1914, first issue	SCWPM 39a
	Printer	Bradbury Wilkinson & Co. Ltd.	
	Total Printed	120000 (only 70000 used for Angola, see † below)	
	Colour	Purple on multicoloured underprint. Reverse blue	
	Obverse Design	Value in guilloche at left, arms at right, green steamship seal at lower centre, black overprint LOANDA	
	Reverse Design	Allegorical maiden looking at ships	
	Size	122 x 72 mm	
	Signatures	G5, VG10	
	Ship Seal	Type 2	

AN29a

				Issued Notes			Archival Specimens
AN29	Start of Print Run	End of Print Run	Overprint Type	VG	VF	Unc	AU
a	0000001	0120000†	28mm black overprint with serifs	$80	$200	$650	$500

† 50000 of the serial number run 000001 to 120000 were overprinted "LOURENÇO MARQUES" for use in Mozambique. See MZ51a

N.B. Printer's archival specimens exist for the initial Order Dated 11. 11. 1914 for 400000 notes with serial number range 000001 to 0400000, and these made no reference to the colony where they would be put in circulation

AN29 (N.B.)

AN30	**10 Centavos**	5 November 1914, first issue	SCWPM unlisted
	Printer	Bradbury Wilkinson & Co. Ltd.	
	Total Printed	44000	
	Colour	Purple on multicoloured underprint. Reverse blue	
	Obverse Design	Value in guilloche at left, arms at right, green steamship seal at lower centre, black overprint LOANDA	
	Reverse Design	Allegorical maiden looking at ships	
	Size	122 x 72 mm	
	Signatures	G5, VG10	
	Ship Seal	Type 2	

AN30a

				Issued Notes			Archival Specimens
AN30	Start of Print Run	End of Print Run	Overprint Type	VG	VF	Unc	AU
a	0190001	0234000	19mm black overprint without serifs	$100	$250	$800	$500

AN31	**10 Centavos**	5 November 1914, first issue — SCWPM 39b
	Printer	Bradbury Wilkinson & Co. Ltd.
	Total Printed	1556000
	Colour	Purple on multicoloured underprint. Reverse blue
	Obverse Design	Value in guilloche at left, arms at right, green steamship seal at lower centre, green overprint LOANDA
	Reverse Design	Allegorical maiden looking at ships
	Size	122 x 72 mm
	Signatures	G5, VG10
	Ship Seal	Type 2

AN31c

				Issued Notes			Archival Specimens
AN31	Start of Print Run	End of Print Run	Overprint Type	VG	VF	Unc	AU
a	0234001	0490000					
b	0700001	1200000	23mm green overprint without serifs	$50	$120	$400	$400
c	3200001	4000000					

AN32	**10 Centavos**	5 November 1914, second issue	SCWPM 40
	Printer	Bradbury Wilkinson & Co. Ltd.	
	Total Printed	2000000	
	Colour	Purple on multicoloured underprint. Reverse blue	
	Obverse Design	Value in guilloche at left, arms at right, green steamship seal at lower centre, green overprint LOANDA	
	Reverse Design	Allegorical maiden looking at ships	
	Size	122 x 72 mm	
	Signatures	G5, VG10	
	Ship Seal	Type 3	

AN32a

				Issued Notes			Archival Specimens
AN32	Start of Print Run	End of Print Run	Overprint Type	VG	VF	Unc	AU
a	4000001	5980000	With counterfoil, 23mm green overprint without serifs	$40	$100	$350	$500
b	5980001	6000000	Without counterfoil, 23mm green overprint without serifs	$100	$250	$800	

N.B. The printer's archival specimen for this issue is with counterfoil and numbered from 4,000,001 to 6,000,000. See scan below.

AN32s

AN33	**20 Centavos**	5 November 1914, first issue	SCWPM 42a
	Printer	Bradbury Wilkinson & Co. Ltd.	
	Total Printed	590000 (only 340000 used for Angola, see † below)	
	Colour	Blue on multicoloured underprint. Reverse purple	
	Obverse Design	Value in guilloche at left, arms at right, red steamship seal at lower centre, black overprint LOANDA	
	Reverse Design	Allegorical maiden looking at ships	
	Size	122 x 72 mm	
	Signatures	G5, VG10	
	Ship Seal	Type 2	

AN33a

AN33	Start of Print Run	End of Print Run	Overprint Type	Issued Notes VG	Issued Notes VF	Issued Notes Unc	Archival Specimens AU
a	0000001	0590000†	28mm black overprint with serifs	$150	$350	$900	$550

† 340000 of the serial number run 0000001 to 0590000 were overprinted "LOURENÇO MARQUES" for use in Mozambique. See MZ54a

N.B. Printer's archival specimens exist for the initial Order Dated 11. 11. 1914 for 1800000 notes with serial number range 000001 to 1800000, and these made no reference to the colony where they would be put in circulation

AN33 (N.B.)

AN34	**20 Centavos**	5 November 1914, first issue	SCWPM unlisted
	Printer	Bradbury Wilkinson & Co. Ltd.	
	Total Printed	250000	
	Colour	Blue on multicoloured underprint. Reverse purple	
	Obverse Design	Value in guilloche at left, arms at right, red steamship seal at lower centre, black overprint LOANDA	
	Reverse Design	Allegorical maiden looking at ships	
	Size	122 x 72 mm	
	Signatures	G5, VG10	
	Ship Seal	Type 2	

AN34a

				Issued Notes			Archival Specimens
AN34	Start of Print Run	End of Print Run	Overprint Type	VG	VF	Unc	AU
a	0650001	0900000	19mm black overprint without serifs	$175	$400	$1,000	$550

AN35	**20 Centavos**	5 November 1914, first issue	SCWPM 42b
	Printer	Bradbury Wilkinson & Co. Ltd.	
	Total Printed	2250000	
	Colour	Blue on multicoloured underprint. Reverse purple	
	Obverse Design	Value in guilloche at left, arms at right, red steamship seal at lower centre, red overprint LOANDA	
	Reverse Design	Allegorical maiden looking at ships	
	Size	122 x 72 mm	
	Signatures	G5, VG10	
	Ship Seal	Type 2	

AN35b

				Issued Notes			Archival Specimens
AN35	Start of Print Run	End of Print Run	Overprint Type	VG	VF	Unc	AU
a	1026001	1276000	23mm red overprint without serifs				
b	1770001	2520000	23mm red overprint without serifs	$70	$180	$450	$450
c	4120001	5370000	23mm red overprint without serifs				

AN36	**20 Centavos**	5 November 1914, second issue	SCWPM 43
	Printer	Bradbury Wilkinson & Co. Ltd.	
	Total Printed	2500000	
	Colour	Blue on multicoloured underprint. Reverse purple	
	Obverse Design	Value in guilloche at left, arms at right, red steamship seal at lower centre, red overprint LOANDA	
	Reverse Design	Allegorical maiden looking at ships	
	Size	122 x 72 mm	
	Signatures	G5, VG10	
	Ship Seal	Type 3	

AN36a

				Issued Notes			Archival Specimens
AN36	Start of Print Run	End of Print Run	Overprint Type	VG	VF	Unc	AU
a	5370001	7521000	With counterfoil, 23mm red overprint without serifs	$70	$180	$450	$550
b	7521001	7870000	Without counterfoil, 23mm red overprint without serifs	$100	$250	$700	

N.B. The printer's archival specimen for this issue is with counterfoil and numbered from 5,370,001 to 7,870,000

AN36s

AN37	**50 Centavos**	5 November 1914, first issue	SCWPM 45
	Printer	Bradbury Wilkinson & Co. Ltd.	
	Total Printed	450000 (only 250000 used for Angola, see † below)	
	Colour	Green on multicoloured underprint. Reverse brown	
	Obverse Design	Value in guilloche at left, arms at right, blue steamship seal at lower centre, black overprint LOANDA	
	Reverse Design	Allegorical maiden looking at ships	
	Size	122 x 72 mm	
	Signatures	G5, VG10	
	Ship Seal	Type 2	

AN37a

AN37	Start of Print Run	End of Print Run	Overprint Type	Issued Notes VG	Issued Notes VF	Issued Notes Unc	Archival Specimens AU
a	0000001	0450000†	28mm black overprint with serifs	$150	$375	$1,000	$650

† 250000 of the serial number run 0000001 to 0450000 were overprinted "LOURENÇO MARQUES" for use in Mozambique. See MZ57a

N.B. Printer's archival specimens exist for the initial Order Dated 11. 11. 1914 for 1300000 notes with serial number range 000001 to 1300000, and these made no reference to the colony where they would be put in circulation

AN37 (N.B.)

AN38	**50 Centavos**	5 November 1914, first issue	SCWPM unlisted
	Printer	Bradbury Wilkinson & Co. Ltd.	
	Total Printed	140000	
	Colour	Green on multicoloured underprint. Reverse brown	
	Obverse Design	Value in guilloche at left, arms at right, blue steamship seal at lower centre, black overprint LOANDA	
	Reverse Design	Allegorical maiden looking at ships	
	Size	122 x 72 mm	
	Signatures	G5, VG10	
	Ship Seal	Type 2	

AN38a

				Issued Notes			Archival Specimens
AN38	Start of Print Run	End of Print Run	Overprint Type	VG	VF	Unc	AU
a	0450001	0590000	19mm black overprint without serifs	$175	$425	$1,100	$650

AN39	**50 Centavos**	5 November 1914, first issue	SCWPM unlisted
	Printer	Bradbury Wilkinson & Co. Ltd.	
	Total Printed	540000	
	Colour	Green on multicoloured underprint. Reverse brown	
	Obverse Design	Value in guilloche at left, arms at right, blue steamship seal at lower centre, black overprint LOANDA	
	Reverse Design	Allegorical maiden looking at ships	
	Size	122 x 72 mm	
	Signatures	G5, VG10	
	Ship Seal	Type 2	

AN39a

				Issued Notes			Archival Specimens
AN39	Start of Print Run	End of Print Run	Overprint Type	VG	VF	Unc	AU
a	1210001	1410000	23mm black overprint without serifs	$80	$200	$550	$600
b	3490001	3830000	23mm black overprint without serifs				

AN40 **50 Centavos** 5 November 1914, second issue SCWPM unlisted

Printer Bradbury Wilkinson & Co. Ltd.

Total Printed 600000

Colour Green on multicoloured underprint. Reverse brown

Obverse Design Value in guilloche at left, arms at right, blue steamship seal at lower centre, black overprint LOANDA

Reverse Design Allegorical maiden looking at ships

Size 122 x 72 mm

Signatures G5, VG10

Ship Seal Type 3

AN40a

				Issued Notes			Archival Specimens
AN40	Start of Print Run	End of Print Run	Overprint Type	VG	VF	Unc	AU
a	3830001	4390000	With counterfoil, 23mm black overprint without serifs	$80	$200	$550	$600
b	4390001	4430000	Without Counterfoil, 23mm black overprint without serifs	$120	$275	$800	

N.B.1 The printer's archival specimen for this issue is with counterfoil and numbered from 3,830,001 to 4,430,001

N.B.2 Neither SCWPM 46a (28mm blue overprint) nor SCWPM 46b (23mm red overprint) exist

AN40s

1914 PROVISIONAL ISSUE

AN41	**50 Centavos**	5 November 1914	SCWPM 47
	Printer	Bradbury Wilkinson & Co. Ltd.	
	Overprint	"PAGAVEL NA FILIAL DE LOANDA" in red on St Thomas and Prince ST27 (SCWPM 15)	
	Total Overprinted	Unknown	
	Colour	Green on multicoloured underprint. Reverse brown	
	Obverse Design	Value in guilloche at left, arms at right, blue steamship seal at lower centre, black overprint S. THOMÉ	
	Reverse Design	Allegorical maiden looking at ships	
	Size	122 x 72 mm	
	Signatures	G5, VG10	
	Ship Seal	Type 2	

AN41a

			Issued Notes		
AN41	Start of Print Run	End of Print Run	VG	VF	Unc
a	Unknown	Unknown	Rare	Rare	Rare

AN42	**50 Centavos**	5 November 1914	SCWPM 48
	Printer	Bradbury Wilkinson & Co. Ltd.	
	Overprint	"Loanda" in blue on St Thomas and Prince ST27 (SCWPM 15)	
	Total Overprinted	Unknown	
	Colour	Green on multicoloured underprint. Reverse brown	
	Obverse Design	Value in guilloche at left, arms at right, blue steamship seal at lower centre, black overprint S. THOMÉ	
	Reverse Design	Allegorical maiden looking at ships	
	Size	122 x 72 mm	
	Signatures	G5, VG10	
	Ship Sea	Type 2	

AN42a

AN42	Start of Print Run	End of Print Run	Issued Notes		
			VG	VF	Unc
a	Unknown	Unknown	Rare	Rare	Rare

1918 CEDULA ISSUE

AN43	**5 Centavos**	19 April 1918	SCWPM 49
	Printer	Casa da Moeda, Lisbon	
	Total Printed	Unknown	
	Colour	Grey-black on yellow underprint	
	Obverse Design	Value at left, steamship seal at right	
	Reverse Design	Steamship seal at centre, value on each side, anchor at lower centre	
	Size	99 x 63 mm	
	Signatures	G7 only	

AN43a

AN43a

AN43	Start of Print Run	End of Print Run	Issued Notes VG	Issued Notes VF	Issued Notes Unc
a	Unknown	Unknown	$15	$60	$500

AN44	**20 Centavos**	19 April 1918	SCWPM 50
	Printer	Casa da Moeda, Lisbon	
	Total Printed	Unknown	
	Colour	Brown-purple on yellow-orange underprint	
	Obverse Design	Pillars at left and right, value at left, Mercury seated at right	
	Reverse Design	Steamship seal at centre, value on each side, anchor at lower centre	
	Size	99 x 63 mm	
	Signatures	G7 only	

AN44a

AN44a

				Issued Notes		
AN44	Start of Print Run	End of Print Run		VG	Fine	VF
a	Unknown	Unknown		$250	$650	$1,500

1918 PROVISIONAL ISSUE

AN45	**2500 reis**	1 March 1909 (Introduced 1918)	SCWPM 25
	Printer	Bradbury Wilkinson & Co. Ltd.	
	Overprint	"Pagaval na Filial de Loanda" in red on St Thomas and Prince ST12 (SCWPM 8a)	
	Total Overprinted	Unknown	
	Colour	Black on green and yellow underprint. Reverse blue	
	Obverse Design	Vasco da Gama and his passage round The Cape, overprint S. THOMÉ	
	Reverse Design	Allegorical maiden looking at ships	
	Size	148 x 94 mm	
	Signatures	G4 and VG6, VG9 or VG10	
	Ship Seal	Type 1	

AN45a

AN45a

AN45	Start of Print Run	End of Print Run	Issued Notes VG	Issued Notes Fine	Issued Notes VF
a	Unknown	Unknown	$800	$1,500	Rare

AN46	**5 mil reis**	1 March 1909 (Introduced 1918)	SCWPM 26
	Printer	Bradbury Wilkinson & Co. Ltd.	
	Overprint	"PAGAVEL NA FILIAL DE BENGUELA" in red on St Thomas and Prince ST14 (SCWPM 9a)	
	Total Overprinted	Unknown	
	Colour	Black on blue and multicoloured underprint. Reverse green	
	Obverse Design	Vasco da Gama and his passage round The Cape, overprint S. THOMÉ	
	Reverse Design	Allegorical maiden looking at ships	
	Size	160 x 100 mm	
	Signatures	G4 and VG6, VG9 or VG10	
	Ship Seal	Type 1	

AN46a

AN46a

			Issued Notes		
AN46	Start of Print Run	End of Print Run	VG	Fine	VF
a	Unknown	Unknown	Rare	Rare	Rare

1920 EMERGENCY 'PORTO' ISSUE

AN47	**10 Centavos**	1 January 1920	SCWPM 51
	Printer	Litografia Nacional, Lda, Porto	
	Total Printed	Unknown	
	Circulation	Withdrawn in stages on 16. 08. 1934, 26. 05. 1937 and 29. 09. 1937	
	Colour	Red. Reverse brown-purple	
	Obverse Design	Sailing ships at left and right	
	Reverse Design	Value in central guilloche	
	Size	105 x 65 mm	
	Signatures	G7, VG14	

AN47a

AN47a

AN47	Start of Print Run	End of Print Run	Issued Notes VG	Issued Notes Fine	Issued Notes EF
a	Unknown	Unknown	$60	$225	$900

AN48	**20 Centavos**	1 January 1920	SCWPM 52
	Printer	Litografia Nacional, Lda, Porto	
	Total Printed	Unknown	
	Circulation	Withdrawn in stages on 16. 08. 1934, 26. 05. 1937 and 29. 09. 1937	
	Colour	Green	
	Obverse Design	Two cherubs above sailing ships at left and right, value at upper left and right	
	Reverse Design	Value in central guilloche	
	Size	105 x 65 mm	
	Signatures	G7, VG14	

AN48a

AN48a

				Issued Notes		
AN48	Start of Print Run	End of Print Run		VG	Fine	EF
a	Unknown	Unknown		$75	$275	$1,000

AN49	**50 Centavos**	1 January 1920	SCWPM 53
	Printer	Litografia Nacional, Lda, Porto	
	Total Printed	Unknown	
	Circulation	Withdrawn in stages on 16. 08. 1934, 26. 05. 1937 and 29. 09. 1937	
	Colour	Blue. Reverse brown	
	Obverse Design	Mercury and ship at left, allegorical female representing industry, and male farmer at right	
	Reverse Design	Ship in roundel at centre, value in four corners set in ornate borders	
	Size	120 x 75 mm	
	Signatures	G7, VG14	

AN49a

AN49a

AN49	Start of Print Run	End of Print Run	Issued Notes VG	Issued Notes Fine	Issued Notes VF
a	Unknown	Unknown	$125	$400	$1,250

AN50	**50 Escudos**	1 January 1920	SCWPM 54
	Printer	Litografia Nacional, Lda, Porto	
	Total Printed	Unknown	
	Circulation	Withdrawn in stages on 16. 08. 1934, 26. 05. 1937 and 29. 09. 1937	
	Colour	Blue on pale green underprint. Reverse brown on yellow-orange underprint	
	Obverse Design	Arms at upper centre, value at lower centre and in each corner	
	Reverse Design	Palm trees and coastline in ornate oval at centre, eagles at left and right, value at lower centre	
	Size	200 x 125 mm	
	Signatures	G7, VG14	

AN50a

AN50a

			Issued Notes		
AN50	Start of Print Run	End of Print Run	Good	Fine	EF
a	Unknown	Unknown	$4,500	$7,000	Rare
s	Specimen perforated and overprinted Specimen in manuscript on obverse				AU - Rare

AN50s

1921 CHAMIÇO ISSUE

By the Decree No. 5809, dated 30 May 1919, which instituted a new banking regime for the overseas colonies, a new issue of notes to replace the Vasco da Gama issues was authorised. This new omnibus series, which circulated in all five of the Portuguese African colonies from 1 August 1922 until 30 November 1950, featured a portrait of the founder and first Governor of the BNU, Francisco de Oliveira Chamiço (1819-88). This new issue consisted of values of 1$00, 2$50, 5$00, 10$00, 20$00, 50$00 and 100$00 escudos, all dated 1 January 1921.

Reverses of the Chamiço Issue

AN51

AN52

AN53

AN54

AN55

AN56

AN57

AN51 **1 escudo** 1 January 1921 SCWPM 55

Printer	Bradbury Wilkinson & Co. Ltd.
Total Printed	60000000
Colour	Green on multicoloured underprint
Obverse Design	Portrait of Francisco de Oliveira Chamiço at left, steamship seal at right, red overprint ANGOLA
Reverse Design	Allegorical maiden looking at ships
Size	128 x 82 mm
Signatures	G7, VG14

AN51a

				Issued Notes			Archival Specimens	Specimens
AN51	Start of Print Run	End of Print Run	Order Date (If Known)	VG	VF	Unc	AU	Unc
a	000001	800000	25.8.20					
b	800001	1600000	3.11.21					
c	1600001	1980000	15.11.21	$30	$75	$350	$350	$300
d	1980001	3150000	22.2.23					
e	3150001	6000000	25.5.23					

AN52	**2½ escudos**	1 January 1921	SCWPM 56
	Printer	Thomas De La Rue & Co. Ltd.	
	Total Printed	2500000*	
	Colour	Blue on multicoloured underprint	
	Obverse Design	Portrait of Francisco de Oliveira Chamiço at left, steamship seal at right	
	Reverse Design	Allegorical maiden looking at ships	
	Size	136 x 69 mm	
	Signatures	G7, VG14	

AN52a

AN52	Start of Print Run	End of Print Run	Order Date (If Known)	Issued Notes Fine	Issued Notes VF	Issued Notes EF	Specimens Unc
a	000001	2500000*		$120	$375	$800	$500
ct	Colour trial in dark green on orange, yellow and pink underprint, no serial numbers, specimen no in lower left margin						$650
ctp	Colour trial uniface obverse proof in brown on multicoloured underprint, blue 000000 serial numbers, black De La Rue oval						$450

AN52s

AN52ct

AN52ct

AN52ctp

AN53	**5 escudos**	1 January 1921	SCWPM 57
	Printer	Bradbury Wilkinson & Co. Ltd.	
	Total Printed	2000000	
	Colour	Black on multicoloured underprint	
	Obverse Design	Portrait of Francisco de Oliveira Chamiço at left, steamship seal at right, red overprint ANGOLA	
	Reverse Design	Allegorical maiden looking at ships	
	Size	154 x 92 mm	
	Signatures	G7, VG14	

AN53a

				Issued Notes			Archival Specimens	Specimens
AN53	Start of Print Run	End of Print Run	Order Date (If Known)	Fine	VF	EF	AU	Unc
a	000001	240000*	25.8.20					
b	240001	260000	3.11.21					
c	260001	754000	15.11.21	$125	$400	$950	$450	$350
d	754001	900000	23.2.23					
e	900001	2000000	23.5.23					

AN54 **10 escudos** 1 January 1921 SCWPM 58

Printer	Bradbury Wilkinson & Co. Ltd.
Total Printed	1200000
Colour	Brown on multicoloured underprint
Obverse Design	Portrait of Francisco de Oliveira Chamiço at left, steamship seal at right, red overprint ANGOLA
Reverse Design	Allegorical maiden looking at ships
Size	160 x 105 mm
Signatures	G7, VG14

AN54a

				Issued Notes			Archival Specimens	Specimens
AN54	Start of Print Run	End of Print Run	Order Date (If Known)	Fine	VF	EF	AU	Unc
a	000001	150000	25.8.20					
b	150001	300000	3.11.21	$140	$450	$1,100	$700	$600
c	300001	642000	15.11.21					
d	642001	1200000	25.5.23					

AN55	**20 escudos**	1 January 1921 SCWPM 59
	Printer	Bradbury Wilkinson & Co. Ltd.
	Total Printed	650000
	Colour	Blue on multicoloured underprint
	Obverse Design	Portrait of Francisco de Oliveira Chamiço at left, steamship seal at right, red overprint ANGOLA
	Reverse Design	Allegorical maiden looking at ships
	Size	170 x 115 mm
	Signatures	G7, VG14

AN55a

				Issued Notes			Archival Specimens	Specimens
AN55	Start of Print Run	End of Print Run	Order Date (If Known)	VG	Fine	VF	AU	Unc
a	000001	100000	25.8.20	$250	$550	$1,500	$700	$600
b	100001	350000	3.11.21					
c	350001	464000	15.11.21					
d	464001	650000	25.5.23					

AN56 **50 escudos** 1 January 1921 SCWPM 60

Printer Bradbury Wilkinson & Co. Ltd.

Total Printed 217000* (An unknown quantity of notes were overprinted for use in Mozambique, see MZ76)

Colour Brownish-red on multicoloured underprint

Obverse Design Portrait of Francisco de Oliveira Chamiço at left, steamship seal at right, red overprint ANGOLA

Reverse Design Allegorical maiden looking at ships

Size 185 x 120 mm

Signatures G7, VG14

AN56a

				Issued Notes			Archival Specimens	Specimens
AN56	Start of Print Run	End of Print Run	Order Date (If Known)	VG	Fine	VF	AU	Unc
a	000001	040000	25.8.20	$400	$750	$2,000	$800	$700
b	040001	160000	3.11.21					
c	160001	217000	15.11.21					
d	217001	Unknown						

AN57 **100 escudos** 1 January 1921 SCWPM 61

Printer Bradbury Wilkinson & Co. Ltd.

Total Printed 300000

Colour Slate-purple on multicoloured underprint

Obverse Design Portrait of Francisco de Oliveira Chamiço at left, steamship seal at right, red overprint ANGOLA

Reverse Design Allegorical maiden looking at ships

Size 193 x 126 mm

Signatures G7, VG14

AN57a

AN57	Start of Print Run	End of Print Run	Order Date (If Known)	Issued Notes VG	Issued Notes Fine	Issued Notes VF	Archival Specimens AU	Specimens Unc
a	000001	030000*	25.8.20*	$1,000	$2,750	Rare	$1,000	$850
b	030001	120000	3.11.21					
c	120001	160000	25.5.23					
d	160001	300000	3.11.24*					

Cape Verde

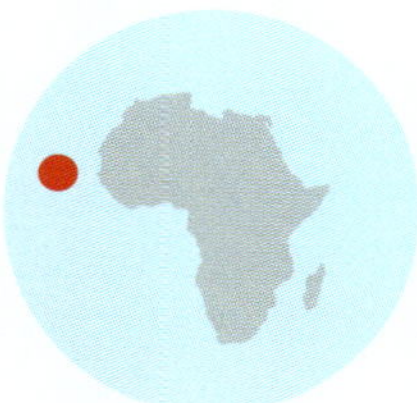

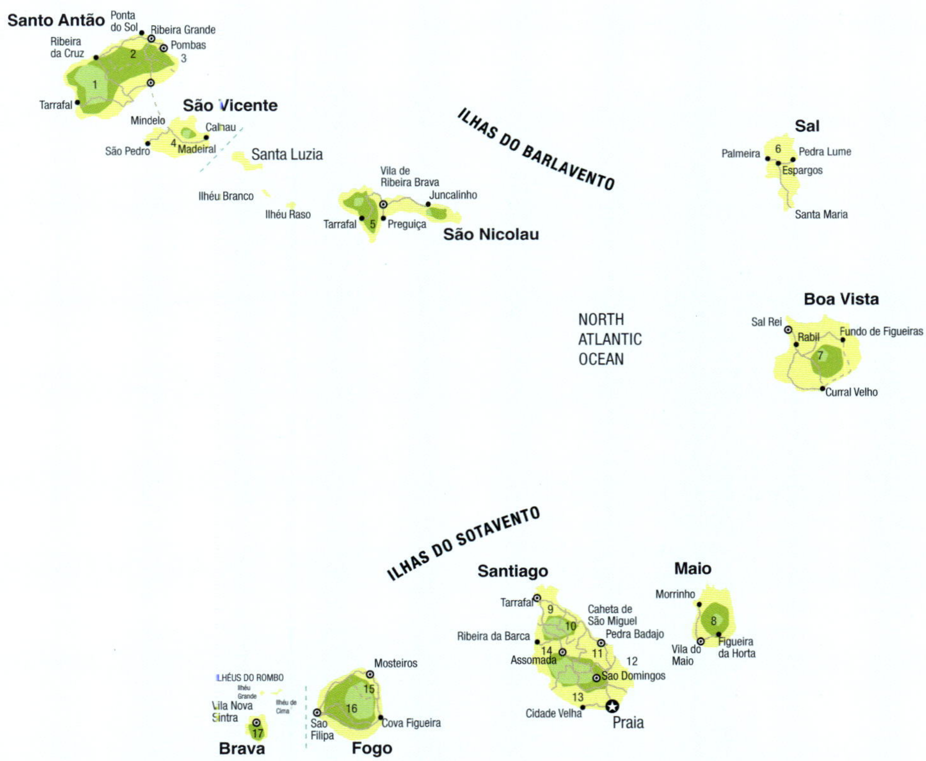

The Municipalities of Cape Verde are numbered 1 to 17 above

INTRODUCTION

Portuguese sailors discovered the fourteen volcanic islands of Cape Verde in 1456 and six years later established a settlement on the island of Santiago, which they named Ribeira Grande (modern day Cidade Velha). It was to become the first European town in the tropics and although the islands were initially regarded as part of Portugal, they can be considered as the starting point of her colonial empire. The archipelago later developed into a trading post for the transportation of enslaved people from Guinea-Bissau to Brazil and also as a stopover for supplies to other Portuguese colonies established in Africa and Asia. The abolition of slavery meant that by the 1840s the economy of the islands was in rapid decline and this continued throughout the latter part of the 19th century. Increasingly ignored by Portugal, repeated droughts caused significant hardship. As starvation became more and more commonplace, mass emigration occurred to other countries, particularly the United States of America.

The population of the archipelago increased from 178,000 in 1950 to 270,000 at independence in 1975 and throughout this period over half the population resided on the main island Santiago. As a result of the rise of tourism in the latter half of the last century, the population has doubled to over half a million, standing at 543,000 in 2018. However more Cape Verdeans now live overseas than in the home country.

The BNU established a branch in Praia, the national capital, in October 1865 under the management of Clarimundo Martins (1835-95). With a small capital of only 30,000 escudos, it took deposits at interest rates varying from 3% to 5%, took letters of credit and managed withdrawals throughout the islands. Rapid expansion of its operations led to the opening of an agency on the island of Såo Vicente in 1894 and later on the island of Sal in 1948, in addition to representative offices in all of the municipal capitals of the seventeen municipalities (see map above).

The first paper money was issued by the BNU in 1897 and all subsequent issues up until 1914 were denominated in reis (singular real), being the currency unit of Portugal until replaced in the colonies by the escudo. Thereafter the Portuguese escudo was used until the grant of independence in 1975. The earlier omnibus colonial issues were overprinted "S. THIAGO". Owing to the very low population, the total number of banknotes issued has always been relatively small and this means many of the notes are correspondingly rare. Collectors should note only 2000 copies of the 50 mil reis 1909 steamship seal I (CV15) were ever issued, making it the rarest issued note of the Vasco da Gama omnibus series.

The principal office of the BNU in Cape Verde. Address: Praça do Infante D. Henrique with Rua Sá da Bandeira, Praia.

1897 ISSUE

CV1	**1000 reis**	2 January 1897	SCWPM 1
	Printer	Casa da Moeda, Lisbon	
	Total Printed	Unknown	
	Colour	Brown. Reverse blue	
	Obverse Design	Ship at upper centre, crowned arms at top left, man with bow and arrow at left	
	Reverse Design	Bank name and value set in leaves and berries, caduceus on either side of value at centre	
	Size	122 x 88 mm	
	Signatures	G3, VG6 and VG8 and manuscript signatures of two managers	

CV1a

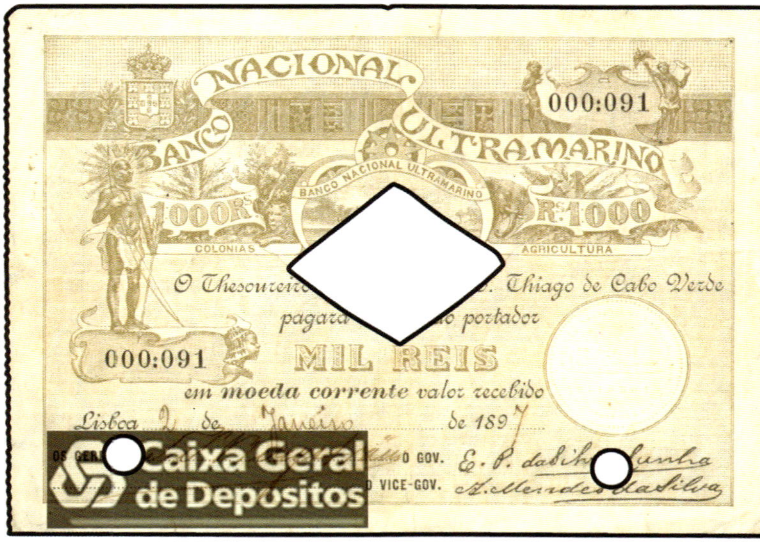

CV1a

CV1	Start of Print Run	End of Print Run	VG	Fine	VF
a	Unknown	Unknown	$6,000	from $10,000	Rare

CV2	**2500 reis**	2 January 1897	SCWPM 2
	Printer	Casa da Moeda, Lisbon	
	Total Printed	Unknown	
	Colour	Blue-grey	
	Obverse design	Steamship at left, crowned arms at top centre, woman at centre right, Mercury at far right	
	Reverse Design	Bank name and value set in leaves	
	Size	143 x 105 mm	
	Signatures	G3, VG6 and VG8 and manuscript signatures of two managers	

CV2a

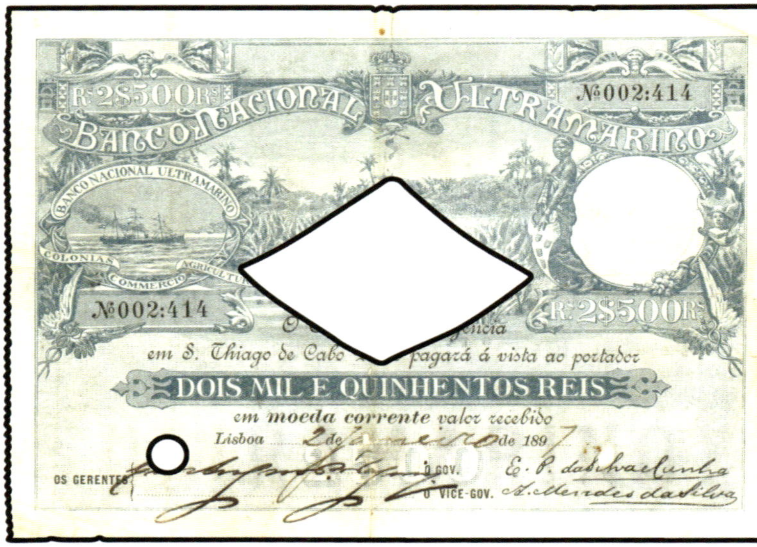

CV2a

CV2	Start of Print Run	End of Print Run	VG	Fine	VF
a	Unknown	Unknown	Rare	Rare	Rare

CV3	**5000 reis**	2 January 1897	SCWPM 3
	Printer	Casa da Moeda, Lisbon	
	Total Printed	Unknown	
	Colour	Blue. Reverse brown-purple	
	Obverse Design	Bush set in pillared arch at left, crowned arms at top centre left, ship at upper centre	
	Reverse Design	Bank name and value set in leaves and berries	
	Size	170 x 124 mm	
	Signatures	G3, VG6 and VG8 and manuscript signatures of two managers	

CV3a

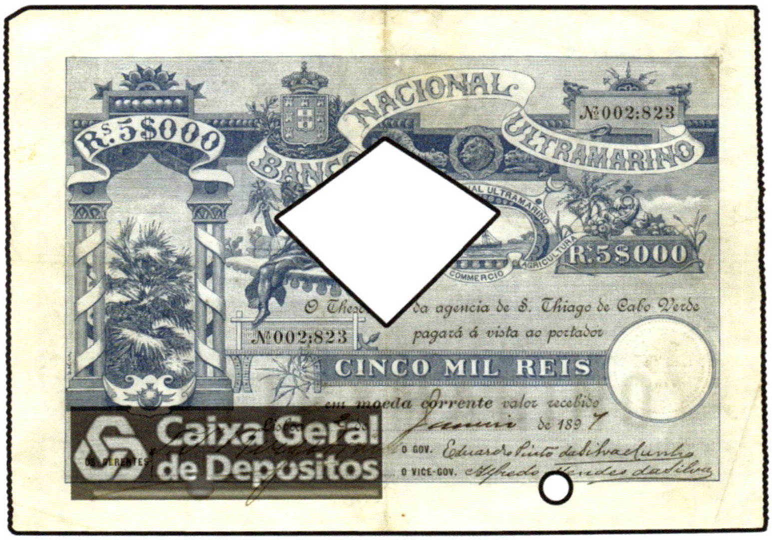

CV3a

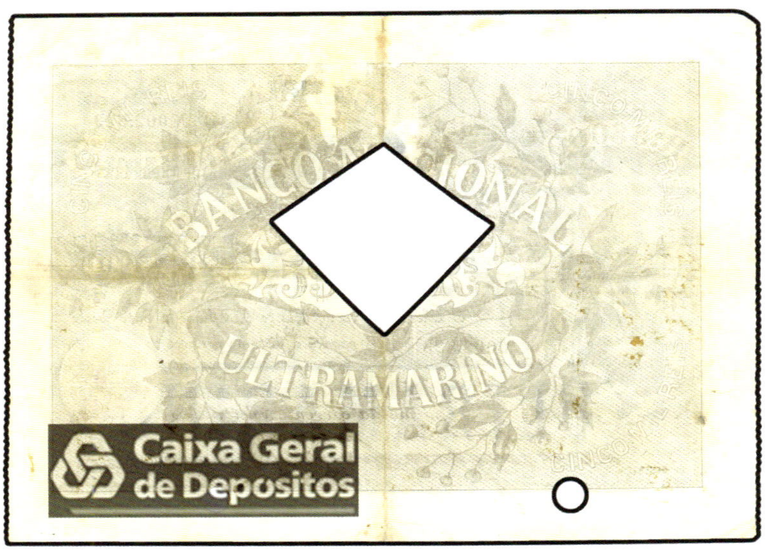

CV3	Start of Print Run	End of Print Run	VG	Fine	VF
a	Unknown	Unknown	Rare	Rare	Rare

CV4	**50000 reis**	2 January 1897	SCWPM unlisted
	Printer	Casa da Moeda, Lisbon	
	Total Printed	Unknown	
	Colour	Orange-brown	
	Obverse Design	Mercury with caduceus at centre, steamship at upper left, lion and elephant at lower left, crowned arms at top centre	
	Reverse Design	Portuguese text, trident, caduceus, seashells and fish	
	Size	198 x 140 mm	
	Signatures	G3, VG6 and VG8 and manuscript signatures of two managers	

CV4p

CV4	Start of Print Run	End of Print Run	VG	Fine	VF
a	Unknown	Unknown	Rare	Rare	Rare
p	Uniface proof		Rare	Rare	Rare

1909 VASCO DE GAMA ISSUE

By the Law of 27 April 1901, a new legal framework for banking activity in the Portuguese Colonial Empire was established. The new legislation divided banking operations into two groups; the issuance of paper money and the grant of loans secured by real estate. Although the banknote issue was open to competitive tendering, each colony could only have one bank and the BNU was the only bidder for Cape Verde and the other four African colonies. Under this new contract, the BNU prepared a new issue of notes, which were known as the Vasco da Gama Issue.

The notes issued under the new contract for Cape Verde were all dated 1 March 1909 with denominations of 1$000, 2$500, 5$000, 10$000, 20$000 and 50$000 reis, all being signed by the Governor Antonio Teixeira de Sousa (G4) and various Vice Governors (VG6, VG9 and VG10) and with a manuscript or facsimile signature of a manager. Two different types of steamship seal were used: the earlier issues used Type 1 and the later issues used Type 3.

See also "A Summary of the Main Banknote Issues of the Banco Nacional Ultramarino" on page 7 and "A Brief History of the Rise of the Portuguese Empire" on page 11 for further information on Vasco da Gama.

Steamship seal Type 1

Steamship seal Type 3

Reverses of the Vasco da Gama Issue

CV5 and CV6

CV7 and CV8

CV9 and CV10

CV11 and CV12

CV13 and CV14

CV15 and CV16

CV5	**1000 reis**	1 March 1909	SCWPM 4a
	Printer	Bradbury Wilkinson & Co. Ltd.	
	Total Printed	35000	
	Colour	Black on green and yellow underprint	
	Obverse design	Crowned arms at upper centre, value in guilloches, overprint S. THIAGO	
	Reverse Design	Allegorical maiden looking at ships	
	Size	138 x 80 mm	
	Ship Seal	Type 1	

CV5b

					Issued Notes			Archival Specimens
CV5	Start of Print Run	End of Print Run	Order Date (If Known)	Signatures	VG	Fine	VF	AU
a	00001	08334		G4, VG9	$450	$700	$1,000	$1,000
b	08335	16667		G4, VG6	$300	$500	$750	$700
c	16668	25000		G4, VG10				
d	25001	30000		G4, VG6				
e	30001	35000	14.11.17	G4, VG10				

CV6 **1000 reis** 1 March 1909 SCWPM 4b

Printer	Bradbury Wilkinson & Co. Ltd.
Total Printed	100000 (50000 notes were overprinted in 1924, see CV33)
Colour	Black on green and yellow underprint
Obverse design	Crowned arms at upper centre, value in guilloches, overprint S. THIAGO
Reverse Design	Allegorical maiden looking at ships
Size	138 x 80 mm
Ship Seal	Type 3

CV6bs

CV6	Start of Print Run	End of Print Run	Order Date (If Known)	Signatures	Issued Notes			Archival Specimens
					VG	Fine	VF	AU
a	35001	60000	18.5.20	G4, VG6				
b	60001	85000	18.5.20	G4, VG10	$250	$450	$700	$850
c	85001	135000	9.11.21	G4, VG6				

CV7	**2500 reis**	1 March 1909	SCWPM 5a
	Printer	Bradbury Wilkinson & Co. Ltd.	
	Total Printed	400000 (40000 notes were overprinted for use in Portuguese Guinea, see PG13)	
	Colour	Black on green and yellow underprint. Reverse blue	
	Obverse Design	Vasco de Gama and his passage round The Cape, overprint S. THIAGO	
	Reverse Design	Allegorical maiden looking at ships	
	Size	148 x 94 mm	
	Ship Seal	Type 1	

CV7a

					Issued Notes			Archival Specimens
CV7	Start of Print Run	End of Print Run	Order Date (If Known)	Signatures	VG	Fine	VF	AU
a	000001	133334		G4, VG9	$450	$800	$2,000	$1,100
b	133335	266667		G4, VG6	$350	$600	$1,600	$750
c	266668	400000		G4, VG10				

CV8	**2500 reis**	1 March 1909	SCWPM 5b
	Printer	Bradbury Wilkinson & Co. Ltd.	
	Total Printed	70000 (50480 notes were overprinted in 1924, see CV34)	
	Colour	Black on green and yellow underprint. Reverse blue	
	Obverse Design	Vasco de Gama and his passage round The Cape, overprint S. THIAGO	
	Reverse Design	Allegorical maiden looking at ships	
	Size	148 x 94 mm	
	Ship Seal	Type 3	

CV8as

					Issued Notes			Archival Specimens
CV8	Start of Print Run	End of Print Run	Order Date (If Known)	Signatures	VG	Fine	VF	AU
a	400001	425000	18.5.20	G4, VG6				
b	425001	450000	18.5.20	G4, VG10	$500	$1,000	$2,500	$850
c	450001	470000	9.11.21	G4, VG6				

CV9	**5 mil reis**	1 March 1909	SCWPM 6a
	Printer	Bradbury Wilkinson & Co. Ltd.	
	Total Printed	105000*	
	Colour	Black on blue and multicoloured underprint. Reverse green	
	Obverse Design	Vasco da Gama and his passge round The Cape, overprint S. THIAGO	
	Reverse Design	Allegorical maiden looking at ships	
	Size	160 x 100 mm	
	Ship Seal	Type 1	

CV9d

CV9	Start of Print Run	End of Print Run	Order Date (If Known)	Signatures	Issued Notes VG	Issued Notes Fine	Issued Notes VF	Archival Specimens AU
a	00001	08334		G4, VG9	$1,200	$2,750	Rare	$1,200
b	08335	016667*		G4, VG6*	$1,000	$2,200	Rare	$850
c	016668*	033334		G4, VG10*				
d	033335	066667		G4, VG6				
e	066668	100000		G4, VG10				
f	100001	102500	14.11.17	G4, VG6				
g	102501	105000		G4, VG10				

CV10	**5 mil reis**	1 March 1909	SCWPM 6b
	Printer	Bradbury Wilkinson & Co. Ltd.	
	Total Printed	135000* (An unknown quantity of notes were overprinted for use in Portuguese Guinea, see PG14, and 37333 notes were overprinted in 1924, see CV35)	
	Colour	Black on blue and multicoloured underprint. Reverse green	
	Obverse Design	Vasco da Gama and his passge round The Cape, overprint S. THIAGO	
	Reverse Design	Allegorical maiden looking at ships	
	Size	160 x 100 mm	
	Ship Seal	Type 3	

CV10cs

CV10	Start of Print Run	End of Print Run	Order Date (If Known)	Signatures	Issued Notes VG	Issued Notes Fine	Issued Notes VF	Archival Specimens AU
a	105001*	123000*		G4, VG6*				
b	123001	141000	29.12.19	G4, VG10				
c	141001	146000		G4, VG6				
d	146001	151000	23.4.20	G4, VG10	$800	$2,000	Rare	$850
e	151001	180000	1.11.21	G4, VG6				
f	181001	211000	1.11.21	G4, VG10				
g	211001*	240000*		G4, VG6*				

CV11	**10 mil reis**	1 March 1909	SCWPM 7a
	Printer	Bradbury Wilkinson & Co. Ltd.	
	Total Printed	30000	
	Colour	Black on yellow and multicoloured underprint. Reverse brown	
	Obverse Design	Vasco da Gama and his passage round The Cape, overprint S. THIAGO	
	Reverse Design	Allegorical maiden looking at ships	
	Size	175 x 105 mm	
	Ship Seal	Type 1	

CV11e

					Issued Notes			Archival Specimens
CV11	Start of Print Run	End of Print Run	Order Date (If Known)	Signatures	VG	Fine	VF	AU
a	00001	08334		G4, VG9	$3,000	Rare	Rare	$1,250
b	08335	16667*		G4, VG6*	$2,500	Rare	Rare	$950
c	16668*	25000*		G4, VG10*				
d	25001*	27500		G4, VG6*				
e	27501	30000	14.11.17	G4, VG10				

CV12	**10 mil reis**	1 March 1909	SCWPM 7b
	Printer	Bradbury Wilkinson & Co. Ltd.	
	Total Printed	60000 (8136 notes were overprinted in 1924, see CV36)	
	Colour	Black on yellow and multicoloured underprint. Reverse brown	
	Obverse Design	Vasco da Gama and his passage round The Cape, overprint S. THIAGO	
	Reverse Design	Allegorical maiden looking at ships	
	Size	175 x 105 mm	
	Ship Seal	Type 3	

CV12fs

					Issued Notes			Archival Specimens
CV12	Start of Print Run	End of Print Run	Order Date (If Known)	Signatures	VG	Fine	VF	AU
a	30001	37500	29.12.19	G4, VG6				
b	37501	45000	29.12.19	G4, VG10				
c	45001	52500		G4, VG6				
d	52501	60000	21.1.20	G4, VG10				
e	60001	65000	23.4.20	G4, VG6				
f	65001	70000	23.4.20	G4, VG10	$2,000	Rare	Rare	$900
g	70001	75000 (85000 deleted)	9.1.21	G4, VG6				
h	75001	80000*		G4, VG10*				
i	80001*	85000*		G4, VG6*				
j	85001	90000		G4, VG10				

CV13	**20 mil reis**	1 March 1909	SCWPM 8a
	Printer	Bradbury Wilkinson & Co. Ltd.	
	Total Printed	42000	
	Colour	Black on blue and yellow underprint. Reverse brown-red and orange	
	Obverse Design	Vasco de Gama and his embarkation, overprint S. THIAGO	
	Reverse Design	Allegorical maiden looking at ships	
	Size	180 x 112 mm	
	Ship Seal	Type 1	

CV13es

CV13	Start of Print Run	End of Print Run	Order Date (If Known)	Signatures	Issued Notes			Archival Specimens
					VG	Fine	VF	AU
a	00001	10000*		G4, VG9*	Rare	Rare	Rare	$1,500
b	10001	11000	14.11.17	G4, VG6				
c	11001	12000	14.11.17	G4, VG10	Rare	Rare	Rare	$1,100
d	12001	27000	5.8.19	G4, VG6				
e	27001	42000	5.8.19	G4, VG10				

CV14	**20 mil reis**	1 March 1909	SCWPM 8b
	Printer	Bradbury Wilkinson & Co. Ltd.	
	Total Printed	55000 (18719 notes were overprinted in 1924, see CV37)	
	Colour	Black on blue and yellow underprint. Reverse brown-red and orange	
	Obverse Design	Vasco de Gama and his embarkation, overprint S. THIAGO	
	Reverse Design	Allegorical maiden looking at ships	
	Size	180 x 112 mm	
	Ship Seal	Type 3	

CV14d

					Issued Notes			Archival Specimens
CV14	Start of Print Run	End of Print Run	Order Date (If Known)	Signatures	VG	Fine	VF	AU
a	42001	47000	29.12.19	G4, VG6				
b	47001	52000	29.12.19	G4, VG10				
c	52001	54500	21.1.20	G4, VG6				
d	54501	57000	21.1.20	G4, VG10	Rare	Rare	Rare	$950
e	57001	67000	18.5.20	G4, VG6				
f	67001	77000	18.5.20	G4, VG10				
g	77001	82000	9.11.21	G4, VG6				
h	82001	97000	9.11.21*	G4, VG10				

CV15	**50 mil reis**	1 March 1909	SCWPM 9a
	Printer	Bradbury Wilkinson & Co. Ltd.	
	Total Printed	2000	
	Colour	Black on yellow, green and multicoloured underprint. Reverse green, blue, yellow and pink	
	Obverse Design	Vasco de Gama and his embarkation, overprint S. THIAGO	
	Reverse Design	Allegorical maiden looking at ships	
	Size	198 x 120 mm	
	Ship Seal	Type 1	

CV15cs

					Issued Notes			Archival Specimens
CV15	Start of Print Run	End of Print Run	Order Date (If Known)	Signatures	VG	Fine	VF	EF
a	0001	0667		G4, VG9	Rare	Rare	Rare	$2,500
b	0668	1000		G4, VG10				
c	1001	1500	14.11.17	G4, VG6	Rare	Rare	Rare	$2,000
d	1501	2000	14.11.17	G4, VG10				

CV16	**50 mil reis**	1 March 1909	SCWPM 9b
	Printer	Bradbury Wilkinson & Co. Ltd.	
	Total Printed	15000 (1954 notes were overprinted in 1924, see CV38)	
	Colour	Black on yellow, green and multicoloured underprint. Reverse green, blue, yellow and pink	
	Obverse Design	Vasco de Gama and his embarkation, overprint S. THIAGO	
	Reverse Design	Allegorical maiden looking at ships	
	Size	198 x 120 mm	
	Ship Seal	Type 3	

CV16a

					Issued Notes			Archival Specimens
CV16	Start of Print Run	End of Print Run	Order Date (If Known)	Signatures	VG	Fine	VF	EF
a	2001	4500		G4, VG6				
b	4501	7000	29.12.19	G4, VG10	Rare	Rare	Rare	$1,750
c	7001	12000*		G4, VG6*				
d	12001	17000	21.1.20	G4, VG10*				

1914 CEDULA ISSUES

The fractional notes issued by the BNU for the Portuguese African colonies, all dated 5 November 1914, are known as the Cedula Issues and in Portugal as "the London Issue". They were emergency notes printed in London during World War I, as a substitute for metal coinage in short supply. They were issued in denominations of 4cts and 5cts for Cape Verde only and for all five African colonies in denominations of 10cts, 20cts and 50cts. Each colony had its own overprint, with S. Tiago used for Cape Verde.

It is important to recognise that the issue of these notes, like metallic coins, was a privilege of the state, which was never transferred to the BNU. Accordingly, to be legal tender every issue had to be the subject of specific legislation proposed by the Minister of Colonies and approved by the Council of Ministers and Parliament in Lisbon. Furthermore, the fulfilment of the orders for the notes experienced all the constraints of a world at war. Among the difficulties encountered, which led to serious delays, were the lack of proper materials (appropriate paper and ink), the absence of skilled workers and the disruption of regular maritime transport. Shortages in the supply of the 10cts and 50cts denominations led to notes of Mozambique being overprinted for use in Cape Verde.

Two types of steamship seal were used for these issues: the earlier issues used Type 2 and the later issues Type 3. The seals were red for the 4cts, 5cts and 20cts, green for the 10cts and blue for the 50 cts.

Steamship seal Type 2

Steamship seal Type 3

Reverses of the 1914 Cedula Issues

CV17

CV18

CV19, CV20,
CV25 and CV31

CV21, CV22 and CV26

CV23, CV24 and CV32

CV17	**4 centavos**	5 November 1914	SCWPM 10
	Printer	Bradbury Wilkinson & Co. Ltd.	
	Total Printed	500000	
	Colour	Blue-green on multicoloured underprint. Reverse purple	
	Obverse Design	Value in guilloche at left, arms at right, brown steamship seal at lower centre, red overprint S. TIAGO	
	Reverse Design	Allegorical maiden looking at ships	
	Size	122 x 72 mm	
	Signatures	G5, VG10	
	Ship Seal	Type 3	

CV17a

			Issued Notes			Archival Specimens
CV17	Start of Print Run	End of Print Run	Good	Fine	EF	AU
a	0000001	0500000	$80	$220	$600	$600

CV18 **5 centavos** 5 November 1914 SCWPM 11B

Printer	Bradbury Wilkinson & Co. Ltd.
Total Printed	400000
Colour	Bluish-purple on multicoloured underprint. Reverse blue-green
Obverse Design	Value in guilloche at left, arms at right, red steamseal at lower centre, red overprint S. TIAGO
Reverse Design	Allegorical maiden looking at ships
Size	122 x 72 mm
Signatures	G5, VG10
Ship Seal	Type 3

CV18a

CV18	Start of Print Run	End of Print Run	Issued Notes Good	Fine	EF	Archival Specimens AU
a	0000001	0400000	$100	$300	$800	$700

N.B. Neither the 5 centavos rose, steamship seal type 1, nor the 5 centavos rose, steamship seal type 3, listed as SCWPM 11 and 11A respectively, exist

CV19	**10 centavos**	5 November 1914, first issue	SCWPM 12A
	Printer	Bradbury Wilkinson & Co. Ltd.	
	Total Printed	200000	
	Colour	Purple on multicoloured underprint. Reverse blue	
	Obverse Design	Value in guilloche at left, arms at right, green steamship seal at lower centre, green overprint S. TIAGO	
	Reverse Design	Allegorical maiden looking at ships	
	Size	122 x 72 mm	
	Signatures	G5, VG10	
	Ship Seal	Type 2	

CV19bs

			Issued Notes			Archival Specimens
CV19	Start of Print Run	End of Print Run	Good	Fine	EF	AU
a	1350000	1450000	$80	$250	$650	$450
b	2700001	2800000				
ph	Sepia and white reverse archival photograph, dated 29. 10. 1914, with "PAGAVEL NA FILIAL EM S. THIAGO" at upper centre					One Copy Known

CV19ph

CV20	**10 centavos**	5 November 1914, second issue	SCWPM 13
	Printer	Bradbury Wilkinson & Co. Ltd.	
	Total Printed	200000	
	Colour	Purple on multicoloured underprint. Reverse blue	
	Obverse Design	Value in guilloche at left, arms at right, green steamship seal at lower centre, green overprint S. TIAGO	
	Reverse Design	Allegorical maiden looking at ships	
	Size	122 x 72 mm	
	Signatures	G5, VG10	
	Ship Seal	Type 3	

CV20b

<table>
<tr><th></th><th></th><th></th><th colspan="3">Issued Notes</th><th>Archival Specimens</th></tr>
<tr><th>CV20</th><th>Start of Print Run</th><th>End of Print Run</th><th>Good</th><th>Fine</th><th>EF</th><th>AU</th></tr>
<tr><td>a</td><td>6500001</td><td>6620000</td><td rowspan="2">$80</td><td rowspan="2">$250</td><td rowspan="2">$650</td><td rowspan="2">$450</td></tr>
<tr><td>b</td><td>8320001</td><td>8400000</td></tr>
</table>

CV21	**20 centavos**	5 November 1914, first issue	SCWPM 14
	Printer	Bradbury Wilkinson & Co. Ltd.	
	Total Printed	200000	
	Colour	Blue on multicoloured underprint. Reverse purple	
	Obverse Design	Value in guilloche at left, arms at right, red steamship seal at centre, red overprint S. TIAGO	
	Reverse Design	Allegorical maiden looking at ships	
	Size	122 x 72 mm	
	Signatures	G5, VG10	
	Ship Seal	Type 2	

CV21bs

			Issued Notes			Archival Specimens
CV21	Start of Print Run	End of Print Run	Good	Fine	EF	AU
a	2645001	2745000	$100	$300	$750	$450
b	3970001	4070000				

CV22	**20 centavos**	5 November 1914, second issue	SCWPM 15
	Printer	Bradbury Wilkinson & Co. Ltd.	
	Total Printed	100000	
	Colour	Blue on multicoloured underprint. Reverse purple	
	Obverse Design	Value in guilloche at left, arms at right, red steamship seal at centre, red overprint S. TIAGO	
	Reverse Design	Allegorical maiden looking at ships	
	Size	122 x 72 mm	
	Signatures	G5, VG10	
	Ship Seal	Type 3	

CV22a

			Issued Notes			Archival Specimens
CV22	Start of Print Run	End of Print Run	Good	Fine	EF	EF
a	8370001	8470000	$120	$350	$900	$550

CV23	**50 centavos**	5 November 1914, first issue — SCWPM 16
	Printer	Bradbury Wilkinson & Co. Ltd.
	Total Printed	300000
	Colour	Green on multicoloured underprint. Reverse brown
	Obverse Design	Value in guilloche at left, arms at right, blue steamship seal at centre, blue overprint S. TIAGO
	Reverse Design	Allegorical maiden looking at ships
	Size	122 x 72 mm
	Signatures	G5, VG10
	Ship Seal	Type 2

CV23c

			Issued Notes			Archival Specimens
CV23	Start of Print Run	End of Print Run	Good	Fine	EF	AU
a	0880001	0980000				
b	1530001	1590000	$90	$275	$700	$500
c	3050001	3190000				

CV24	**50 centavos**	5 November 1914, second issue	SCWPM 17
	Printer	Bradbury Wilkinson & Co. Ltd.	
	Total Printed	60000	
	Colour	Green on multicoloured underprint. Reverse brown	
	Obverse Design	Value in guilloche at left, arms at right, blue steamship seal at centre, blue overprint S. TIAGO	
	Reverse Design	Allegorical maiden looking at ships	
	Size	122 x 72 mm	
	Signatures	G5, VG10	
	Ship Seal	Type 3	

CV24as

CV24	Start of Print Run	End of Print Run	Issued Notes Good	Issued Notes Fine	Issued Notes EF	Archival Specimens EF
a	5130001	5190000	$100	$300	$800	$600

1914 PROVISIONAL ISSUE

CV25 **10 centavos** 5 November 1914 SCWPM 9A

Printer Bradbury Wilkinson & Co. Ltd.

Overprint "PAGAVEL EM S. TIAGO" on Portuguese Guinea PG15 (SCWPM 6)

Total Overprinted Unknown

Colour Purple on multicoloured underprint. Reverse blue

Obverse Design Value in guilloche at left, arms at right, green steamship seal at lower centre

Reverse Design Allegorical maiden looking at ships

Size 122 x 72 mm

Signatures G5, VG10

Ship Seal Type 2

CV25a

Issued Notes

CV25	Start of Print Run	End of Print Run	Good	Fine	EF
a	Unknown	Unknown	$200	$900	Rare

CV26	**20 centavos**	5 November 1914	SCWPM unlisted
	Printer	Bradbury Wilkinson & Co. Ltd.	
	Overprint	"PAGAVEL EM S. TIAGO" on Portuguese Guinea PG17 (SCWPM 7)	
	Total Overprinted	Unknown	
	Colour	Blue on multicoloured underprint. Reverse purple	
	Obverse Design	Value in guilloche at left, arms at right, red steamship seal at lower centre	
	Reverse Design	Allegorical maiden looking at ships	
	Size	122 x 72 mm	
	Signatures	G5, VG10	
	Ship Seal	Type 2	

CV26a

			Issued Notes		
CV26	Start of Print Run	End of Print Run	Good	Fine	EF
a	circa 3060000	Unknown	Rare	Rare	Rare

1920 EMERGENCY "PORTO" ISSUE

CV27	**10 centavos**	1 January 1920	SCWPM 18
	Printer	Litografia Nacional, Lda. Porto	
	Total Printed	Unknown	
	Colour	Red. Reverse brown-purple	
	Obverse Design	Sailing ships at left and right	
	Reverse Design	Value in central guilloche	
	Size	105 x 65 mm	
	Signatures	G7, VG14	

CV27a

CV27a

			Issued Notes		
CV27	Start of Print Run	End of Print Run	Good	Fine	EF
a	Unknown	Unknown	$350	$1,200	$3,000

CV28	**20 centavos**	1 January 1920	SCWPM unlisted
	Printer	Litografia Nacional, Lda. Porto	
	Total Printed	Unknown	
	Colour	Green	
	Obverse Design	Two cherubs above sailing ships at left and right, value at upper left and right	
	Reverse Design	Value in central guilloche	
	Size	105 x 65 mm	
	Signatures	G7, VG14	

CV28a

CV28a

Issued Notes

CV28	Start of Print Run	End of Print Run	Good	Fine	EF
a	Unknown	Unknown	Rare	Rare	Rare

N.B. A single copy of CV28, serial number 938693 has been reported, but the whereabouts of the original is unknown

CV29	**50 centavos**	1 January 1920	SCWPM 19
	Printer	Litografia Nacional, Lda. Porto	
	Total Printed	Unknown	
	Colour	Blue. Reverse brown	
	Obverse Design	Mercury at left, ships at lower left, allegorical female representing industry, and male farmer at right	
	Reverse Design	Ship in roundel at centre, value in four corners set in ornate borders	
	Size	120 x 75 mm	
	Signatures	G7, VG14	

CV29a

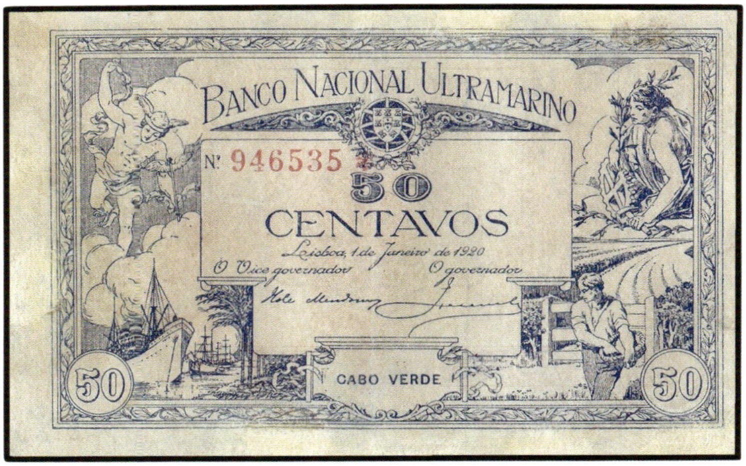

CV29a

Issued Notes

CV29	Start of Print Run	End of Print Run	Good	Fine	EF
a	Unknown	Unknown	$450	$1,500	Rare

CV30	**50 escudos**	1 January 1920 SCWPM 19A
	Printer	Litografia Nacional, Lda. Porto
	Total Printed	Unknown
	Colour	Dark blue on pale green underprint. Reverse brown on yellow-orange underprint
	Obverse Design	Arms at upper centre, value at lower centre and in each corner
	Reverse Design	Palm trees and coastline in ornate oval at centre, eagles at left and right, value at lower centre
	Size	200 x 125 mm
	Signatures	G7, VG14

CV30a

CV30a

			Issued Notes		
CV30	Start of Print Run	End of Print Run	Good	Fine	EF
a	Unknown	Unknown	Rare	Rare	Rare

1923 PROVISIONAL ISSUE

CV31	**10 centavos**	ND (1923) - old date 5 November 1914	SCWPM 20
	Printer	Bradbury Wilkinson & Co. Ltd.	
	Overprint	"CABO VERDE" in black on Mozambique MZ53 (SCWPM 59)	
	Total Overprints	550000	
	Colour	Purple on multicoloured underprint. Reverse blue	
	Obverse Design	Value in guilloche at left, arms at right, green steamship seal at lower centre	
	Reverse Design	Allegorical maiden looking at ships	
	Size	122 x 72 mm	
	Signatures	G5, VG10	
	Ship Seal	Type 3	

CV31a

			Issued Notes		
CV31	Start of Print Run	End of Print Run	Good	Fine	EF
a	circa A3300000	circa A3800000	$25	$100	$350

N.B.1 20 Centavos ND (1923) listed as SCWPM 21 does not exist and any copies appearing on the market are recent forgeries. Forgeries of the 10 centavos and 50 centavos also exist

N.B.2 Numerous high quality and deceptive modern fakes of the above overprint, on genuine examples of Mozambique MZ53, have appeared on the market

CV32	**50 centavos**	ND (1923) - old date 5 November 1914	SCWPM 22
	Printer	Bradbury Wilkinson & Co. Ltd.	
	Overprint	"CABO VERDE" in black on Mozambique MZ59 (SCWPM 61)	
	Total Overprints	80000	
	Colour	Green on multicoloured underprint. Reverse brown	
	Obverse Design	Value in guilloche at left, arms at right, blue steamship seal at lower centre	
	Reverse Design	Allegorical maiden looking at ships	
	Size	122 x 72 mm	
	Signatures	G5, VG10	
	Ship Seal	Type 3	

CV32a

Issued Notes

CV32	Start of Print Run	End of Print Run	Good	Fine	EF
a	circa A2900000		$60	$220	$900

N.B. 1 50 Centavos ND (1923) with overprint "CABO VERDE" on Portugese Guinea PG19 (SCWPM 11) listed as SCWPM 22A has not been traced by the authors and may either be a forged overprint or not exist.

N.B. 2 Numerous high quality and deceptive modern fakes of the above overprint, on genuine examples of Mozambique MZ59, have appeared on the market

1924 PROVISIONAL ISSUE

CV33	**1000 reis**	ND (1924) - old date 1 March 1909	SCWPM 23
	Printer	Bradbury Wilkinson & Co. Ltd.	
	Overprint	Purple or black overprint “Emissão Chamiço” in rectangular frame on CV6	
	Total Overprints	50000	
	Colour	Black on green and yellow underprint	
	Obverse design	Crowned arms at upper centre, value in guilloches, overprint S. THIAGO	
	Reverse Design	Allegorical maiden looking at ships	
	Size	138 x 80 mm	
	Signatures	As CV6	
	Ship Seal	Type 3	

CV33a

			Issued Notes		
CV33	Start of Print Run	End of Print Run	VG	Fine	VF
a	Unknown	Unknown	$800	$1,400	$2,500

CV34	**2500 reis**	ND (1924) - old date 1 March 1909	SCWPM 24
	Printer	Bradbury Wilkinson & Co. Ltd.	
	Overprint	Red, purple or black overprint "Emissão Chamiço" in rectangular frame on CV8	
	Total Overprints	50480	
	Colour	Black on green and yellow underprint. Reverse blue	
	Obverse design	Vasco de Gama and his passage round The Cape, overprint S. THIAGO	
	Reverse Design	Allegorical maiden looking at ships	
	Size	148 x 94 mm	
	Signatures	As CV8	
	Ship Seal	Type 3	

CV34a
(Red Overprint)

CV34a
(Purple Overprint)

			Issued Notes		
CV34	Start of Print Run	End of Print Run	VG	Fine	VF
a	Unknown	Unknown	Rare	Rare	Rare

CV35 **5 mil reis** ND (1924) - old date 1 March 1909 SCWPM 25

Printer Bradbury Wilkinson & Co. Ltd.

Overprint Purple or black overprint "Emissão Chamiço" in rectangular frame on CV10

Total Overprints 37333

Colour Black on blue and multicoloured underprint. Reverse green

Obverse design Vasco da Gama and his passge round The Cape, overprint S. THIAGO

Reverse Design Allegorical maiden looking at ships

Size 160 x 100 mm

Signatures As CV10

Ship Seal Type 3

CV35a

			Issued Notes		
CV35	Start of Print Run	End of Print Run	VG	Fine	VF
a	Unknown	Unknown	Rare	Rare	Rare

CV36 **10 mil reis** ND (1924) - old date 1 March 1909 SCWPM 26

Printer Bradbury Wilkinson & Co. Ltd.

Overprint Purple or black overprint "Emissão Chamiço" in rectangular frame on CV12

Total Overprints 8136

Colour Black on yellow and multicoloured underprint. Reverse brown

Obverse design Vasco da Gama and his passage round The Cape, overprint S. THIAGO

Reverse Design Allegorical maiden looking at ships

Size 175 x 105 mm

Signatures As CV12

Ship Seal Type 3

			Issued Notes		
CV36	Start of Print Run	End of Print Run	VG	Fine	VF
a	Unknown	Unknown	Rare	Rare	Rare

CV37	**20 mil reis**	ND (1924) - old date 1 March 1909	SCWPM 27
	Printer	Bradbury Wilkinson & Co. Ltd.	
	Overprint	Purple or black overprint "Emissão Chamiço" in rectangular frame on CV14	
	Total Overprints	18719	
	Colour	Black on blue and yellow underprint. Reverse brown-red and orange	
	Obverse design	Vasco de Gama and his embarkation, overprint S. THIAGO	
	Reverse Design	Allegorical maiden looking at ships	
	Size	180 x 112 mm	
	Signatures	As CV14	
	Ship Seal	Type 3	

CV37a

Issued Notes

CV37	Start of Print Run	End of Print Run	VG	Fine	VF
a	Unknown	Unknown	Rare	Rare	Rare

CV38	**50 mil reis**	ND (1924) - old date 1 March 1909	SCWPM 28
	Printer	Bradbury Wilkinson & Co. Ltd.	
	Overprint	Purple or black overprint “Emissão Chamiço” in rectangular frame on CV16	
	Total Overprints	1954	
	Colour	Black on yellow, green and multicoloured underprint. Reverse green, blue, yellow and pink	
	Obverse design	Vasco de Gama and his embarkation, overprint S. THIAGO	
	Reverse Design	Allegorical maiden looking at ships	
	Size	198 x 120 mm	
	Signatures	As CV16	
	Ship Seal	Type 3	

CV38a

Issued Notes

CV38	Start of Print Run	End of Print Run	VG	Fine	VF
a	Unknown	Unknown	Rare	Rare	Rare

INTRODUCTION TO THE CHAMIÇO ISSUES

By the Decree No. 5809, dated 30 May 1919, which instituted a new banking regime for the overseas colonies, a new issue of notes to replace the Vasco da Gama issues was authorised. This new omnibus series, which circulated in all five of the Portuguese African colonies from 1 August 1922 until 30 November 1950, featured a portrait of the founder and first Governor of the BNU, Francisco de Oliveira Chamiço (1819-88). This new issue consisted of values of 1$00, 5$00, 10$00, 20$00, 50$00 and 100$00 escudos with dates ranging from 1 January 1921 to 1 August 1941, It should be noted that no 2$50 Chamiço note was ever issued for Cape Verde and a shortage of the 5$00 note led to the 1$00 note being overprinted "CINCO ESCUDOS".

Reverses of the Chamico Issues

CV39
and CV40

CV41

CV42

CV43

CV44
and CV53

CV45
and CV54

1921 CHAMIÇO ISSUES

CV39	**1 escudo**	1 January 1921	SCWPM 32
	Printer	Bradbury Wilkinson & Co. Ltd.	
	Total Printed	1000000*	
	Colour	Green on multicoloured underprint	
	Obverse Design	Portrait of Francisco de Oliveira Chamiço at left, steamship seal at right, red overprint CABO VERDE	
	Reverse Design	Allegorical maiden looking at ships	
	Size	128 x 82 mm	
	Signatures	G7, VG14	

CV39b

					Issued Notes		Archival Specimens	Specimens
CV39	Start of Print Run	End of Print Run	Order Date (If Known)	Fine	VF	EF	AU	AU
a	000001	200000*	25.8.20					
b	200001	240000	3.11.21					
c	240001	290000	15.11.21	$60	$140	$350	$350	$300
d	290001	775000	23.2.23					
e	775001	1000000	15.10.24					
ph	Sepia and white obverse and reverse archival photographs, dated 26. 06. 1920, of undated issued note but with counterfoil and larger signatures, serial number 0000000							One Pair Known

CV39ph

CV40	**5 escudos**	ND 1937 - old date 1 January 1921	SCWPM 33
	Printer	Bradbury Wilkinson & Co. Ltd.	
	Overprint	"CINCO ESCUDOS" in silver rectangular panel on CV39	
	Total Overprints	500000	
	Colour	Green on multicoloured underprint	
	Obverse Design	Portrait of Francisco de Oliveira Chamiço at left, steamship seal at right, black overprint CABO VERDE	
	Reverse Design	Allegorical maiden looking at ships	
	Size	128 x 82 mm	
	Signatures	G7, VG14	

CV40as

				Issued Notes			Specimens
CV40	Start of Print Run	End of Print Run	Order Date (If Known)	Fine	VF	EF	AU
a	A000001	A500000	31.15.35	$180	$350	$800	$700

N.B. The reverse of this note was not overprinted "CINCO ESCUDOS" and is identical to the reverse of CV39

CV40a

BANCO NACIONAL ULTRAMARINO
PROVINCIA DE
DECRETO Nº 17.154
Nº A105.184
CABO VERDE
CINCO ESCUDOS
PAGAVEL NAS DEPENDENCIAS DA PROVINCIA DE
CABO VERDE
Nº A105.184
LISBOA, 1 de Janeiro de 1921
O VICE GOVERNADOR
O GOVERNADOR

CV40a

PAGAVEL NAS DEPENDENCIAS DA PROVINCIA DE
CABO VERDE
BANCO NACIONAL ULTRAMARINO

CV41	**5 escudos**	1 January 1921	SCWPM 34
	Printer	Bradbury Wilkinson & Co. Ltd.	
	Total Printed	340000*	
	Colour	Black on multicoloured underprint	
	Obverse Design	Portrait of Francisco de Oliveira Chamiço at left, steamship seal at right, red overprint CABO VERDE	
	Reverse Design	Allegorical maiden looking at ships	
	Size	154 x 90 mm	
	Signatures	G7, VG14	

CV41a

				Issued Notes			Archival Specimens	Specimens
CV41	Start of Print Run	End of Print Run	Order Date (If Known)	Fine	VF	EF	AU	AU
a	000001	080000*	25.8.20					
b	080001	084000	3.11.21					
c	084001	149000	15.11.21	$240	$450	$1,000	$450	$400
d	149001	300000	23.2.23					
e	300001	340000	23.2.23					
ph	Sepia and white obverse and reverse archival photographs, dated 09. 09. 1920, of undated issued note but with larger signatures, serial number 0000000							One Pair Known

CV42	**10 escudos**	1 January 1921	SCWPM 35
	Printer	Bradbury Wilkinson & Co. Ltd.	
	Total Printed	300000*	
	Colour	Brown on multicoloured underprint	
	Obverse Design	Portrait of Francisco de Oliveira Chamiço at left, steamship seal at right, red overprint CABO VERDE	
	Reverse Design	Allegorical maiden looking at ships	
	Size	160 x 105 mm	
	Signatures	G7, VG14	

CV42f

				Issued Notes			Archival Specimens	Specimens
CV42	Start of Print Run	End of Print Run	Order Date (If Known)	VG	Fine	VF	AU	AU
a	000001	060000*	25.8.20					
b	060001	110000	3.11.21					
c	110001	155000	15.11.21	$200	$450	$1,000	$550	$500
d	155001	180000	15.10.24					
e	180001	200000	15.10.24					
f	200001	300000*	18.8.28*					
ph	Sepia and white obverse and reverse archival photographs, dated 13. 09. 1920, of undated issued note but with larger signatures, serial number 0000000							One Pair Known

CV43	**20 escudos**	1 January 1921	SCWPM 36
	Printer	Bradbury Wilkinson & Co. Ltd.	
	Total Printed	150000*	
	Colour	Dark blue on multicoloured underprint	
	Obverse Design	Portrait of Francisco de Oliveira Chamiço at left, steamship seal at right, red overprint CABO VERDE	
	Reverse Design	Allegorical maiden looking at ships	
	Size	170 x 115 mm	
	Signatures	G7, VG14	

CV43f

				Issued Notes			Archival Specimens	Specimens
CV43	Start of Print Run	End of Print Run	Order Date (If Known)	VG	Fine	VF	AU	AU
a	000001	035000*	25.8.20					
b	035001	055000	3.11.21					
c	055001	070000	15.11.21	$450	$1,000	$2,200	$750	$650
d	070001	100000	15.10.24					
e	100001	115000	29.10.24					
f	115001	150000*	18.8.28*					
ph	Sepia and white obverse and reverse archival photographs, dated 09. 09. 1920, of undated issued note but with larger signatures, serial number 0000000							One Pair Known

CV44	**50 escudos**	1 January 1921	SCWPM 37
	Printer	Bradbury Wilkinson & Co. Ltd.	
	Total Printed	70000*	
	Colour	Brownish-red on multicoloured underprint	
	Obverse Design	Portrait of Francisco de Oliveira Chamiço at left, steamship seal at right, red overprint CABO VERDE	
	Reverse Design	Allegorical maiden looking at ships	
	Size	185 x 120 mm	
	Signatures	G7, VG14	

CV44a

				Issued Notes			Archival Specimens	Specimens
CV44	Start of Print Run	End of Print Run	Order Date (If Known)	VG	Fine	VF	AU	AU
a	000001	020000	25.8.20					
b	020001	034000	3.11.21					
c	034001	041500	15.11.21	$1,500	$4000	Rare	$850	$750
d	041501	042000	15.10.24					
e	042001	050000	29.10.24					
f	050001	070000	18.8.28					
ph	Sepia and white obverse and reverse rem archival photographs, dated 17. 09. 1920, of undated issued note but with larger signatures, serial number 0000000							One Pair Known

CV44es

CV45	**100 escudos**	1 January 1921	SCWPM 38
	Printer	Bradbury Wilkinson & Co. Ltd.	
	Total Printed	72000	
	Colour	Slate-purple on multicoloured underprint	
	Obverse Design	Portrait of Francisco de Oliveira Chamiço at left, steamship seal at right, red overprint CABO VERDE	
	Reverse Design	Allegorical maiden locking at ships	
	Size	193 x 126 mm	
	Signtures	G7, VG14	

CV45cs

CV45	Start of Print Run	End of Print Run	Order Date (If Known)	Issued Notes VG	Issued Notes Fine	Issued Notes VF	Archival Specimens AU	Specimens AU
a	000001	010000	25.8.20	Rare	Rare	Rare	$1,000	$900
b	010001	016000	3.11.21					
c	016001	027000	29.10.24					
d	027001	035000	18.8.28					
e	035001	042000*						
f	042001	072000	2.9.32					
ct	Colour trial in orange and multicoloured, reverse orange on green underprint. Believed only 3 copies known							AU - Rare
p	Proof with Decreto No. 17,154 in red added at upper left, pencil date 24. 10. 29 in lower right hand margin. Believed to be unique							VF - Rare
ph	Sepia and white obverse and reverse archival photographs, dated 26. 06. 1920, of undated issued note but with counterfoil and larger signatures, serial number 0000000							One Pair Known

CV45ph

CV45ct

CV45ct

CV45p

1924 CIRCULATING BEARER CHEQUE ISSUE

CV46	**50 escudos**	1 July 1924	SCWPM unlisted
	Printer	Litografia E. Barrault, Lisboa	
	Total Printed	Unknown	
	Colour	Blue and white	
	Obverse Design	Steamship seal set in two ornate semi-ovals at left. Bank legend at upper centre and as microprint	
	Reverse Design	Uniface.	
	Size	165 x 80 mm	
	Signature	Fernando Arvelos as Gerente	

CV46a

CV46a

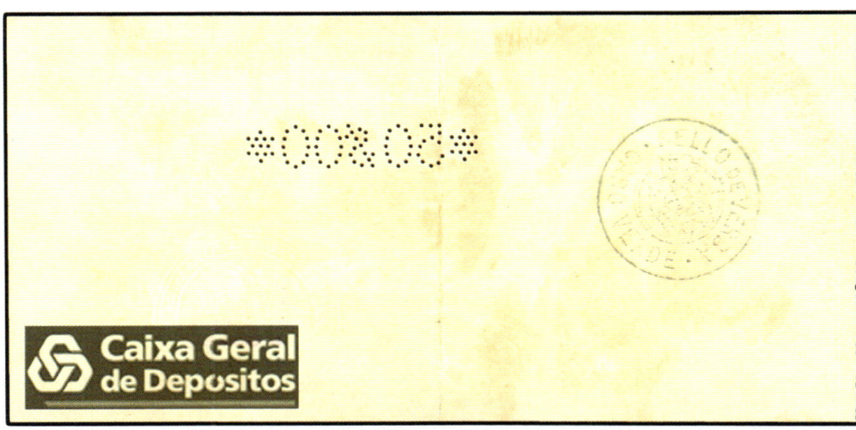

CV46	Start of Print Run	End of Print Run	VG	Fine	VF
a	Unknown	Unknown	Rare	Rare	Rare

CV47	**100 escudos**	30 June 1924	SCWPM unlisted
	Printer	Litografia E. Barrault, Lisboa	
	Total Printed	Unknown	
	Colour	Blue and white	
	Obverse Design	Steamship seal set in two ornate semi-ovals at left. Bank legend at upper centre and as microprint	
	Reverse Design	Uniface.	
	Size	165 x 80 mm	
	Signature	Fernando Arvelos as Gerente	

CV47a

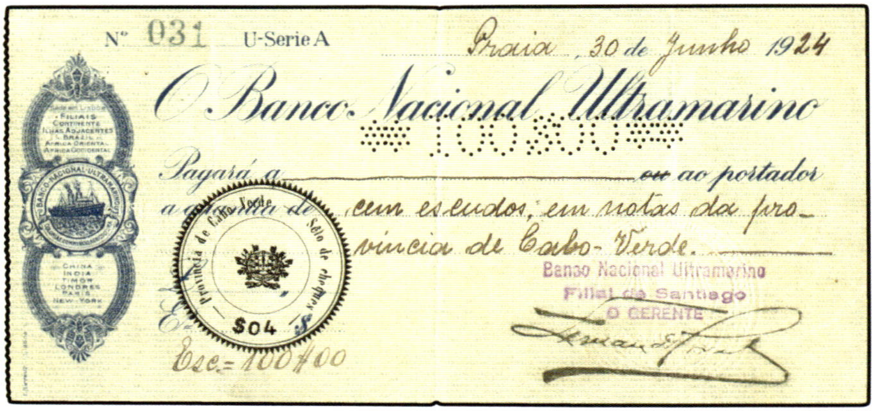

CV47a

CV47	Start of Print Run	End of Print Run	VG	Fine	VF
a	Unknown	Unknown	Rare	Rare	Rare

CV48	**500 escudos**	30 June 1924	SCWPM unlisted
	Printer	Litografia E. Barrault, Lisboa	
	Total Printed	Unknown	
	Colour	Blue and white	
	Obverse Design	Steamship seal set in two ornate semi-ovals at left. Bank legend at upper centre and as microprint	
	Reverse Design	Uniface.	
	Size	165 x 80 mm	
	Signature	Fernando Arvelos as Gerente	

CV48a

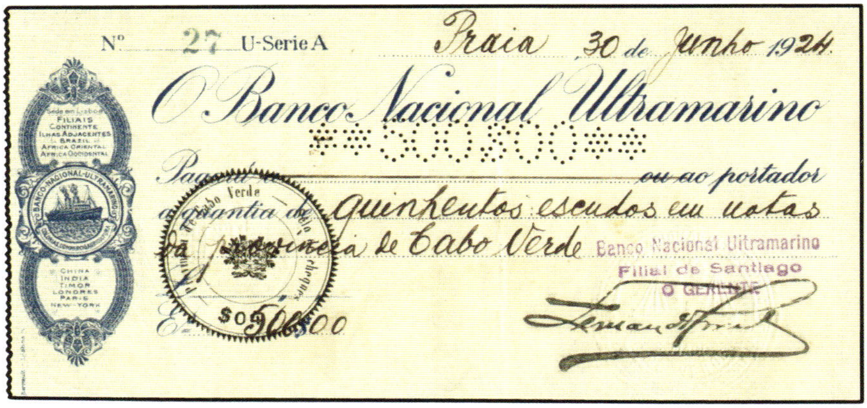

CV48a

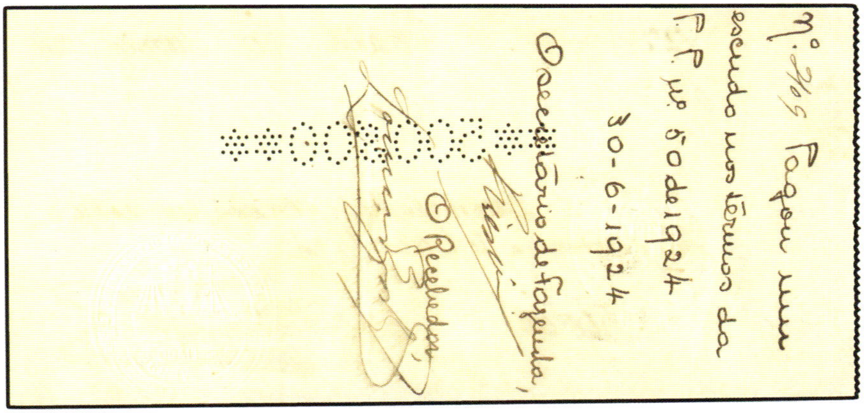

CV48	Start of Print Run	End of Print Run	VG	Fine	VF
a	Unknown	Unknown	Rare	Rare	Rare

CV49	**1000 escudos**	4 July 1924	SCWPM unlisted
	Printer	Litografia E. Barrault, Lisboa	
	Total Printed	Unknown	
	Colour	Blue and white	
	Obverse Design	Steamship seal set in two ornate semi-ovals at left. Bank legend at upper centre and as microprint	
	Reverse Design	Uniface.	
	Size	165 x 80 mm	
	Signature	Fernando Arvelos as Gerente	

CV49a

CV49a

CV49	Start of Print Run	End of Print Run	VG	Fine	VF
a	Unknown	Unknown	Rare	Rare	Rare

1932 PROVISIONAL ISSUE

CV50	**20 escudos**	ND (1932) - old date 1 January 1921	SCWPM 29
	Printer	Bradbury Wilkinson & Co. Ltd.	
	Overprint	"CABO VERDE" on Portuguese Guinea PG28 (SCWPM 16) with manuscript validation signature at upper right	
	Total Overprints	20000	
	Colour	Dark blue on multicoloured underprint	
	Obverse Design	Portrait of Francisco de Oliveira Chamiço at left, steamship seal at right	
	Reverse Design	Allegorical maiden looking at ships	
	Size	170 x 115 mm	
	Signatures	G7, VG14	

CV50a

CV50a

Issued Notes

CV50	Start of Print Run	End of Print Run	VG	Fine	VF
a	Unknown	Unknown	$2,800	Rare	Rare

CV51	**50 escudos**	ND (1932) - old date 1 January 1921	SCWPM 30
	Printer	Bradbury Wilkinson & Co. Ltd.	
	Overprint	"CABO VERDE" on Portuguese Guinea PG29 (SCWPM 17), with manuscript validation signature at upper right	
	Total Overprints	16000	
	Colour	Brownish-red on multicoloured underprint	
	Obverse Design	Portrait of Francisco de Oliveira Chamiço at left, steamship seal at right	
	Reverse Design	Allegorical maiden looking at ships	
	Size	185 x 120 mm	
	Signatures	G7, VG14	

CV51a

CV51a

Issued Notes

CV51	Start of Print Run	End of Print Run	VG	Fine	VF
a	Unknown	Unknown	$4,000	Rare	Rare

CV52	**100 escudos**	ND (1932) - old date 1 January 1921	SCWPM 31
	Printer	Bradbury Wilkinson & Co. Ltd.	
	Overprint	"CABO VERDE" on Portuguese Guinea PG30 (SCWPM 18), with manuscript validation signature at upper right	
	Total Overprints	8000	
	Colour	Slate-purple on multicoloured underprint	
	Obverse Design	Portrait of Francisco de Oliveira Chamiço at left, steamship seal at right	
	Reverse Design	Allegorical maiden looking at ships	
	Size	192 x 122 mm	
	Signatures	G7, VG14	

CV52a

CV52a

			Issued Notes		
CV52	Start of Print Run	End of Print Run	VG	Fine	VF
a	Unknown	Unknown	Rare	Rare	Rare

1941 CHAMIÇO ISSUE

CV53	**50 escudos**	1 August 1941	SCWPM 39
	Printer	Bradbury Wilkinson & Co. Ltd.	
	Total Printed	100000	
	Colour	Brownish-red on multicoloured underprint	
	Obverse Design	Portrait of Francisco de Oliveira Chamiço at left, steamship seal at right, red overprint CABO VERDE	
	Reverse Design	Allegorical maiden looking at ships	
	Size	185 x 120 mm	

CV53as

CV53	Start of Print Run	End of Print Run	Order Date (If Known)	Signatures	Issued Notes Fine	Issued Notes VF	Issued Notes EF	Archival Specimens AU	Specimens AU
a	A00001	A10000	26.7.41	PCA8, A25	$900	$2,000	Rare	$600	$500
b	A10001	A20000	26.7.41	PCA8, A29					
c	A20001	A30000	26.7.41	PCA8, A26					
d	A30001	A40000	26.7.41	PCA8, A19					
e	A40001	A50000	26.7.41	PCA8, A27					
f	A50001	A60000	26.7.41	PCA8, A26					
g	A60001	A70000	26.7.41	PCA8, A27					
h	A70001	A80000	26.7.41	PCA8, A29					
i	A80001	A90000	26.7.41	PCA8, A25					
j	A90001	A100000	26.7.41	PCA8, A19					

CV54 **100 escudos** 1 August 1941 SCWPM 40

Printer Bradbury Wilkinson & Co. Ltd.

Total Printed 50000

Colour Slate-purple on multicoloured underprint

Obverse Design Portrait of Francisco de Oliveira Chamiço at left, steamship seal at right, red overprint CABO VERDE

Reverse Design Allegorical maiden looking at ships

Size 192 x 122 mm

CV54as

					Issued Notes			Archival Specimens	Specimens
CV54	Start of Print Run	End of Print Run	Order Date (If Known)	Signatures	Fine	VF	EF	EF	AU
a	A00001	A05000	26.7.41	PCA8, A29	Rare	Rare	Rare	$700	$600
b	A05001	A10000	26.7.41	PCA8, A25					
c	A10001	A15000	26.7.41	PCA8, A19					
d	A15001	A20000	26.7.41	PCA8, A26					
e	A20001	A25000	26.7.41	PCA8, A27					
f	A25001	A30000	26.7.41	PCA8, A19					
g	A30001	A35000	26.7.41	PCA8, A26					
h	A35001	A40000	26.7.41	PCA8, A27					
i	A40001	A45000	26.7.41	PCA8, A29					
j	A45001	A50000	26.7.41	PCA8, A25					

CV54g

1945 DIAS ISSUE

Bartolomeu Dias (1450-1500) was a nobleman of the Portuguese royal household and in 1488 was the first European navigator to sail round the Cape of Good Hope, thus opening up the sea route to Mozambique and India. Later he used his maritime experience to assist in the construction of the ships used by Vasco da Gama in his 1497 voyage to India. He accompanied him on that voyage, but only on the first leg of the journey as far as the Cape Verde islands. His portrait appeared on the notes of the colony from 1945-1958.

Reverses of the Dias issue

CV55

CV56

CV57

CV58

CV59

CV60

CV55	**5 escudos**	16 November 1945	SCWPM 41
	Printer	Bradbury Wilkinson & Co. Ltd.	
	Total Printed	800000	
	Circulation	Withdrawn 30 September 1960	
	Colour	Deep grey-green and multicoloured	
	Obverse Design	Portrait of Bartolomeu Dias at right, steamship seal at left	
	Reverse Design	Allegorical maiden looking at ships	
	Size	140 x 75 mm	

CV55f

					Issued Notes			Archival Specimens	Specimens
CV55	Start of Print Run	End of Print Run	Order Date (If Known)	Signatures	VF	EF	Unc	EF	Unc
a	000001	100000	21.11.45	PCA8, A25					
b	100001	200000	21.11.45	PCA8, A18					
c	200001	300000	21.11.45	PCA8, A30					
d	300001	500000	21.11.45	PCA8, A26	$60	$200	$450	$220	$200
e	500001	600000	21.11.45	PCA8, A27					
f	600001	700000	21.11.45	PCA8, A29					
g	700001	800000	21.11.45	PCA8, A19					
ct	Specimen colour trial in purple on pale green underprint, overprinted SPECIMEN diagonally in red on obverse and SPECIMEN OF NO VALUE in red in top margin on reverse								Unc - $600
dp	Obverse and reverse die proof in issued colour deep grey-green								AU - $350 (pair)
p	Proof in issued colours deep grey-green and multicoloured, with large signatures PCA8, A26. Endorsed, "small signatures to be used" and hand-signed by PCA8a								One Copy Known

CV55p

CV55ct

CV55ct

CV56 **10 escudos** 16 November 1945 SCWPM 42

Printer	Bradbury Wilkinson & Co. Ltd.
Total Printed	500000
Circulation	Withdrawn 30 September 1960
Colour	Violet and multicoloured
Obverse Design	Portrait of Bartolomeu Dias at right, steamship seal at left
Reverse Design	Allegorical maider looking at ships
Size	146 x 77 mm

CV56f

						Issued Notes		Archival Specimens	Specimens
CV56	Start of Print Run	End of Print Run	Order Date (If Known)	Signatures	VF	EF	Unc	AU	AU
a	000001	070000	21.11.45	PCA8, A29					
b	070001	140000	21.11.45	PCA8, A30					
c	140001	210000	21.11.45	PCA8, A27					
d	210001	290000	21.11.45	PCA8, A18	$100	$250	$550	$300	$250
e	290001	360000	21.11.45	PCA8, A26					
f	360001	430000	21.11.45	PCA8, A19					
g	430001	500000	21.11.45	PCA8, A25					
ct	Specimen colour trial in purple on pale blue underprint, overprinted SPECIMEN diagonally in red on obverse and SPECIMEN OF NO VALUE in red in top margin on reverse								Unc - $650
dp	Obverse and reverse die proof in issued colour violet								AU - $350 (pair)
p	Proof in issued colours violet and multicoloured, with large signatures PCA8, A26. Endorsed, "small signatures to be used" and hand-signed by A18								One Copy Known

CV56dp

CV56p

CV57	**20 escudos**	16 November 1945 — SCWPM 43
	Printer	Bradbury Wilkinson & Co. Ltd.
	Total Printed	800000
	Circulation	Withdrawn 30 September 1960
	Colour	Green and multicoloured
	Obverse Design	Portrait of Bartolomeu Dias at right, steamship seal at left
	Reverse Design	Allegorical maiden looking at ships
	Size	151 x 80 mm

CV57h

					Issued Notes			Archival Specimens	Specimens
CV57	Start of Print Run	End of Print Run	Order Date (If Known)	Signatures	Fine	VF	EF	AU	AU
a	000001	050000	21.11.45	PCA8, A18	$120	$350	$800	$400	$350
b	050001	100000	21.11.45	PCA8, A27					
c	100001	140000	21.11.45	PCA8, A19					
d	140001	180000	21.11.45	PCA8, A29					
e	180001	220000	21.11.45	PCA8, A26					
f	220001	260000	21.11.45	PCA8, A25					
g	260001	300000	21.11.45	PCA8, A30					
h	300001	370000	7.4.48	PCA8, A30					
i	370001	450000	7.4.48	PCA8, A25					
j	450001	510000	7.4.48	PCA8, A26					
k	510001	600000	7.4.48	PCA8, A29					
l	600001	660000	7.4.48	PCA8, A19					
m	660001	740000	7.4.48	PCA8, A28					
n	740001	800000	7.4.48	PCA8, A18					
ct	Specimen colour trial in magenta on multicoloured underprint, overprinted SPECIMEN diagonally in red on obverse and SPECIMEN OF NO VALUE in red in top margin on reverse								Unc - $750
dp	Obverse and reverse die proof in issued colour green								AU - $400 (pair)
p	Proof in issued colours green and multicoloured, with large signatures PCA8, A26. Endorsed, "small signatures to be used" and hand-signed by PCA8a								One Copy Known

CV57ct

CV57ct

CV57dp

CV57p

CV58	**50 escudos**	16 November 1945	SCWPM 44
	Printer	Bradbury Wilkinson & Co. Ltd.	
	Total Printed	200000	
	Circulation	Withdrawn 30 September 1960	
	Colour	Blue and multicoloured	
	Obverse Design	Portrait of Bartolomeu Dias at right, steamship seal at left	
	Reverse Design	Allegorical maiden looking at ships	
	Size	156 x 82 mm	

CV58l

<table>
<tr><th colspan="5"></th><th colspan="3">Issued Notes</th><th>Archival Specimens</th><th>Specimens</th></tr>
<tr><th>CV58</th><th>Start of Print Run</th><th>End of Print Run</th><th>Order Date (If Known)</th><th>Signatures</th><th>Fine</th><th>VF</th><th>EF</th><th>EF</th><th>AU</th></tr>
<tr><td>a</td><td>000001</td><td>020000</td><td>21.11.45</td><td>PCA8, A19</td><td rowspan="14">$350</td><td rowspan="14">$900</td><td rowspan="14">Rare</td><td rowspan="14">$500</td><td rowspan="14">$450</td></tr>
<tr><td>b</td><td>020001</td><td>040000</td><td>21.11.45</td><td>PCA8, A25</td></tr>
<tr><td>c</td><td>040001</td><td>060000</td><td>21.11.45</td><td>PCA8, A26</td></tr>
<tr><td>d</td><td>060001</td><td>080000</td><td>21.11.45</td><td>PCA8, A30</td></tr>
<tr><td>e</td><td>080001</td><td>100000</td><td>21.11.45</td><td>PCA8, A18</td></tr>
<tr><td>f</td><td>100001</td><td>120000</td><td>21.11.45</td><td>PCA8, A27</td></tr>
<tr><td>g</td><td>120001</td><td>140000</td><td>21.11.45</td><td>PCA8, A29</td></tr>
<tr><td>h</td><td>140001</td><td>145000</td><td>7.4.48</td><td>PCA8, A29</td></tr>
<tr><td>i</td><td>145001</td><td>150000</td><td>7.4.48</td><td>PCA8, A18</td></tr>
<tr><td>j</td><td>155001</td><td>160000</td><td>7.4.48</td><td>PCA8, A30</td></tr>
<tr><td>k</td><td>160001</td><td>170000</td><td>7.4.48</td><td>PCA8, A26</td></tr>
<tr><td>l</td><td>170001</td><td>185000</td><td>7.4.48</td><td>PCA8, A25</td></tr>
<tr><td>m</td><td>185001</td><td>190000</td><td>7.4.48</td><td>PCA8, A19</td></tr>
<tr><td>n</td><td>190001</td><td>200000</td><td>7.4.48</td><td>PCA8, A28</td></tr>
<tr><td>ct</td><td colspan="8">Specimen colour trial in brown on pale blue underprint, overprinted SPECIMEN diagonally in red on obverse and SPECIMEN OF NO VALUE in red in top margin on reverse</td><td>Unc - $800</td></tr>
<tr><td>dp</td><td colspan="8">Obverse and reverse die proof in issued colour blue</td><td>AU - $450 (pair)</td></tr>
<tr><td>p</td><td colspan="8">Proof in issued colours blue and multicoloured, with large signatures PCA8, A26. Endorsed, “small signatures to be used” and hand-signed by PCA8a</td><td>One Copy Known</td></tr>
</table>

CV58dp

CV58p

CV59 **100 escudos** 16 November 1945 SCWPM 45

Printer	Bradbury Wilkinson & Co. Ltd.
Total Printed	150000
Circulation	Withdrawn 30 September 1960
Colour	Red and multicoloured
Obverse Design	Portrait of Bartolomeu Dias at right, steamship seal at left
Reverse Design	Allegorical maiden looking at ships
Size	161 x 85 mm

CV59m

					Issued Notes			Archival Specimens	Specimens
CV59	Start of Print Run	End of Print Run	Order Date (f Known)	Signatures	Fine	VF	EF	EF	AU
a	000001	010000	21.11.45	PCA8, A26					
b	010001	020000	21.11.45	PCA8, A19					
c	020001	030000	21.11.45	PCA8, A30					
d	030001	045000	21.11.45	PCA8, A27					
e	045001	060000	21.11.45	PCA8, A18					
f	060001	070000	21.11.45	PCA8, A25					
g	070001	080000	21.11.45	PCA8, A29					
h	080001	090000	7.4.48	PCA8, A19	$1,000	$2,500	Rare	$600	$550
i	090001	100000	7.4.48	PCA8, A28					
j	100001	115000	7.4.48	PCA8, A25					
k	115001	120000	7.4.48	PCA8, A26					
l	120001	130000	7.4.48	PCA8, A30					
m	130001	140000	7.4.48	PCA8, A18					
n	140001	150000	7.4.48	PCA8, A29					
ct	Specimen colour trial in deep green on orange underprint, overprinted SPECIMEN diagonally in red on obverse and SPECIMEN OF NO VALUE in red in top margin on reverse								Unc - $1000
dp	Obverse and reverse die proof in issued colour red								AU - $550 (pair)
p	Proof in issued colours red and multicoloured, with large signatures PCA8, A26. Endorsed, "small signatures to be used" and hand-signed by PCA8a								One Copy Known

CV59ct

CV59ct

CV59dp

CV59dp

CV59p

CV60	**500 escudos**	16 November 1945	SCWPM 46
	Printer	Bradbury Wilkinson & Co. Ltd.	
	Total Printed	30000	
	Circulation	Withdrawn 30 September 1960	
	Colour	Brown-violet and multicoloured	
	Obverse Design	Portrait of Bartolomeu Dias at right, steamship seal at left	
	Reverse Design	Allegorical young woman looking out at ships from various eras	
	Size	166 x 87 mm	

CV60as

					Issued Notes			Archival Specimens	Specimens
CV60	Start of Print Run	End of Print Run	Order Date (If Known)	Signatures	Fine	VF	EF	EF	AU
a	000001	005000	21.11.45	PCA8, A27					
b	005001	010000	21.11.45	PCA8, A18					
c	010001	015000	21.11.45	PCA8, A29					
d	015001	020000	21.11.45	PCA8, A25					
e	020001	021470	7.4.48	PCA8, A26					
f	021471	022880	7.4.48	PCA8, A19	Rare	Rare	Rare	$1,000	$800
g	022881	024300	7.4.48	PCA8, A30					
h	024301	025700	7.4.48	PCA8, A28					
i	025701	027120	7.4.48	PCA8, A18					
j	027121	028600	7.4.48	PCA8, A25					
k	028600	030000	7.4.48	PCA8, A29					
dp	Obverse and reverse die proof in issued colour brown-violet								AU - $750 (pair)
p	Proof in issued colours brown-violet and multicoloured, with large signatures PCA8, A26. Endorsed, “small signatures to be used” and hand-signed by PCA8a								One Copy Known

CV60dp

CV60dp

CV60p

1958 SERPA PINTO ISSUE

Alexandre Alberto da Rocha de Serpa Pinto, Viscount of Serpa Pinto (1846-1900) was a Portuguese explorer of southern Africa and colonial administrator. Born near Viseu in northern Portugal, at the age of ten he entered the Colégio Militar, a military school in Lisbon, which trained young men for service in Portugal's colonies. In 1864, the year of the founding of the BNU, he was sent to Mozambique, where he saw action as a soldier. From 1869 he took part in three major exploratory expeditions in southern Africa, with the aim of colonising a continuous stretch of territory linking Mozambique in the east with Angola in the west. The scramble for Africa by Portugal and other colonial powers led to opposition from the British and an ultimatum from them in 1890, which forced the Portuguese to withdraw. Serpa Pinto then returned to Portugal, dying there soon afterwards. World famous in his day, he is now largely forgotten, except in Portugal where his name lives on in streets named "Rua Serpa Pinto" throughout the country.

Reverses of the Serpa Pinto and Prince Henry Issues

CV61
and CV66

CV62
and CV67

CV63

CV64

CV65

CV61	**20 escudos**	16 June 1958	SCWPM 47
	Printer	Bradbury Wilkinson & Co. Ltd.	
	Total Printed	800000	
	Colour	Green and muticoloured	
	Obverse Design	Portrait of Serpa Pinto at right, ship seal at left	
	Reverse Design	Allegorical maiden looking at ships	
	Size	150 x 79 mm	

CV61fs

CV61	Start of Print Run	End of Print Run	Order Date (If Known)	Signatures	Issued Notes VG	Issued Notes VF	Issued Notes Unc	Archival Specimens EF	Specimens Unc
a	000001	135000	10.10.58	G9, A19	$15	$50	$200	$200	$180
b	135001	265000	10.10.58	G9, A36					
c	265001	400000	10.10.58	G9, A34					
d	400001	533000	10.10.58	G9, A37					
e	533001	660000	10.10.58	G9, A38					
f	660001	800000	10.10.58	G9, A35					
ct	Specimen colour trial in blue on multicoloured underprint, overprinted SPECIMEN diagonally in red on obverse								Unc - $225
dp	Obverse and reverse die proof in issued colour green								AU - $300 (pair)
p	Specimen proof in issued colours green on multiocoloured underprint, serial number 123456 at lower left and 789012 at upper right, signatures G9 and A34, one punch hole								Rare

CV61ct

CV61ct

CV61p

CV62	**50 escudos**	16 June 1958	SCWPM 48
	Printer	Bradbury Wilkinson & Co. Ltd.	
	Total Printed	500000	
	Colour	Blue and multicoloured	
	Obverse Design	Portrait of Serpa Pinto at right, ship seal at left	
	Reverse Design	Allegorical maiden looking at ships	
	Size	156 x 82 mm	

CV62fs

					Issued Notes			Archival Specimens	Specimens
CV62	Start of Print Run	End of Print Run	Order Date (If Known)	Signatures	VG	VF	Unc	EF	Unc
a	000001	080000	9.10.58	G9, A34	$30	$140	$500	$250	$225
b	080001	165000	9.10.58	G9, A37					
c	165001	250000	9.10.58	G9, A19					
d	250001	330000	9.10.58	G9, A38					
e	330001	410000	9.10.58	G9, A35					
f	410001	500000	9.10.58	G9, A36					
ct	Specimen colour trial in green on multicoloured underprint, overprinted SPECIMEN diagonally in red on obverse								Unc - $275
dp	Obverse and reverse die proof in issued colour blue								AU - $350 (pair)
p	Specimen proof in issued colours blue on multicoloured underprint, serial number 123456 at lower left and 789012 at upper right, signatures G9 and A34, one punch hole								Rare
ph	Black and white obverse and reverse archival photographs, dated 29. 08. 1958, of issued note dated 16 November 1945, serial number 000,000, signatures G8, A25								One Pair Known

CV62p

CV62ct

CV62ct

CV62ph

CV62ph

CV63	**100 escudos**	16 June 1958	SCWPM 49
	Printer	Bradbury Wilkinson & Co. Ltd.	
	Total Printed	1600000	
	Colour	Red and multicoloured	
	Obverse Design	Portrait of Serpa Pinto at right, ship seal at left	
	Reverse Design	Allegorical maiden looking at ships	
	Size	160 x 86 mm	

CV63as

					Issued Notes			Archival Specimens	Specimens
CV63	Start of Print Run	End of Print Run	Order Date (If Known)	Signatures	VG	VF	Unc	EF	Unc
a	000001	050000	9.10.58	G9, A37					
b	050001	100000	9.10.58	G9, A36					
c	100001	140000	9.10.58	G9, A35					
d	140001	195000	9.10.58	G9, A19					
e	195001	240000	9.10.58	G9, A38					
f	240001	300000	9.10.58	G9, A34					
g	300001	360000	10.5.66	G9, A38	$20	$70	$250	$180	$140
h	360001	420000	10.5.66	G9, A41					
i	420001	480000	10.5.66	G9, A36					
j	480001	540000	10.5.66	G9, A40					
k	540001	600000	10.5.66	G9, A37					
l	600001	1100000	10.5.75	G9, A38					
m	1100001	1600000	10.5.75	G9, A36					
ct	Specimen colour trial in brown on multicoloured underprint, overprinted SPECIMEN diagonally in red on obverse								Unc - $200
dp	Obverse and reverse die proof in issued colour red								AU - $350 (pair)
p	Specimen proof in issued colours brown on multicoloured underprint, serial number 123456 at lower left and 789012 at upper right, signatures G9 and A34, one punch hole								Rare

CV63p

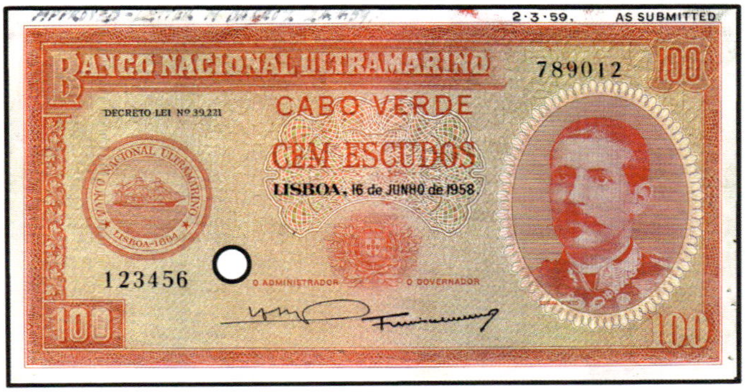

CV63ct

CV63ct

CV64	**500 escudos**	16 June 1958	SCWPM 50
	Printer	Bradbury Wilkinson & Co. Ltd.	
	Total Printed	500000	
	Colour	Brown-violet and multicoloured	
	Obverse Design	Portrait of Serpa Pinto at right, ship seal at left	
	Reverse Design	Allegorical maiden looking at ships	
	Size	166 x 86 mm	

CV64as

					Issued Notes			Archival Specimens	Specimens
CV64	Start of Print Run	End of Print Run	Order Date (If Known)	Signatures	VG	VF	Unc	AU	Unc
a	00001	08600	9.10.58	G9, A38					
b	08601	16300	9.10.58	G9, A35					
c	16301	24000	9.10.58	G9, A34					
d	24001	33000	9.10.58	G9, A38					
e	33001	40000	9.10.58	G9, A37					
f	40001	50000	9.10.58	G9, A19					
g	50001	60000	10.5.66	G9, A38					
h	60001	70000	10.5.66	G9, A41	$25	$90	$300	$250	$180
i	70001	80000	10.5.66	G9, A36					
j	80001	90000	10.5.66	G9, A40					
k	90001	100000	10.5.66	G9, A37					
l	100001	150000	10.5.66	G9, A38					
m	150001	200000	20.11.70	G9, A36					
n	200001	350000	23.4.75	G9, A38					
o	350001	500000	23.4.75	G9, A36					
ct	Specimen colour trial in red on multicoloured underprint, overprinted SPECIMEN diagonally in red on obverse								Unc - $275
dp	Obverse and reverse die proof in issued colour brown-violet								AU - $400 (pair)
p	Specimen proof in issued colours brown-violet and multicoloured, serial number 123456 at lower left and 789012 at upper right, signatures G9 and A34, one punch hole								Rare

CV64ct

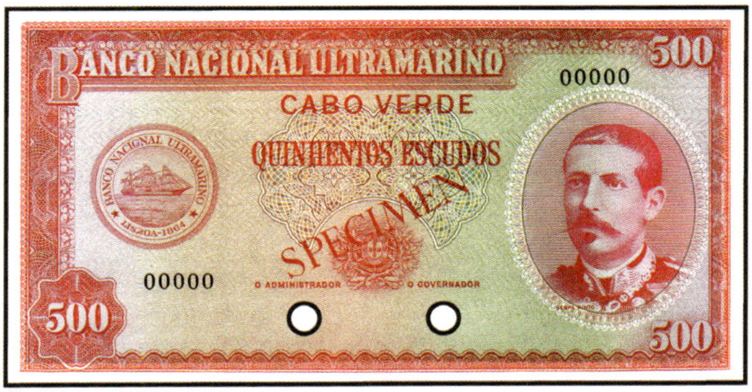

CV64ct

CV64p

1971 PRINCE HENRY ISSUE

Infante Dom Henrique of Portugal (aka Prince Henry the Navigator) (1394-1460) was an important figure in the early days of the Portuguese Empire, particularly through his initiation, administration and patronage of several major voyages of discovery in the mid-15th century. See also, "A Brief History of the Rise of the Portuguese Empire" on page 11, for a brief account of these early maritime voyages.

CV65	**500 escudos**	29 June 1971	SCWPM 53A
	Printer	Bradbury Wilkinson & Co. Ltd.	
	Total Printed	300000	
	Colour	Olive-green and multicoloured	
	Obverse Design	Portrait of Infante D. Henrique at right	
	Reverse Design	Allegorical maiden looking at ships	
	Watermark	Infante D. Henrique	
	Size	166 x 86 mm	

CV65as

					Issued Notes			Archival Specimens	Specimens
CV65	Start of Print Run	End of Print Run	Order Date (If Known)	Signatures	VG	VF	Unc	AU	Unc
a	000001	040000	4.1.72	G9, A38	$60	$200	$500	$450	$350
b	040001	080000	4.1.72	G9, A36					
c	080001	120000	4.1.72	G9, A44					
d	120001	160000	4.1.72	G9, A45					
e	160001	200000	4.1.72	G9, A43					
f	200001	250000	4.1.72	G9, A41					
g	250001	300000	4.1.72	G9, A42					
ct1	Colour trial proof, pale blue and multicoloured with star decoration at right on reverse, signatures G9 and A38, 000000 serial number, one punch hole								Rare
ct2	Colour trial proof, pale blue and multicoloured without star decoration at right on reverse, signatures G9 and A38, 000000 serial number, one punch hole								Rare
ct3	Colour trial in deep blue and multicoloured, signatures G9 and A45, overprinted SPECIMEN diagonally in red on obverse and reverse								Unc - $400
dp	Obverse and reverse die proof in issued colour olive green								AU - $600 (pair)

CV65ct1

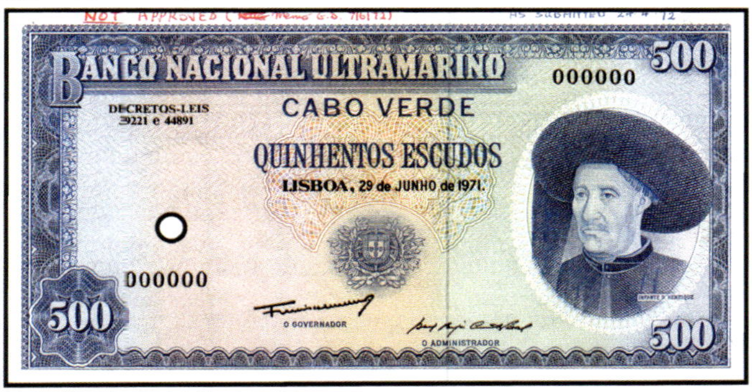

CV65ct1

CV65ct2

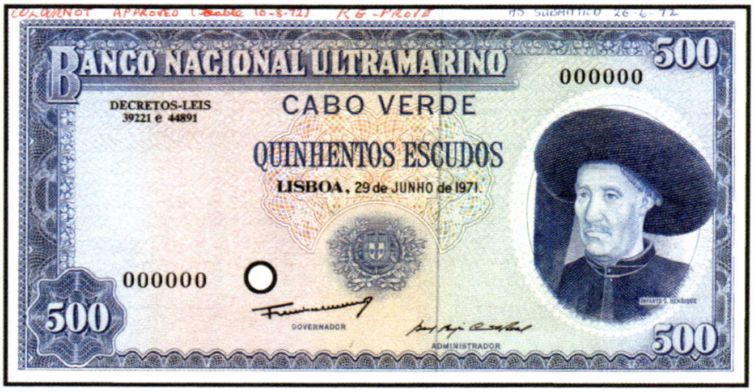

CV65ct2

CV65ct3

CV65ct3

1972 SERPA PINTO ISSUE

CV66	**20 escudos**	4 April 1972 — SCWPM 52
	Printer	Bradbury Wilkinson & Co. Ltd.
	Total Printed	1500000
	Colour	Green and multicoloured
	Obverse Design	Portrait of Serpa Pinto at right, ship seal at left
	Reverse Design	Allegorical maiden looking at ships
	Size	150 x 79 mm

CV66as

					Issued Notes			Archival Specimens	Specimens
CV66	Start of Print Run	End of Print Run	Order Date (If Known)	Signatures	VG	VF	Unc	EF	Unc
a	800001	1000000	6.6.72	VG27, A38					
b	1000001	1200000	6.6.72	VG27, A36					
c	1200001	1400000	6.6.72	VG27, A44					
d	1400001	1600000	6.6.72	VG27, A45	$10	$35	$180	$180	$160
e	1600001	1800000	6.6.72	VG27, A43					
f	1800001	2000000	6.6.72	VG27, A41					
g	2000001	2300000	6.6.72	VG27, A42					
p	Proof in issued colours green and multicoloured, no serial numbers, no signatures, no Decretos-Leis numbers								Rare

CV66p

CV67 **50 escudos** 4 April 1972 SCWPM 53

Printer Bradbury Wilkinson & Co. Ltd.

Total Printed 1200000

Colour Blue and multicoloured

Obverse design Portrait of Serpa Pinto at right, ship seal at left

Reverse Design Allegorical maiden looking at ships

Size 156 x 82 mm

CV67as

					Issued Notes			Archival Specimens	Specimens
CV67	Start of Print Run	End of Print Run	Order Date (If Known)	Signatures	VG	VF	Unc	EF	Unc
a	500001	600000	24.4.72	VG27, A38					
b	600001	700000	24.4.72	VG27, A36					
c	700001	900000	24.4.72	VG27, A44					
d	900001	1100000	24.4.72	VG27, A45	$12	$45	$220	$240	$200
e	1100001	1300000	24.4.72	VG27, A43					
f	1300001	1500000	24.4.72	VG27, A41					
g	1500001	1700000	24.4.72	VG27, A42					
p	Proof in issued colours blue and multicoloured, no serial numbers, no signatures, no Decretos-Leis numbers								Rare

CV67p

MOZAMBIQUE

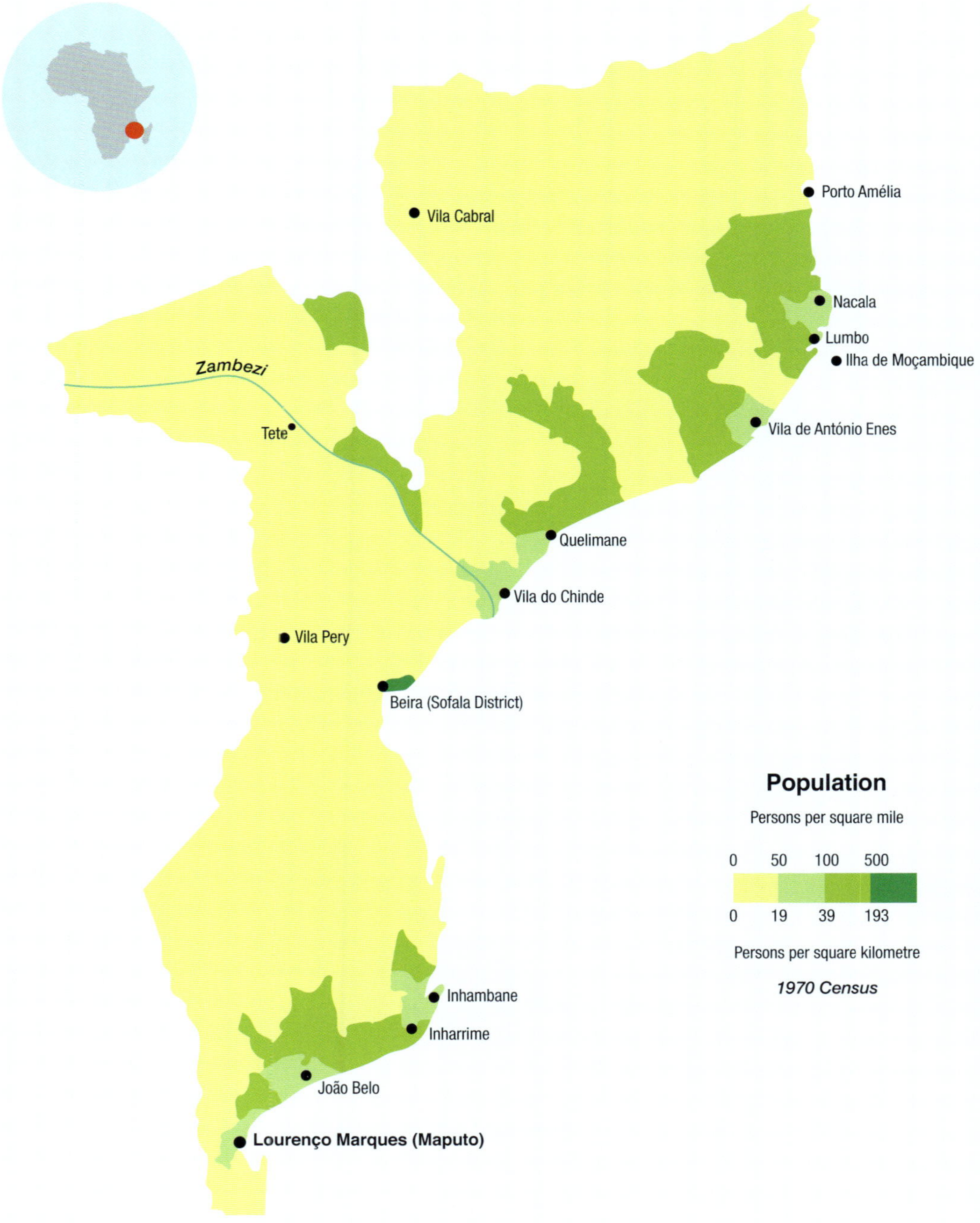
Porto Amélia
Vila Cabral
Nacala
Lumbo
Ilha de Moçambique
Zambezi
Tete
Vila de António Enes
Quelimane
Vila do Chinde
Vila Pery
Beira (Sofala District)
Population
Persons per square mile
0 50 100 500
0 19 39 193
Persons per square kilometre
1970 Census
Inhambane
Inharrime
João Belo
Lourenço Marques (Maputo)

INTRODUCTION

Portuguese Mozambique originally consisted of a group of settlements along the south eastern African coast. Vasco da Gama on his voyage to India discovered the mouth of the Zambezi River and then in March 1498 made landfall on the Ilha de Moçambique, a small coral island at the mouth of Mossuril Bay on the Nacala coast in the north of the country. Here in 1507 a settlement was established to serve as a way station to India. Meanwhile in 1500, Pedro Alvares Cabral (1467-1520) had landed at Sofala, also on his way to India, and a settlement was established there in 1502 with the purpose of exploiting the fabled gold trade in the empire of Mwene Matapa, which was centred far inland, in present day Zimbabwe. In order to further facilitate control of the gold trade, settlements were then established on the banks of the Zambezi at Sena and Tete, 160 and 260 miles upstream respectively. In 1544, Lourenço Marques, a Portuguese explorer and trader, founded a post at Quelimane to guard the river delta and the Portuguese began to trade at Inhambane and Maputo Bay, renamed Lourenço Marques Bay by King João III. Portuguese involvement with the gold trade brought them into conflict with the Arabs and the Swahili and a Jesuit mission in 1561 resulted in its leader being murdered. This led to the dispatch of an expedition from Lisbon in 1569 to seize the main gold mine at Mwene Matapa, which ended unsuccessfully in 1575. Nevertheless the Zambezi river valley and the Mwene Matapa area remained the focus of Portuguese attention until the 19th century.

In 1629, the Portuguese negotiated a vassalage treaty with Mavura, emperor of Mwane Matapa, who converted to Christianity and recognised the sovereignty of the king of Portugal. It led to the establishment of missionary and trading stations all the way into Central Africa. In 1752, Mozambique having been subordinated to the Portuguese administration in Goa, was separated and acquired its own governor. The slave trade became important during the 18th century, with demand coming from French slave traders in the Mascarene Islands and later from Brazil.

Until the early 20th century, Portugal never gained complete control of the interior, although prior to the Berlin Conference of 1884-5, it maintained rights based on the discovery of most of the African coast. The Berlin Conference established the doctrine of effective occupation with the result that colonial rule in the interior began in the 1890s, with complete control achieved after the Treaty of Versailles in 1919. Railway building led to a rapid growth of Mozambique's economy which was largely based on agriculture, cashew nuts, cotton, sugar, copra and tea being exported.

The BNU Ilha de Moçambique Branch. Address: Rua Alexandre Herculano with Travessa da Saudade.

In 1951 the colony was designated an overseas province of Portugal and this is reflected in the change in the description of Mozambique from a colony to a province on her paper money (e.g. compare MZ107 issued in 1950 and describing it as a colony with MZ109 issued in 1953 describing it as a province).

Nationalism came to the fore in the 1950s and evolved into an armed revolutionary force, known as Frelimo, led by Eduardo Mondlane (1920-69) in the 1960s. He was assassinated in 1969 and the cause was subsequently fronted by Samora Machel (1933-86). Portugal tried to stem the flow of nationalism by instigating various reforms, but it was too little, too late and the sheer cost of the war and opposition to the Portuguese government led to an army revolt in 1974. The continued rise in nationalism coincided with the 1974 Carnation Revolution in Portgual and resulted in Mozambique's independence in June 1975.

The BNU Lourenço Marques Branch. Address: Rua das Laranjeiras. Fourth installation. 1914 to 1958

The BNU opened its first Portuguese East African branch on Mozambique Island on 2nd April 1877. This island was initially the base for a factory and later became a fort, which ruled the colony from the early 17th century until 1898. At the same time the BNU provided the new branch with 18,000 notes of 5000 reis and 8,500 notes of 20,000 reis, which were sent from Lisbon, being the first Luanda issues of Angola overprinted "Payable in Mozambique". It is thought a certain number of notes of 10,000 reis from the same issue were also overprinted, but this requires confirmation (see MZ1-MZ3). The first issue specially designed for the branch were put in circulation on 29th January 1878 and notes were issued with various hand-written dates until 2nd January 1897 (see MZ4-MZ16).

At the same time the BNU operated an agency in Lourenço Marques, which closed briefly and was then reopened as a fully-fledged branch in 1883. Initially the new branch was supplied with notes from Mozambique Island overprinted, "Payable in Lourenço Marques". The increased traffic on the railways and the widening of commercial relations with the Transvaal led to an increase in circulation of the BNU's notes. So on 2nd January 1897, a year before the capital was transferred to Lourenço Marques, the BNU issued a new set of notes produced expressly for that town with a second issue dated 20th February 1906 (see MZ17-MZ23). Thereafter the BNU's omnibus African issues – the Vasco da Gama, Cedula and Chamiço series - were used with the overprint "LOURENÇO MARQUES" for the colony, until the Ennes series was released exclusively for Mozambique from 1937 (see MZ77-MZ106).

1877 PROVISIONAL ISSUE

MZ1 **5000 reis** 2 April 1877, partly hand-written. SCWPM 1

Printer	Chambers & Sons, London
Overprint	"PAGÁVAL EM MOÇAMBIQUE" on Angola AN1 (SCWPM 10)
Total Overprinted	18000
Circulation	Introduced 02. 04. 1877. 12000 withdrawn on 10. 04. 1884, remainder on 30. 09. 1907
Colour	Black
Obverse Design	Sailing ship at upper centre, value in figures in oval at upper right and in word in panel at lower left
Reverse Design	Uniface
Watermark	BANCO NACIONAL / ULTRAMARINO
Size	178 x 111 mm
Signatures	Facsimile signature of G1 and manuscript signatures of two managers

MZ1	Start of Print Run	End of Print Run	VG	Fine	VF
a	Unknown	Unknown	Rare	Rare	Rare

MZ2 **10000 reis** 2 April 1877, partly hand-written. SCWPM 1A

Printer	Chambers & Sons, London
Overprint	"PAGÁVAL EM MOÇAMBIQUE" on Angola AN2 (SCWPM 11)
Total Overprinted	Unknown
Circulation	Unknown
Colour	Black
Obverse Design	Sailing ship at upper centre, value in figures in oval at upper right and in word in panel at lower left
Reverse Design	Uniface
Watermark	BANCO NACIONAL / ULTRAMARINO
Size	178 x 111 mm
Signatures	Facsimile signature of G1 and manuscript signatures of two managers

MZ2	Start of Print Run	End of Print Run	VG	Fine	VF
a	Unknown	Unknown	Rare	Rare	Rare

N.B. No copies of this note have been traced and it is unclear whether it was ever issued

MZ3 **20000 reis** 2 April 1877, partly hand-written. SCWPM 2

Printer	Chambers & Sons, London
Overprint	"PAGÁVAL EM MOÇAMBIQUE" on Angola AN3 (SCWPM 12)
Total Overprinted	8500
Circulation	Introduced 02. 04. 1877. 7750 withdrawn on 10. 04. 1884, remainder on 15. 12. 1899
Colour	Black
Obverse Design	Sailing ship at upper centre, value in figures in oval at upper right and in word in panel at lower left
Reverse Design	Uniface
Watermark	BANCO NACIONAL / ULTRAMARINO
Size	178 x 111 mm
Signatures	Facsimile signature of G1 and manuscript signatures of two managers

MZ3	Start of Print Run	End of Print Run	VG	Fine	VF
a	Unknown	Unknown	Rare	Rare	Rare

1877-84 ISSUES

With text 'Succursal em Moçambque' (Island of Mozambique Branch)

MZ4	**1000 reis**	a. 20 March 1877, b. 29 January 1878, c. 28 January 1884 and possibly other dates, all partly hand-written	SCWPM 3 and 9
	Printer	Nissen & Arnold, London	
	Total Printed	40000	
	Circulation	Introduced 29. 01. 1878. Withdrawn 06. 04. 1909	
	Colour	Green	
	Obverse Design	Sailing ship at upper centre, value in figures at left and right and in words at lower centre	
	Reverse Design	Decorated rectangular panel with micro-lettering	
	Watermark	SUCCARSAL DO / 1$00 / BANCO NACIONAL / ULTRAMARINO	
	Size	173 x 120 mm	
	Signatures	Facsimile signature of G1 and manuscript signatures of two managers	

MZ4a

MZ4a

MZ4	Start of Print Run	End of Print Run	VG	Fine	VF
a 1877	Unknown	Unknown	Rare	Rare	Rare
b 1878	Unknown	Unknown	Rare	Rare	Rare
c 1884	Unknown	Unknown	$10,000	Rare	Rare

MZ4c

MZ5 **2000 reis** a. 20 March 1877, b. 29 January 1878 and c. 28 January 1884 and possibly other dates, all partly hand-written — SCWPM 4 and unlisted

Printer Nissen & Arnold, London

Total Printed 30000

Circulation Introduced 29. 01. 1878. Withdrawn 06. 04. 1909

Colour Blue-green

Obverse Design Sailing ship at upper centre, value in figures at left and right and in words at lower centre

Reverse Design Decorated rectangular panel with micro-lettering

Watermark SUCCARSAL DO / 2$00 / BANCO NACIONAL / ULTRAMARINO

Size 173 x 120 mm

Signatures Facsimile signature of G1 and manuscript signatures of two managers

MZ5	Start of Print Run	End of Print Run	VG	Fine	VF
a 1877	Unknown	Unknown	Rare	Rare	Rare
b 1878	Unknown	Unknown	Rare	Rare	Rare
c 1884	Unknown	Unknown	Rare	Rare	Rare

MZ6 **2500 reis** a. 20 March 1877, b. 29 January 1878 and c. 28 January 1884 and possibly other dates, all partly hand-written — SCWPM 5 and unlisted

Printer Nissen & Arnold, London

Total Printed 20000

Circulation Introduced 29. 01. 1878. Withdrawn 06. 04. 1909

Colour Purple

Obverse Design Sailing ship at upper centre, value in figures at left and right and in words at lower centre

Reverse Design Decorated rectangular panel with micro-lettering

Watermark SUCCARSAL DO / 2$50 / BANCO NACIONAL / ULTRAMARINO

Size 173 x 120 mm (unconfirmed)

Signatures Facsimile signature of G1 and manuscript signatures of two managers

MZ6a

MZ6a

v

MZ6	Start of Print Run	End of Print Run	VG	Fine	VF
a 1877	Unknown	Unknown	Rare	Rare	Rare
b 1878	Unknown	Unknown	Rare	Rare	Rare
c 1884	Unknown	Unknown	Rare	Rare	Rare

MZ7	**5000 reis**	a. 29 January 1878 and b. 28 January 1884 and possibly other dates, all partly hand-written	SCWPM 6 and unlisted
	Printer	Nissen & Arnold, London	
	Total Printed	10000	
	Circulation	Introduced 29. 01. 1878. Withdrawn 06. 04. 1909	
	Colour	Blue	
	Obverse Design	Sailing ship at upper centre, value in figures at left and right and in words at lower centre	
	Reverse Design	Decorated rectangular panel with micro-lettering	
	Watermark	SUCCARSAL DO / 5$00 / BANCO NACIONAL / ULTRAMARINO	
	Size	173 x 120 mm (unconfirmed)	
	Signatures	Facsimile signature of G1 and manuscript signatures of two managers	

MZ7	Start of Print Run	End of Print Run	VG	Fine	VF
a 1878	Unknown	Unknown	Rare	Rare	Rare
b 1884	Unknown	Unknown	Rare	Rare	Rare

MZ8	**10000 reis**	a. 29 January 1878 and b. 28 January 1884 and possibly other dates, all partly hand-written				SCWPM 7 and unlisted
	Printer	Nissen & Arnold, London				
	Total Printed	10000				
	Circulation	Introduced 29. 01. 1878. Withdrawn 06. 04. 1909				
	Colour	Unknown				
	Obverse Design	Sailing ship at upper centre, value in figures at left and right and in words at lower centre				
	Reverse Design	Decorated rectangular panel with micro-lettering				
	Watermark	SUCCARSAL DO / 10$00 / BANCO NACIONAL / ULTRAMARINO				
	Size	173 x 120 mm (unconfirmed)				
	Signatures	Facsimile signature of G1 and manuscript signatures of two managers				

MZ8	Start of Print Run	End of Print Run	VG	Fine	VF
a 1878	Unknown	Unknown	Rare	Rare	Rare
b 1884	Unknown	Unknown	Rare	Rare	Rare

MZ9	**20000 reis**	a. 29 January 1878 and b. 28 January 1884 and possibly other dates, all partly hand-written				SCWPM 8 and unlisted
	Printer	Nissen & Arnold, London				
	Total Printed	10000				
	Circulation	Introduced 29. 01. 1878. Withdrawn 06. 04. 1909				
	Colour	Unknown				
	Obverse Design	Sailing ship at upper centre, value in figures at left and right and in words at lower centre				
	Reverse Design	Decorated rectangular panel with micro-lettering				
	Watermark	SUCCARSAL DO / 20$00 / BANCO NACIONAL / ULTRAMARINO				
	Size	173 x 120 mm (unconfirmed)				
	Signatures	Facsimile signature of G1 and manuscript signatures of two managers				

MZ9	Start of Print Run	End of Print Run	VG	Fine	VF
a 1878	Unknown	Unknown	Rare	Rare	Rare
b 1884	Unknown	Unknown	Rare	Rare	Rare

1897 FIRST ISSUE

With text 'Succursal em Moçambque' (Island of Mozambique Branch)

MZ10	**1000 reis**	2 January 1897	SCWPM 9
	Printer	Casa da Moeda, Lisbon	
	Total Printed	6500	
	Circulation	Withdrawn 17. 02. 1912	
	Colour	Orange-brown	
	Obverse Design	Man with bow and arrows at left, sailing ship at centre, elephant's head, arms at upper left	
	Reverse Design	Bank name and value in words and figures	
	Watermark	Unknown	
	Size	125 x 91 mm	
	Signatures	G3, VG6 or VG8 and manuscript signatures of one or two managers	

MZ10a

MZ10a

MZ10 a	Start of Print Run	End of Print Run	VG	Fine	VF
	Unknown	Unknown	$10,000	Rare	Rare

MZ11	**2000 reis**	2 January 1897	SCWPM 10
	Printer	Casa da Moeda, Lisbon	
	Total Printed	Unknown	
	Circulation	Withdrawn 17. 02. 1912	
	Colour	Unknown	
	Obverse Design	Unknown	
	Reverse Design	Unknown	
	Watermark	Unknown	
	Size	Unknown	
	Signatures	G3, VG6 or VG8 and manuscript signatures of one or two managers	

MZ11 a	Start of Print Run	End of Print Run	VG	Fine	VF
	Unknown	Unknown	Rare	Rare	Rare

MZ12 **2500 reis** 2 January 1897 SCWPM 11
Printer Casa da Moeda, Lisbon
Total Printed 12500
Circulation Withdrawn 17. 02. 1912
Colour Mauve and black
Obverse Design Steamship at left, field at centre, woman standing at centre right
Reverse Design Large winged vessel, waves, seadogs and seaweed
Watermark Unknown
Size 170 x 125 mm
Signatures G3, VG6 or VG8 and manuscript signatures of one or two managers

MZ12	Start of Print Run	End of Print Run	VG	Fine	VF
a	Unknown	Unknown	$12,000	Rare	Rare
s	specimen, serial number 000,000		Rare	Rare	Rare

MZ13 **5000 reis** 2 January 1897 SCWPM 12
Printer Casa da Moeda, Lisbon
Total Printed 10000
Circulation Withdrawn 17. 02. 1912
Colour Obverse blue, reverse brown
Obverse Design Bush set in columns at left, seated woman holding caduceus, steamship and flora at right
Reverse Design Bank name and value in foliate surround
Watermark Unknown
Size 170 x 125 mm
Signatures G3, VG6 or VG8 and manuscript signatures of one or two managers

MZ13	Start of Print Run	End of Print Run	VG	Fine	VF
a	Unknown	Unknown	Rare	Rare	Rare

MZ14 10000 reis 2 January 1897 SCWPM 13
Printer Casa da Moeda, Lisbon
Total Printed 5000
Circulation Withdrawn 17. 02. 1912
Colour Blue-green. Reverse green
Obverse Design Woman representing agriculture at left, steamship at centre, Mercury at right
Reverse Design Bank name and value in foliate surround
Watermark Unknown
Size 170 x 125 mm
Signatures G3, VG6 or VG8 and manuscript signatures of one or two managers

MZ14a

MZ14a

MZ14	Start of Print Run	End of Print Run	VG	Fine	VF
a	Unknown	Unknown	Rare	Rare	Rare

MZ15 **20000 reis** 2 January 1897 SCWPM 14

Printer Casa da Moeda, Lisbon
Total Printed 17500
Circulation Withdrawn 17. 02. 1912
Colour Unknown
Obverse Design Unknown
Reverse Design Unknown
Watermark Unknown
Size Unknown
Signatures G3, VG6 or VG8 and manuscript signatures of one or two managers

MZ15	Start of Print Run	End of Print Run	VG	Fine	VF
a	Unknown	Unknown	Rare	Rare	Rare

MZ16 **50000 reis** 2 January 1897 SCWPM 15

Printer Casa da Moeda, Lisbon
Total Printed Unknown
Circulation Withdrawn 17. 02. 1912
Colour Red-orange
Obverse Design Reclining figure of Mercury with caduceus at centre, steamship at upper left, elephant and lion at lower left, arms at top centre
Reverse Design Value in words at centre, trident, seashells and fish
Watermark Unknown
Size 198 x 140 mm
Signatures G3, VG6 or VG8 and manuscript signatures of one or two managers

MZ16	Start of Print Run	End of Print Run	VG	Fine	VF
a	Unknown	Unknown	Rare	Rare	Rare

1897 SECOND ISSUE AND 1906 ISSUE

With text 'Succursal em Lourenço Marques' (Lourenço Marques Branch)

MZ17 **1000 reis** a. 2 January 1897, b. 20 February 1906 SCWPM 16 and 23

Printer	Casa da Moeda, Lisbon
Total Printed	Unknown
Circulation	Withdrawn 17. 02. 1912
Colour	Purple. Reverse olive-green
Obverse Design	Man with bow and arrows at left, sailing ship at centre, elephant's head, arms at upper left
Reverse Design	Bank name and value in words and figures
Watermark	Unknown
Size	125 x 91 mm
Signatures	G3, VG6 or VG8 and manuscript signatures of one or two managers

MZ17b

MZ17b

MZ17	Start of Print Run	End of Print Run	VG	Fine	VF
a 1897	Unknown	Unknown	$6,000	from $9,000	Rare
b 1906	Unknown	Unknown	$5,000	from $8,000	Rare

MZ18 **2000 reis** a. 2 January 1897, b. 20 February 1906 SCWPM 17 and 24

Printer Casa da Moeda, Lisbon

Total Printed Unknown

Circulation Withdrawn 17. 02. 1912

Colour Unknown

Obverse Design Unknown

Reverse Design Unknown

Watermark Unknown

Size Unknown

Signatures G3, VG6 or VG8 and manuscript signatures of one or two managers

MZ18	Start of Print Run	End of Print Run	VG	Fine	VF
a 1897	Unknown	Unknown	Rare	Rare	Rare
b 1906	Unknown	Unknown	Rare	Rare	Rare

MZ19 **2500 reis** a. 2 January 1897, b. 20 February 1906 SCWPM 18 and 25

Printer Casa da Moeda, Lisbon

Total Printed Unknown

Circulation Withdrawn 17. 02. 1912

Colour Greyish blue

Obverse Design Steamship at left, field at centre, woman standing at centre right

Reverse Design Large winged vessel, waves, seadogs and seaweed

Watermark Unknown

Size 170 x 125 mm

Signatures G3, VG6 or VG8 and manuscript signatures of one or two managers

MZ19a

MZ19a

MZ19	Start of Print Run	End of Print Run	VG	Fine	VF
a 1897	Unknown	Unknown	Rare	Rare	Rare
b 1906	Unknown	Unknown	Rare	Rare	Rare

MZ20 **5000 reis** a. 2 January 1897, b. 20 February 1906 SCWPM 19 and 26

Printer	Casa da Moeda, Lisbon
Total Printed	Unknown
Circulation	Withdrawn 17. 02. 1912
Colour	Greyish blue. Reverse bistre
Obverse Design	Bush set in columns at left, seated woman holding caduceus, steamship and flora at right
Reverse Design	Bank name and value in floral surround
Watermark	Unknown
Size	170 x 125 mm
Signatures	G3, VG6 or VG8 and manuscript signatures of one or two managers

MZ20b

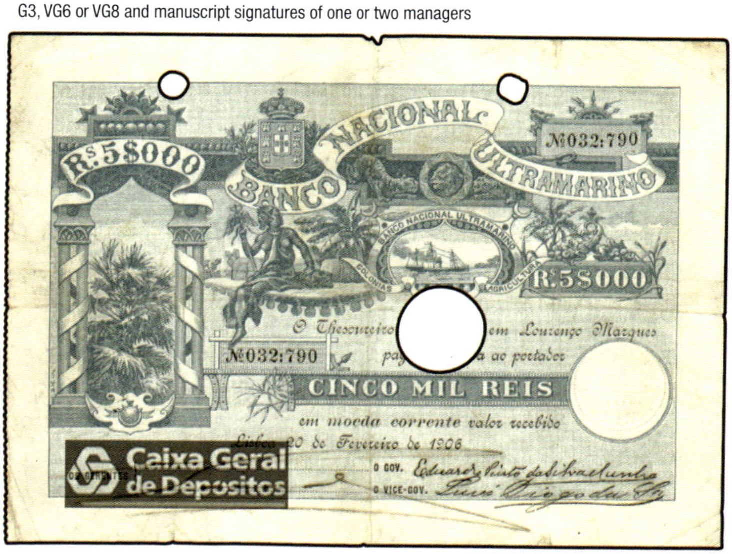

MZ20b

MZ20	Start of Print Run	End of Print Run	VG	Fine	VF
a 1897	Unknown	Unknown	Rare	Rare	Rare
b 1906	Unknown	Unknown	Rare	Rare	Rare

MZ21 **10000 reis** a. 2 January 1897, b. 20 February 1906 SCWPM 19 and 26

Printer Casa da Moeda, Lisbon

Total Printed Unknown

Circulation Withdrawn 17. 02. 1912

Colour Blue-green. Reverse green

Obverse Design Woman representing agriculture at left, steamship at centre, Mercury at right

Reverse Design Bank name and value in floral surround

Watermark Unknown

Size 170 x 125 mm

Signatures G3, VG6 or VG8 and manuscript signatures of one or two managers

MZ21	Start of Print Run	End of Print Run	VG	Fine	VF
a 1897	Unknown	Unknown	Rare	Rare	Rare
b 1906	Unknown	Unknown	Rare	Rare	Rare

MZ22 **20000 reis** a. 2 January 1897, b. 20 February 1906 SCWPM 21 and 28

Printer Casa da Moeda, Lisbon

Total Printed Unknown

Circulation Withdrawn 17. 02. 1912

Colour Unknown

Obverse Design Unknown

Reverse Design Unknown

Watermark Unknown

Size Unknown

Signatures G3, VG6 or VG8 and manuscript signatures of one or two managers

MZ22	Start of Print Run	End of Print Run	VG	Fine	VF
a 1897	Unknown	Unknown	Rare	Rare	Rare
b 1906	Unknown	Unknown	Rare	Rare	Rare

MZ23	**50000 reis**	a. 2 January 1897, b. 20 February 1906	SCWPM 21 and 28
	Printer	Casa da Moeda, Lisbon	
	Total Printed	Unknown	
	Circulation	Withdrawn 17. 02. 1912	
	Colour	Red-orange	
	Obverse Design	Reclining figure of Mercury with caduceus at centre, steamship at upper left, elephant and lion at lower left, arms at top centre	
	Reverse Design	Value in words at centre, trident, caduceus, seashells and fish	
	Watermark	Unknown	
	Size	198 x 140 mm	
	Signatures	G3, VG6 or VG8 and manuscript signatures of one or two managers	

MZ23b

MZ23b

MZ23	Start of Print Run	End of Print Run	VG	Fine	VF
a 1897	Unknown	Unknown	Rare	Rare	Rare
b 1906	Unknown	Unknown	Rare	Rare	Rare

INTRODUCTION TO THE VASCO DA GAMA ISSUES

By the Law of 27 April 1901, a new legal framework for banking activity in the Portuguese Colonial Empire was established. The new legislation divided banking operations into two groups; the issuance of paper money and the grant of loans secured by real estate. Although the banknote issue was open to competitive tendering, each colony could only have one bank and the BNU was the only bidder for Mozambique and the other four Portuguese African colonies. Under this new contract, the BNU prepared a new issue of notes, which were known as the Vasco da Gama Issue.

In the meantime, before the notes of the new issue had been released, the BNU was authorised to leave in circulation for some time the previous issues and increase the amount in circulation, repeating the designs of 1897, which circulated during the interval with the date 20 February 1906.

The notes issued under the new contract represented silver in denominations of 2$500 and 5$000 reis and were dated 2 January 1908. In addition specimens were prepared for a 1$000 reis note representing copper and 10$000, 20$000 and 50$000 reis notes representing silver. However the Governor of the BNU, Eduardo Pinto da Silva e Cunha (G3) retired on 15 February 1909 and was replaced by Antonio Teixeira de Sousa (G4), so the additional denominations dated 1908 were never issued. Many of the surviving specimens were only discovered in 2014 and all are of the utmost rarity. With the date of 1 March 1909, more notes of 2$500 and 5$000 reis were issued signed by the new Governor (G4) together with notes of 1$000, 10$000, 20$000 and 50$000 reis. All of the issued notes also bear the manuscript or facsimile signature of a manager. Two types of steamship seal were used: the earlier issues used Type 1 and the later issues used Type 3.

See also "A Summary of the Main Banknote Issues of the Banco Nacional Ultramarino" on page 7 and "A Brief History of the Rise of the Portuguese Empire" on page 11 for further information on Vasco da Gama.

Steamship Seal Type 1

Steamship Seal Type 3

Reverses of the Vasco da Gama Issues

MZ24, MZ30 and MZ31

MZ25, MZ32 and MZ33

MZ26, MZ34 and MZ35

MZ27, MZ36 and MZ37

MZ28, MZ38 and MZ39

MZ29, MZ40 and MZ41

1908 VASCO DE GAMA ISSUE

MZ24	**1000 reis**	2 January 1908	SCWPM unlisted
	Printer	Bradbury Wilkinson & Co. Ltd.	
	Total Printed	Specimens only	
	Circulation	Specimens only	
	Colour	Black on green and yellow underprint	
	Obverse Design	Value in guilloches, crowned arms at upper right, overprint LOURENÇO MARQUES	
	Reverse Design	Allegorical maiden looking at ships	
	Size	138 x 80 mm	
	Signatures	G3, VG8	
	Ship seal	Type 1	

MZ24s1

s1	Specimen with counterfoil, no serial numbers, perforated CANCELLED. Believed only two copies known	AU - $3,000
s2	Specimen with counterfoil, hand-written serial numbers 000000 in red, perforated CANCELLED. Believed one copy known	Fine - $1,500
aw	Obverse artwork on pale blue carton paper in pencil, black and red ink, value at left, blank red seal at right	Unique
ph1	Sepia and white obverse photograph, Lisboa 190--, no signatures, serial number 00000 with LOURENÇO MARQUES in larger capitals than issued note	one copy known
ph2	Sepia and white reverse photograph, with crowned arms in circle set in entwined acanthus leaves	one copy known

MZ24aw

MZ24ph1

MZ24ph2

MZ25	2 January 1908	SCWPM 30
Printer	Bradbury Wilkinson & Co. Ltd.	
Total Printed	130000	
Circulation	Withdrawn 27. 07. 1922	
Colour	Black on green and yellow underprint. Reverse blue	
Obverse Design	Vasco da Gama and his passage round The Cape, overprint LOURENÇO MARQUES	
Reverse Design	Allegorical maiden looking at ships	
Size	148 x 94 mm	
Signatures	G3, VG6 or VG8 or VG9	
Ship seal	Type 1	

MZ25a

MZ25	Start of Print Run	End of Print Run	Order Date (If Known)	Good	Fine	EF
a	000001	130000	September 1909	$450	$1,250	Rare
s1	Specimen with counterfoil, one cancelled No at centre, No and red manuscript serial number 000000 at upper centre right, perforated CANCELLED. Believed one copy known					Fine - $1,250
s2	Specimen with counterfoil, one cancelled No at centre, No and red manuscript serial number 000000 at upper centre right, perforated SPECIMEN. Believed one copy known					VF - $1,800
s3	Specimen with counterfoil, no serial numbers, one No at lower left centre and one No at upper centre right, perforated SPECIMEN. Believed two copies known					AU - $2,500
s4	Specimen with counterfoil, no serial numbers, one No only at upper centre right, perforated SPECIMEN. Believed three copies known					AU - $2,500

MZ25s2

MZ26	5 mil reis	2 January 1908	SCWPM 31
	Printer	Bradbury Wilkinson & Co. Ltd.	
	Total Printed	150000*	
	Circulation	Withdrawn 27. 07. 1922	
	Colour	Black on blue and multicoloured underprint. Reverse green	
	Obverse Design	Vasco da Gama and his passage round The Cape, overprint LOURENÇO MARQUES	
	Reverse Design	Allegorical maiden looking at ships	
	Size	160 x 100 mm	
	Ship Seal	Type 1	

MZ26a

MZ26	Start of Print Run	End of Print Run	Order Date (If Known)	Signatures	Good	Fine	EF
a	000001	040000*		G3, VG8	$450	$1,250	Rare
b	040001*	080000*		G3, VG6			
c	080001*	120000*		G3, VG9			
d	120001*	150000		G3, VG6			
s1	Specimen with counterfoil, one cancelled No at lower left centre, one No and manuscript red serial number No 000000 at upper centre perforated CANCELLED. Believed one copy known						Fine - $1,250
s2	Specimen with counterfoil, one cancelled No at lower left centre, No and red manuscript serial number 000000 at upper centre and upper right, perforated SPECIMEN. Believed one copy known						VF - $1,800
s3	Specimen with counterfoil, no serial numbers, one No at lower left centre and one No at upper right, perforated SPECIMEN. Believed two copies known						UNC - $2,500
s4	Specimen with counterfoil, no serial numbers, one No only at upper right, perforated SPECIMEN. Believed three copies known						UNC - $2,500
ct1	Uniface obverse specimen colour trial in unknown colours						EF - $2,000
ct2	Uniface reverse specimen colour trial in dark brown on green underprint						EF - $1,000

MZ26s3

MZ26ct2

MZ27	**10 mil reis**	2 January 1908	SCWPM unlisted
	Printer	Bradbury Wilkinson & Co. Ltd.	
	Total Printed	Specimens only	
	Circulation	Specimens only	
	Colour	Black on yellow and multicoloured underprint. Reverse brown	
	Obverse Design	Vasco da Gama and his passage round the Cape, overprint LOURENÇO MARQUES	
	Reverse Design	Allegorical maiden looking at ships	
	Size	175 x 105 mm	
	Signatures	G3, VG8	
	Ship seal	Type 1	

MZ27s3

s1	Specimen with counterfoil, one cancelled No at upper left centre, one No and manuscript red serial number 000000 at upper centre perforated SPECIMEN. Believed one copy known	EF - $3,500
s2	Specimen with counterfoil, one cancelled No at upper left centre, No and red manuscript serial number 000000 at upper centre and upper right, perforated CANCELLED. Believed one copy known	Fine - $1,500
s3	Specimen with counterfoil, no serial numbers, one No at upper left centre and one No at upper right, perforated SPECIMEN. Believed only two copies known	AU - $3,500
ct1	Uniface obverse specimen colour trial in black on yellow and pink underprint, orange ship seal	EF - $3,000
ct2	Uniface reverse specimen colour trial in aqua on yellow underprint	AU - $1,000

MZ27ct1

MZ27ct2

MZ28	**20 mil reis**	2 January 1908	SCWPM unlisted
	Printer	Bradbury Wilkinson & Co. Ltd.	
	Total Printed	Specimens only	
	Circulation	Specimens only	
	Colour	Black on blue and yellow underprint. Reverse brown-red and orange	
	Obverse Design	Vasco de Gama and his embarkation, overprint LOURENÇO MARQUES	
	Reverse Design	Allegorical maiden looking at ships	
	Size	180 x 112 mm	
	Signatures	G3, VG8	
	Ship seal	Type 1	

MZ28s1

s1	Specimen with counterfoil, no serial numbers. Believed one copy known	AU - $4,500
s2	Specimen with counterfoil, red manuscript serial number 000000 at upper centre and upper right, perforated CANCELLED. Believed one copy known	Fine - $1,800
ct1	Uniface obverse specimen colour trial in black on pale purple and pale green underprint, purple ship seal	EF - $4,000
ct2	Uniface reverse specimen colour trial in brown on green underprint	AU - $1,200

MZ28ct1

MZ28ct2

MZ29	**50 mil reis**	2 January 1908	SCWPM 32A
	Printer	Bradbury Wilkinson & Co. Ltd.	
	Total Printed	Specimens only	
	Circulation	Specimens only	
	Colour	Black on yellow, green and multicoloured underprint. Reverse green, blue, yellow and pink	
	Obverse Design	Vasco de Gama and his embarkation, overprint LOURENÇO MARQUES	
	Reverse Design	Allegorical maiden looking at ships	
	Size	198 x 120 mm	
	Signatures	G3, VG8	
	Ship seal	Type 1	

MZ29s2

s1	Specimen with counterfoil, no serial numbers, perforated SPECIMEN. Believed only two copies known	EF - $6,000
s2	Specimen with counterfoil, with red manuscript serial number 000000 at upper centre left and upper centre right, perforated SPECIMEN. Believed one copy known	VF - $4,500
ct1	Uniface obverse specimen colour trial with counterfoil, no serial numbers, in black on yellow, blue and pink underprint, blue figure '50' at centre, whitened steamship seal	AU - $5,000
ct2	Uniface obverse specimen colour trial with counterfoil, no serial numbers, in black on yellow, blue and pink underprint, green figure '50' at centre, green steamship seal	AU - $5,000
ct3	Uniface reverse specimen colour trial in brown-red on olive-green and yellow underprint	EF - $1,500
ct4	Uniface reverse specimen colour trial in blue-green and purple	EF - $1,500

MZ29ct1

MZ29ct3

MZ29ct4

1909 VASCO DE GAMA ISSUE

MZ30 **1000 reis** 1 March 1909 SCWPM 32

Printer	Bradbury Wilkinson & Co. Ltd.
Total Printed	1250000
Circulation	Withdrawn 27. 07. 1922
Colour	Black on green and yellow underprint
Obverse Design	Value in guilloches, crowned arms at upper right, overprint LOURENÇO MARQUES
Reverse Design	Allegorical maiden looking at ships
Size	138 x 80 mm
Ship Seal	Type 1

MZ30f

					Issued Notes			Archival Specimens
MZ30	Start of Print Run	End of Print Run	Order Date (If Known)	Signatures	VG	VF	Unc	AU
a	00001	25000*		G4, VG9	$90	$300	$1,500	$550
b	25001*	50000*		G4, VG6*	$60	$200	$1,000	$450
c	50001	83333	"Delivered Aug 1910"	G4, VG9	$90	$300	$1,500	$550
d	83334	116667		G4, VG6	$60	$200	$1,000	$450
e	116668	150000		G4, VG10				
f	150001	183333	October 1911	G4, VG9	$90	$300	$1500	$550
g	183334	216667	12 Oct 1911	G4, VG6	$60	$200	$1000	$450
h	216668	250000		G4 VG10	$90	$300	$1500	$550
i	250001	283333	Oct 1913	G4, VG9				
j	283334	316666		G4, VG6				
k	316667	350000		G4, VG10				
l	350001	400000	7. 11.14	G4, VG6				
m	400001	450000	7.11.14*	G4, VG10				
n	450001	500000	10.2.16	G4, VG6				
o	500001	550000	10.2.16	G4, VG10				
p	550001	600000	3.7.16	G4, VG6				
q	600001	650000	3.7.16	G4, VG10				
r	650001	700000	7.5.17	G4, VG6	$60	$200	$1000	$450
s	700001	750000	7.5.17	G4, VG10				
t	750001	800000	15.11.17	G4, VG6				
u	800001	850000	15.11.17	G4, VG10				
v	850001	900000	17.4.18	G4, VG6				
w	900001	950000	17.4.18	G4, VG10				
x	950001	1000000	28.5.18	G4, VG6				
y	1000001	1050000	28.5.18	G4, VG10				
z1	1050001	1150000	26.8.18	G4, VG6				
z2	1150001	1250000	26.8.18	G4, VG10				

MZ31 **1000 reis** 1 March 1909 SCWPM 33

Printer Bradbury Wilkinson & Co. Ltd.
Total Printed 1050000
Circulation Withdrawn 27. 07. 1922
Colour Black on green and yellow underprint
Obverse Design Value in guilloches, crowned arms at upper right, overprint LOURENÇO MARQUES
Reverse Design Allegorical maiden looking at ships
Size 138 x 80 mm
Ship Seal Type 3

MZ31fs

MZ31	Start of Print Run	End of Print Run	Order Date (If Known)	Signatures	Issued Notes VG	Issued Notes VF	Issued Notes Unc	Archival Specimens AU
a	1250001	1380000		G4, VG6				
b	1380001	1550000*		G4, VG10				
c	1550001*	1575000	23.4.20*	G4, VG6				
d	1575001	1600000	23.4.20	G4, VG10	$60	$200	$1,000	$500
e	1600001	1850000	18.5.20	G4, VG6				
f	1850001	2100000	18.5.20	G4, VG10				
g	2100001	2200000	11.8.21	G4, VG6				
h	2200001	2300000	11.8.21	G4, VG10				

MZ32	**2500 reis**	1 March 1909	SCWPM 34
	Printer	Bradbury Wilkinson & Co. Ltd.	
	Total Printed	430000	
	Circulation	Withdrawn 27. 07. 1922	
	Colour	Black on green and yellow underprint. Reverse blue	
	Obverse Design	Vasco da Gama and his passage round The Cape, overprint LOURENÇO MARQUES	
	Reverse Design	Allegorical maiden looking at ships	
	Size	148 x 94 mm	
	Ship Seal	Type 1	

MZ32es

					Issued Notes			Archival Specimens
MZ32	Start of Print Run	End of Print Run	Order Date (If Known)	Signatures	Good	Fine	EF	AU
a	130001	260000		G4, VG11	$750	$1,750	Rare	$1,000
b	260001	390000		G4, VG9	$300	$850	$1,800	$700
c	390001	520000	Sept 1909	G4, VG6				
d	520001	540000	3.9.19	G4, VG6	$250	$700	$1,600	$600
e	540001	560000	3.9.19	G4, VG10				

MZ33	**2500 reis**	1 March 1909	SCWPM 35
	Printer	Bradbury Wilkinson & Co. Ltd.	
	Total Printed	120000	
	Circulation	Withdrawn 27. 07. 1922	
	Colour	Black on green and yellow underprint. Reverse blue	
	Obverse Design	Vasco da Gama and his passage round The Cape, overprint LOURENÇO MARQUES	
	Reverse Design	Allegorical maiden ooking at ships	
	Size	148 x 94 mm	
	Ship Seal	Type 3	

MZ33a

					Issued Notes			Archival Specimens
MZ33	Start of Print Run	End of Print Run	Order Date (If Known)	Signatures	Good	Fine	EF	AU
a	560001	610000	18.5.20	G4, VG6				
b	610001	660000	18.5.20	G4, VG10	$250	$700	$1,600	$700
c	660001	680000	11.8.21	G4, VG6				

MZ34	**5 mil reis**	1 March 1909
	Printer	Bradbury Wilkinson & Co. Ltd.
	Total Printed	110000*
	Circulation	Withdrawn 27. 07. 1922
	Colour	Black on blue and multicoloured underprint. Reverse green
	Obverse Design	Vasco da Gama and his passage round The Cape, overprint LOURENÇO MARQUES
	Reverse Design	Allegorical maiden looking at ships
	Size	160 x 100 mm
	Ship Seal	Type 1

SCWPM 36

MZ34es
(large signatures)

MZ34gs
(small signatures)

					Issued Notes			Archival Specimens
MZ34	Start of Print Run	End of Print Run	Order Date (If Known)	Signatures	Good	Fine	EF	AU
a	150001*	170000*		G4, VG11	$750	$1,750	Rare	$1,200
b	170001*	190000*		G4, VG9*	$325	$850	Rare	$800
c	190001*	200000		G4, VG6*				
d	200001	210000	15.11.17*	G4, VG10				
e	210001	220000	15.11.17	G4, VG10	$275	$750	$1,700	$650
f	220001	240000	3.9.19	G4, VG6				
g	240001	260000	3.9.19	G4, VG10				

N.B. For the 5 mil reis note there are two types of Governor signature G4 and Vice Governor signature VG10. The small versions are 33 mm and 32 mm long respectively and the large versions are 41 mm and 43 mm long respectively.

MZ35	**5 mil reis**	1 March 1909	SCWPM 37
	Printer	Bradbury Wilkinson & Co. Ltd.	
	Total Printed	130000	
	Circulation	Withdrawn 27. 07. 1922	
	Colour	Black on blue and multicoloured underprint. Reverse green	
	Obverse Design	Vasco da Gama and his passage round The Cape, overprint LOURENÇO MARQUES	
	Reverse Design	Allegorical maiden looking at ships	
	Size	160 x 100 mm	
	Ship Seal	Type 3	

MZ35f

					Issued Notes			Archival Specimens
MZ35	Start of Print Run	End of Print Run	Order Date (If Known)	Signatures	Good	Fine	EF	AU
a	260001	270000	30.1.20	G4, VG6	$275	$750	$1,700	$650
b	270001	280000	30.1.20	G4, VG10				
c	280001	290000	23.4.20	G4, VG6				
d	290001	300000	23.4.20*	G4, VG10				
e	300001	325000	18.5.20	G4, VG6				
f	325001	350000	18.5.20	G4, VG10				
g	350001	370000*	13.6.21*	G4, VG6				
h	370001	390000	13.6.21	G4, VG10				

MZ36	**10 mil reis**	1 March 1909	SCWPM 38
	Printer	Bradbury Wilkinson & Co. Ltd.	
	Total Printed	160000	
	Circulation	Withdrawn 27. 07. 1922	
	Colour	Black on yellow and multicoloured underprint. Reverse brown	
	Obverse Design	Vasco da Gama and his passage round The Cape, overprint LOURENÇO MARQUES	
	Reverse Design	Allegorical maiden looking at ships	
	Size	175 x 105 mm	
	Ship Seal	Type 1	

MZ36js

					Issued Notes			Archival Specimens
MZ36	Start of Print Run	End of Print Run	Order Date (If Known)	Signatures	Good	Fine	EF	AU
a	00001	17500	Sept 1909	G4, VG11	$1,500	$3,500	Rare	$1,400
b-h	Information missing for several issues. It is possible that some or all of these notes may have been in the ship sunk by the Germans in 1915 and not subsequently reprinted.							
i	70001	77500	5.10.15	G4, VG6				
j	70001	77500	marked 'Reprint. Originals sunk by Germans'	G4, VG6				
k	77501	85000	5.10.15	G4, VG10				
l	77501	85000	marked 'Reprint. Originals sunk by Germans'	G4, VG10	$500	$1,250	Rare	$850
m	85001	90000	13.2.17	G4, VG6				
n	90001	95000	13.2.17	G4 VG10				
o	95001	102500	15.11.17	G4, VG6				
p	102501	110000	15.11.17	G4, VG10				
q	110001	135000	3.9.19	G4, VG6				
r	135001	160000	3.9.19	G4, VG10				

MZ37	**10 mil reis**	1 March 1909	SCWPM 39
	Printer	Bradbury Wilkinson & Co. Ltd.	
	Total Printed	45000	
	Circulation	Withdrawn 27. 07. 1922	
	Colour	Black on yellow and multicoloured underprint. Reverse brown	
	Obverse Design	Vasco da Gama and his passage round The Cape, overprint LOURENÇO MARQUES	
	Reverse Design	Allegorical maiden looking at ships	
	Size	175 x 105 mm	
	Ship Seal	Type 3	

MZ37cs

MZ37	Start of Print Run	End of Print Run	Order Date (If Known)	Signatures	Issued Notes Good	Issued Notes Fine	Issued Notes EF	Archival Specimens AU
a	160001	170000	23.4.20	G4, VG6				
b	170001	180000		G4, VG10	$500	$1,250	Rare	$950
c	180001	205000	18.5.20	G4, VG6				

MZ38	**20 mil reis**	1 March 1909	SCWPM 40
	Printer	Bradbury Wilkinson & Co. Ltd.	
	Total Printed	172000	
	Circulation	Withdrawn 27. 07. 1922	
	Colour	Black on blue and yellow underprint. Reverse brown-red and orange	
	Obverse Design	Vasco de Gama and his embarkation, overprint LOURENÇO MARQUES	
	Reverse Design	Allegorical maiden looking at ships	
	Size	180 x 112 mm	
	Ship Seal	Type 1	

MZ38w

					Issued Notes			Archival Specimens
MZ38	Start of Print Run	End of Print Run	Order Date (If Known)	Signatures	Good	Fine	EF	AU
a	00001	08750		G4, VG11	$2,750	$6,000	Rare	$1,600
b	08751	17500	Sept 1909	G4, VG9	$1,600	$3,500	Rare	$1,000
c	17501	35000*		G4, Unknown	$1,000	$2,500	Rare	$900
d	35001	38333		G4, VG9	$1,600	$3,500	Rare	$1,000
e	38334	41667	delivered 1910	G4, VG6	$1000	$2500	Rare	$900
f	41668	45000		G4, VG10				
g	45001	48333	October 1911	G4, VG9	$1600	$3500	Rare	$1,000
h	48334	51666*		G4, VG6*	$1000	$2500	Rare	$900
i	51667	55000		G4, VG10				
j	55001	65000	21.7.15	G4, VG6				
k	65001	75000		G4, VG10				
l	75001	82500*		G4, VG6*				
m	82501	90000	17.5.16	G4, VG10				
n	90001	95000*		G4, VG6				
o	95001	100000	13.2.17	G4, VG10				
p	100001	105000	14.6.17	G4, VG6				
q	105001	110000	14.6.17	G4, VG10				
r	110001	116000	15.11.17	G4, VG6				
s	116001	122000*		G4, VG10				
t	122001	134500	15.10.18	G4, VG6				
u	134501	147000	15.10.18	G4, VG10				
v	147001	159500	3.9.19	G4, VG6				
w	159501	172000	3.9.19	G4, VG10				

MZ39	**20 mil reis**	1 March 1909 — SCWPM 41
	Printer	Bradbury Wilkinson & Co. Ltd.
	Total Printed	70000
	Circulation	Withdrawn 27. 07. 1922
	Colour	Black on blue and yellow underprint. Reverse brown-red and orange
	Obverse Design	Vasco de Gama and his embarkation, overprint LOURENÇO MARQUES
	Reverse Design	Allegorical maiden looking at ships
	Size	180 x 112 mm
	Ship Seal	Type 3

MZ39as

					Issued Notes			Archival Specimens
MZ39	Start of Print Run	End of Print Run	Order Date (If Known)	Signatures	Good	Fine	EF	AU
a	172001	182000	23.4.20	G4, VG6				
b	182001	192000	23.4.20	G4, VG10	$1,000	$2,500	Rare	$1,000
c	192001	217000*	18.5.20*	G4, VG6				
d	217001	242000	18.5.20	G4, VG10				

MZ40	**50 mil reis**	1 March 1909	SCWPM 42
	Printer	Bradbury Wilkinson & Co. Ltd.	
	Total Printed	82000	
	Circulation	Withdrawn 27. 07. 1922	
	Colour	Black on yellow, green and multicoloured underprint. Reverse green, blue, yellow and pink	
	Obverse Design	Vasco de Gama and his embarkation, overprint LOURENÇO MARQUES	
	Reverse Design	Allegorical maiden looking at ships	
	Size	198 x 120 mm	
	Ship Seal	Type 1	

MZ40gs

MZ40	Start of Print Run	End of Print Run	Order Date (If Known)	Signatures	Issued Notes Good	Issued Notes Fine	Issued Notes EF	Archival Specimens AU
a	0001	1500	Sept 1909	G4, VG11	Rare	Rare	Rare	$2,500
b	1501	3000*		G4, Unknown				
c	3001*	4500*		G4, Unknown	Rare	Rare	Rare	$1,600
d	4501*	6000		G4, Unknown				
e	6001	7500		G4, VG6	Rare	Rare	Rare	$1,400
f	7501	9000	Oct 1911	G4, VG10				
g	9001	10000	Oct 1913	G4, VG9	Rare	Rare	Rare	$1,600
h	10001	11000		G4, VG6	Rare	Rare	Rare	$1,400
i	11001	12000		G4, VG10				
j	12001	13333	25.11.15	G4, VG9	Rare	Rare	Rare	$1,600
k	13334	14666		G4, VG6				
l	14667	16000		G4, VG10				
m	16001	19000	17. 5. 16	G4, VG6				
n	19001	22000	17. 5. 16	G4, VG10				
o	22001	24500	13.2.17*	G4, VG6				
p	24501	27000	13.2.17	G4, VG10				
q	27001	29500	14. 6. 17	G4, VG6				
r	29501	32000	14. 6. 17	G4, VG10	Rare	Rare	Rare	$1,400
s	32001	37000	15.11.17	G4, VG6				
t	37001	42000	15.11.17	G4, VG10				
u	42001	52000	28.5.18*	G4, VG6				
v	52001	62000	28.5.18	G4, VG10				
w	62001	67000	15.10.18	G4, VG6				
x	67001	72000	15.10.18	G4, VG10				
y	72001	77000	3. 9. 19	G4, VG6				
z	77001	82000	3. 9. 19	G4, VG10				

MZ41 **50 mil reis** 1 March 1909 SCWPM 43

Printer Bradbury Wilkinson & Co. Ltd.

Total Printed 137000

Circulation Withdrawn 27. 07. 1922

Colour Black on yellow, green and multicoloured underprint. Reverse green, blue, yellow and pink

Obverse Design Vasco de Gama and his embarkation, overprint LOURENÇO MARQUES

Reverse Design Allegorical maiden looking at ships

Size 198 x 120 mm

Ship Sea Type 3

MZ41ds

MZ41	Start of Print Run	End of Print Run	Order Date (If Known)	Signatures	Issued Notes Good	Issued Notes Fine	Issued Notes EF	Archival Specimens EF
a	82001	85000	30. 1. 20	G4, VG6	Rare	Rare	Rare	$1,600
b	85001	89000	30. 1. 20	G4, VG10				
c	89001	154000	5. 2. 20	G4, VG6				
d	154001	219000	5. 2. 20	G4, VG10				

INTRODUCTION TO THE LIBRA ESTERLINA ISSUES

Long before the regularisation of the currency in Mozambique, the pound sterling already circulated there. This was not surprising, because the western boundary of the Colony adjoined British colonies and the commerce of the south of the Colony was centred on its ports (particularly Lourenço Marques), which primarily used the gold sovereign as its currency.

The decree which authorised the Libra Issue of 1 April 1905 stated: "The convenience of allowing the circulation of gold in the Province of Mozambique must be recognised and opportunely the increase in the availability of gold in the district of Lourenço Marques, thus seeking to facilitate commercial transactions." Accordingly notes representing 1, 5 and 10 pounds sterling were issued simultaneously with the Vasco da Gama issues. The first 1 pound and 5 pound notes were, like the first Vasco da Gama notes, dated 2 January 1908. However the Governor of the BNU, Eduardo Pinto da Silva e Cunha (G3) retired on 15 February 1909 and was replaced by Antonio Teixeira de Sousa (G4) and these two notes with the 1908 date are only known as very rare specimens. No examples of the 10 pound notes dated 1908 are known. The 20 pound note only ever circulated later from 1929 with a 1000 escudo surcharge (see MZ75), although one or two very rare specimens are known (see MZ50). All the issued notes also bear the manuscript or facsimile signature of a manager. The Libra notes were convertible into gold at BNU branches and changeable for gold coins or bank drafts at all dependencies of the Bank of Mozambique. The issue in circulation at any one time was initially not to exceed 50,000 pounds and the BNU had to maintain a reserve of gold equivalent at least to one third of the total value of the notes in circulation.

Two different types of steamship seal were used, Types 1 and 3 (see Introduction to the Vasco da Gama Issues).

Reverses of the Libra Esterlina Issues

MZ42, MZ44 and MZ45

MZ43, MZ46 and MZ47

MZ48 and MZ49

MZ50

1908 LIBRA ESTERLINA ISSUE

MZ42	**1 libra esterlina**	2 January 1908	SCWPM unlisted
	Printer	Bradbury Wilkinson & Co. Ltd.	
	Total Printed	Specimens only	
	Circulation	Specimens only	
	Colour	Black and blue on yellow underprint	
	Obverse Design	Value at lower centre and in guilloche at left, arms at top centre, steamship seal at right	
	Reverse Design	Brown, value in words in ornate guilloche	
	Size	136 x 75 mm	
	Signatures	G3, VG8	
	Ship seal	Type 1	

MZ42s2

s1	Specimen with counterfoil, no serial numbers, perforated SPECIMEN. Believed two copies known	AU - $3,000
s2	Specimen with counterfoil, hand-written serial numbers 000000 in red, peforated SPECIMEN. Believed one copy known	EF - $2,200
p	Reverse proof in brown with £1 oro in diamond guioches at left and right and 'UNA LIBRA ESTERLINA' in central circular guioche. Believed one copy known	VF - $500
ph1	Obverse and reverse sepia and white archival photographs, with counterfoil, 'UMA LIVRA ESTERLINA' on obverse and reverse, serial number 000000	One Pair Known
ph2	Obverse and reverse sepia and white archival photographs with ''UMA LIBRA ESTERLINA' on obverse and reverse, 19--, serial number 00000	One Pair Known

MZ42p

MZ42ph1

MZ42ph1

MZ42ph2

MZ42ph2

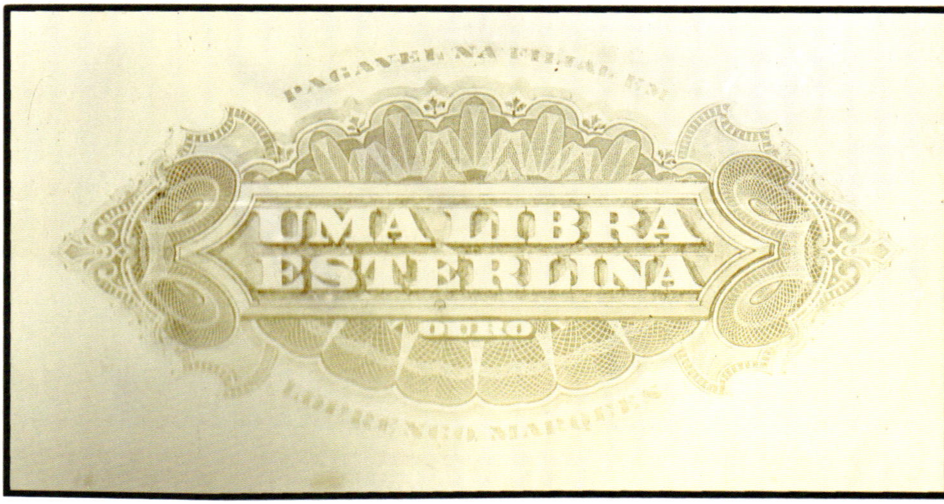

MZ43	**5 libras esterlinas**	2 January 1908	SCWPM unlisted
	Printer	Bradbury Wilkinson & Co. Ltd.	
	Total Printed	Specimens only	
	Circulation	Specimens only	
	Colour	Black on blue, orange and yellow underprint	
	Obverse Design	Value at centre and in guilloche at left, arms at right, steamship seal at lower centre	
	Reverse Design	Green, value in words in ornate guilloche	
	Size	158 x 90 mm	
	Signatures	G3, VG8	
	Ship seal	Type 1	

MZ43s2

s1	Specimen with counterfoil, no serial numbers, perforated SPECIMEN. Believed only two copies known	AU - $4,500
s2	Specimen with counterfoil, hand-written serial numbers 000000 in red, peforated SPECIMEN. Believed one copy known	VF - $2,500
ph1	Reverse sepia and white archival photographs, with counterfoil, 'CINCO LIVRAS ESTERLINAS' in guilloche	One Copy Known
ph2	Obverse and reverse sepia and white archival photographs with "CINCO LIBRAS ESTERLINAS' on obverse and reverse, 19--, serial number 00000	One Pair Known

MZ43ph1

MZ43ph2

MZ43ph2

1909 LIBRA ESTERLINA ISSUE

MZ44 **1 libra esterlina** 1 March 1909 SCWPM 44

Printer Bradbury Wilkinson & Co. Ltd.

Total Printed 83000

Circulation Withdrawn 01. 04. 1926

Colour Black and blue on yellow underprint

Obverse Design Value at lower centre and in guilloche at left, arms at top centre, steamship seal at right

Reverse Design Brown, value in words in ornate guilloche

Size 136 x 75 mm

Ship Seal Type 1

MZ44js

					Issued Notes			Archival Specimens
MZ44	Start of Print Run	End of Print Run	Order Date (If Known)	Signatures	Good	Fine	EF	AU
a	00001*	Unknown		G4, VG11*	$600	$1,500	Rare	$1,000
b-h	information missing for several issues			G4, Unknown	---	---	---	---
i	27001*	30000		G4, VG10				
j	30001	33000	21. 3. 16	G4, VG10	$200	$500	$1,200	$700
k	33001	83000	5. 6. 18	G4, VG10				

MZ45 **1 libra esterlina** 1 March 1909 SCWPM 45

Printer	Bradbury Wilkinson & Co. Ltd.
Total Printed	500000*
Circulation	Withdrawn 01. 04. 1926
Colour	Black and blue on yellow underprint
Obverse Design	Value at lower centre and in guilloche at left, arms at top centre, steamship seal at right
Reverse Design	Brown, value in words in ornate guilloche
Size	136 x 75 mm
Ship Seal	Type 3

MZ45as

MZ45	Start of Print Run	End of Print Run	Order Date (If Known)	Signatures	Issued Notes Good	Fine	EF	Archival Specimens AU
a	83001	133000	22.12.19	G4, VG10				
b	133001	183000	28.11.20	G4, VG10				
c	183001	283000*		G4, VG10*	$200	$500	$1,200	$700
d	283001*	383000		G4, VG10*				
e	383001	483000	7.8.23	G4, VG10				
f	483001	583000*		G4, VG10				

MZ46 **5 libras esterlinas** 1 March 1909 SCWPM 46

Printer	Bradbury Wilkinson & Co. Ltd.
Total Printed	26000
Circulation	Withdrawn 01. 04. 1926
Colour	Black on blue, orange and yellow underprint
Obverse Design	Value at centre and in guilloche at left, arms at right, steamship seal at lower centre
Reverse Design	Green, value in words in ornate guilloche
Size	158 x 90 mm
Ship Seal	Type 1

MZ46as

MZ46	Start of Print Run	End of Print Run	Order Date (If Known)	Signatures	Issued Notes Good	Issued Notes Fine	Issued Notes EF	Archival Specimens AU
a	0001	1000	Sept 1909	G4, VG11	$1,200	$3,000	Rare	$1,800
b	1001	2000		G4, VG9	$1,000	$2,500	Rare	$1,200
c	2001	3000		G4, VG6*	$400	$1,000	Rare	$950
d	3001	4000	Sept 1909	G4, VG10				
e	4001	5666	Oct 1913	G4, VG9	$1,000	$2,500	Rare	$1,200
f	5667	7332		G4, VG6				
g	7333	9000		G4, VG10	$400	$1,000	Rare	$950
h	9001	12000	21.3.16	G4 VG10				
i	12001	26000	5.6.18	G4, VG10				

MZ47 **5 libras esterlinas** 1 March 1909 SCWPM unlisted

Printer Bradbury Wilkinson & Co. Ltd.
Total Printed 100000
Circulation Withdrawn 01. 04. 1926
Colour Black on blue, orange and yellow underprint
Obverse Design Value at centre and in guilloche at left, arms at right, steamship seal at lower centre
Reverse Design Green, value in words in ornate guilloche
Size 158 x 90 mm
Ship Seal Type 3

MZ47as

					Issued Notes			Archival Specimens
MZ47	Start of Print Run	End of Print Run	Order Date (If Known)	Signatures	Good	Fine	EF	AU
a	26001	76000	22.12.19	G4, VG10	$400	$1,000	Rare	$1,200
b	76001	126000	28.11.20	G4, VG10				

MZ48	**10 libras esterlinas**	1 March 1909	SCWPM 47
	Printer	Bradbury Wilkinson & Co. Ltd.	
	Total Printed	14000	
	Circulation	Withdrawn 01. 04. 1926	
	Colour	Blue on pink and olive underprint. Reverse deep blue, pale green and pink	
	Obverse Design	Value at centre, at right in guilloche and in top corners, red steamship seal at lower centre	
	Reverse Design	Value in words in ornate guilloche with acanthus leaves, value in figures at upper left and right	
	Size	160 x 100 mm	
	Ship Seal	Type 1	

MZ48b

MZ48	Start of Print Run	End of Print Run	Order Date (If Known)	Signatures	Issued Notes: Good	Issued Notes: Fine	Issued Notes: EF	Archival Specimens: AU
a	0001	5000	16.6.16	G4, VG10	Rare	Rare	Rare	$2,000
b	5001	14000	5.6.18	G4, VG10				
ct	Uniface reverse colour trial in purple on pale green underprint							Rare
ph	Sepia and white obverse and reverse archival photographs, dated 1 March 1909, serial number 00000, no signatures, on card dated 28. 3. 1916							One Pair Known

MZ48ct

MZ48ph

MZ48ph

MZ49	**10 libras esterlinas**	1 March 1909	SCWPM unlisted
	Printer	Bradbury Wilkinson & Co. Ltd.	
	Total Printed	150000	
	Circulation	Withdrawn 01. 04. 1926	
	Colour	Blue on pink and olive underprint. Reverse deep blue, pale green and pink	
	Obverse Design	Value at centre, at right in guilloche and in top corners, red steamship seal at lower centre	
	Reverse Design	Value in words in ornate guilloche with acanthus leaves, value in figures at upper left and right	
	Size	160 x 100 mm	
	Ship Seal	Type 3	

MZ49as

					Issued Notes			Archival Specimens
MZ49	Start of Print Run	End of Print Run	Order Date (If Known)	Signatures	Good	Fine	EF	AU
a	14001	64000	22.12.19	G4, VG10				
b	64001	114000	28.1.20	G4, VG10	Rare	Rare	Rare	$1,500
c	114001	164000	23.4.20	G4, VG10				

MZ50	**20 libras esterlinas**	1 March 1909	SCWPM 49
	Printer	Bradbury Wilkinson & Co. Ltd.	
	Total Printed	Specimens only	
	Circulation	Specimens only	
	Colour	Brown, purple, orange and pale green. Reverse violet, purple and pale green	
	Obverse Design	Value in words in guilloche at left and in figures at upper and lower right, arms at right	
	Reverse Design	Arms at centre in ornate pattern, value in figures on either side and in words at lower centre	
	Size	160 x 100 mm	
	Signatures	G4, VG10	
	Ship seal	Type 3	

MZ50s2

s1	Specimen with counterfoil, no serial numbers, red steamship seal	AU - Rare
s2	Specimen with counterfoil, no serial numbers, no steamship seal	AU - Rare
ph	Sepia and white obverse and reverse archival photographs, no signatures, dated 18. 2. 1920	One Pair Known

MZ50ph

MZ50ph

1914 CEDULA ISSUES

The fractional notes issued by the BNU for the Portuguese African colonies, all dated 5 November 1914, are known as the Cedula Issues and in Portugal as "the London Issue". They were emergency notes printed in London during World War I, as a substitute for metal coinage in short supply. They were issued in denominations of 10cts, 20cts and 50cts for all five of the African colonies. Each colony had its own overprint, with Lourenço Marques used for Mozambique.

It is important to recognise that the issue of these notes, like metallic coins, was a privilege of the state, which was never transferred to the BNU. Accordingly to be legal tender, every issue had to be the subject of specific legislation proposed by the Minister of Colonies and approved by the Council of Ministers and Parliament in Lisbon. Furthermore, the fulfilment of the orders for the notes experienced all the constraints of a world at war. Among the difficulties encountered, which led to serious delays, were the lack of proper materials (appropriate paper and ink), the absence of skilled workers and the disruption of regular maritime transport.

These notes were issued with two types of steamship seal: the earlier issues used Type 2 and the later issues Type 3. The seals were green for the 10cts, red for the 20cts and blue for the 50cts.

Steamship seal Type 2

Steamship seal Type 3

MZ51-59 Overprint Types

Black overprint with serifs

Black overprint without serifs

Green, Red or Blue overprints without serifs

Reverses of the 1914 Cedula Issues

MZ51, MZ52 and MZ53

MZ54, MZ55 and MZ56

MZ57, MZ58 and MZ59

MZ51	**10 centavos**	5 November 1914, first issue	SCWPM 53
	Printer	Bradbury Wilkinson & Co. Ltd.	
	Total Printed	820000	
	Circulation	Withdrawn 16. 08. 1934	
	Colour	Purple on multicoloured underprint. Reverse blue	
	Obverse Design	Value in guilloche at left, arms at right, green steamship seal at lower centre, black or green overprint LOURENÇO MARQUES	
	Reverse Design	Allegorical maiden looking at ships	
	Size	122 x 72 mm	
	Signatures	G5, VG10	
	Ship seal	Type 2	

MZ51a

MZ51	Start of Print Run	End of Print Run		Issued Notes VG	Issued Notes VF	Issued Notes Unc	Archival Specimens AU
a	0000001†	0120000†	Black overprint with serifs	$100	$250	$800	$400
b	0120001	0160000					
c	0470001	0490000	Green overprint without serifs	$15	$40	$140	$300
d	0490001	0500000					
e	0500001	0700000					
f	1900001	2400000					

† Only 50000 of this print run were overprinted for use in Mozambique, the remaining 70000 were overprinted LOANDA for use in Angola. See AN29a

N.B.1 Printer's archival specimens exist for the initial order dated 11. 11. 1914 for 400000 notes with serial number range 000001 to 0400000, and these made no reference to the colony where they would be put in circulation. For an image of this specimen see Angola AN29 (N.B.)

N.B.2 Some printers archival specimens feature overprints that differ in style and/or colour from the corresponding issued notes

MZ52	**10 centavos**	5 November 1914, second issue — SCWPM 56
	Printer	Bradbury Wilkinson & Co. Ltd.
	Total Printed	1950000
	Circulation	Withdrawn 16. 08. 1934
	Colour	Purple on multicoloured underprint. Reverse blue
	Obverse Design	Value in guilloche at left, arms at right, green steamship seal at lower centre, green overprint LOURENÇO MARQUES
	Reverse Design	Allegorical maiden looking at ships
	Size	122 x 72 mm
	Signatures	G5, VG10
	Ship Seal	Type 3

MZ52b

MZ52	Start of Print Run	End of Print Run		Issued Notes VG	Issued Notes VF	Issued Notes Unc	Archival Specimens AU
a	6000001	6500000	Green overprint, with counterfoil at left	$15	$40	$140	$350
b†	6820001	8270000					

† The printer's archival specimens are actually with serial number range 6820001 to 8320000, because an error was made when distributing these notes. Only two copies are known. See article by Parcidio Campos e Matos, IBNS Journal 55/1 at page 24

MZ53 **10 centavos** 5 November 1914, third issue SCWPM 59

Printer	Bradbury Wilkinson & Co. Ltd.
Total Printed	9550000 (550000 notes were overprinted “CABO VERDE” for use in Cape Verde, see CV31 (SCWPM 20)
Circulation	Withdrawn 16. 08. 1934
Colour	Purple on multicoloured underprint. Reverse blue
Obverse Design	Value in guilloche at left, arms at right, green steamship seal at lower centre, green overprint LOURENÇO MARQUES
Reverse Design	Allegorical maiden looking at ships
Size	122 x 72 mm
Signatures	G5, VG10
Ship Seal	Type 3

MZ53a

				Issued Notes			Archival Specimens
MZ53	Start of Print Run	End of Print Run		VG	VF	Unc	AU
a	8270001	10000000	Green overprint, without counterfoil at left	$15	$40	$140	$350
b	A0000001	A7820000					

N.B. The printer's archival specimens are numbered with serial number range 8320001 to A7820000, because an error was made when distributing these notes. Only two copies are known. See article by Parcidio Campos e Matos, IBNS Journal 55/1 at page 24

MZ54	**20 centavos**	5 November 1914, first issue	SCWPM 54
	Printer	Bradbury Wilkinson & Co. Ltd.	
	Total Printed	1620000	
	Circulation	Withdrawn 16. 08. 1934	
	Colour	Blue on multicoloured underprint. Reverse purple	
	Obverse Design	Value in guilloche at left, arms at right, red steamship seal at lower centre, black or red overprint LOURENÇO MARQUES	
	Reverse Design	Allegorical maiden looking at ships	
	Size	122 x 72 mm	
	Signatures	G5, VG10	
	Ship Seal	Type 2	

MZ54f

				Issued Notes			Archival Specimens
MZ54	Start of Print Run	End of Print Run		VG	VF	Unc	AU
a	0000001	0590000†	Black overprint with serifs	$70	$180	$700	$500
b	0900001	1026000	Black overprint without serifs				
c	1276001	1330000	Red overprint without serifs	$15	$40	$160	$350
d	1330001	1370000					
e	1370001	1770000					
f	3120001	3870000					

† Only 250000 of this print run were overprinted for use in Mozambique, the remaining 340000 were overprinted LOANDA for use in Angola. See AN33a

N.B.1 Printer's archival specimens exist for the initial order dated 11. 11. 1914 for 1800000 notes with serial number range 0000001 to 1800000 and these made no reference to the colony where they would be put in circulation. For an image of this specimen see Angola AN33 (N.B.)

N.B.2 Some printers archival specimens feature overprints that differ in style and/or colour from the corresponding issued notes

MZ55	**20 centavos**	5 November 1914, second issue	SCWPM 57
	Printer	Bradbury Wilkinson & Co. Ltd.	
	Total Printed	197000	
	Circulation	Withdrawn 16. 08. 1934	
	Colour	Blue on multicoloured underprint. Reverse purple	
	Obverse Design	Value in guilloche at left, arms at right, red steamship seal at lower centre, red overprint LOURENÇO MARQUES	
	Reverse Design	Allegorical maiden looking at ships	
	Size	122 x 72 mm	
	Signatures	G5, VG10	
	Ship Seal	Type 3	

MZ55a

				Issued Notes			Archival Specimens
MZ55	Start of Print Run	End of Print Run		VG	VF	Unc	AU
a	7870001	8370000	Red overprint without serifs, counterfoil at left	$18	$50	$220	$400
b	8490001	9960000					

MZ56 **20 centavos** 5 November 1914, third issue SCWPM 60

Printer	Bradbury Wilkinson & Co. Ltd.
Total Printed	4530000
Circulation	Withdrawn 16. 08. 1934
Colour	Blue on multicoloured underprint. Reverse purple
Obverse Design	Value in guilloche at left, arms at right, red steamship seal at lower centre, red overprint LOURENÇO MARQUES
Reverse Design	Allegorical maiden looking at ships
Size	122 x 72 mm
Signatures	G5, VG10
Ship Seal	Type 3

MZ56c

				Issued Notes			Archival Specimens
MZ56	Start of Print Run	End of Print Run		VG	VF	Unc	AU
a	9960001	9990000					
b	9990001	10000000	Red overprint without serifs, without counterfoil at left	$15	$40	$160	$400
c	A000001	A4490000					

MZ57	**50 centavos**	5 November 1914, first issue	SCWPM 55
	Printer	Bradbury Wilkinson & Co. Ltd.	
	Total Printed	1390000	
	Circulation	Withdrawn 16. 08. 1934	
	Colour	Green on multicoloured underprint. Reverse brown	
	Obverse Design	Value in guilloche at left, arms at right, blue steamship seal at lower centre, black or blue overprint LOURENÇO MARQUES	
	Reverse Design	Allegorical maiden looking at ships	
	Size	122 x 72 mm	
	Signatures	G5, VG10	
	Ship Seal	Type 2	

MZ57b

				Issued Notes			Archival Specimens
MZ57	Start of Print Run	End of Print Run		VG	VF	Unc	AU
a	000001†	0450000†	Black overprint with serifs	$70	$180	$700	$650
b	0590001	0750000	Black overprint without serifs				
c	0980001	1010000					
d	1010001	1210000	Blue overprint without serifs	$25	$60	$200	$450
e	1950001	2750000					

† Only 200000 of this print run were overprinted for use in Mozambique, the remaining 250000 were overprinted LOANDA for use in Angola. See AN37a

N.B.1 Printer's archival specimens exist for the initial Order Dated 11. 11. 1914 for 130000 notes with serial number range 000001 to 130000, and these made no reference to the colony where they would be put in circulation. For an image of this specimen see Angola AN37 (N.B.)

N.B.2 Some printers archival specimens feature overprints that differ in style and/or colour from the corresponding issued notes

MZ58	**50 centavos**	5 November 1914, second issue	SCWPM 58
	Printer	Bradbury Wilkinson & Co. Ltd.	
	Total Printed	2614000	
	Circulation	Withdrawn 16. 08. 1934	
	Colour	Green on multicoloured underprint. Reverse brown	
	Obverse Design	Value in guilloche at left, arms at right, blue steamship seal at lower centre, blue overprint LOURENÇO MARQUES	
	Reverse Design	Allegorical maiden looking at ships	
	Size	122 x 72 mm	
	Signatures	G5, VG10	
	Ship Seal	Type 3	

MZ58b

				Issued Notes			Archival Specimens
MZ58	Start of Print Run	End of Print Run		VG	VF	Unc	AU
a	4430001	5130000	Blue overprint without serifs, counterfoil at left	$18	$50	$220	$450
b	5390001	7304000					

MZ59 **50 centavos** 5 November 1914, third issue SCWPM 61

Printer	Bradbury Wilkinson & Co. Ltd.
Total Printed	5686000 (80000 notes were overprinted "CABO VERDE" for use in Cape Verde, see CV32 (SCWPM 22)
Circulation	Withdrawn 16. 08. 1934
Colour	Green on multicoloured underprint. Reverse brown
Obverse Design	Value in guilloche at left, arms at right, blue steamship seal at lower centre, blue overprint LOURENÇO MARQUES
Reverse Design	Allegorical maiden looking at ships
Size	122 x 72 mm
Signatures	G5, VG10
Ship Seal	Type 3

MZ59b

MZ59	Start of Print Run	End of Print Run		Issued Notes VG	Issued Notes VF	Issued Notes Unc	Archival Specimens AU
a	7304001	7490000	Blue overprint without serifs, without counterfoil at left	$18	$50	$220	$450
b	7490001	10000000					
c	A0000001	A2990000					

1920 EMERGENCY "PORTO" ISSUE

MZ60	**10 centavos**	1920	SCWPM 62
	Printer	Litografia Nacional, Lda, Porto	
	Total Printed	1500000	
	Circulation	Withdrawn in stages on 16. 08. 1934, 26. 05. 1937 and 29. 09. 1937	
	Colour	Red. Reverse brown-purple	
	Obverse Design	Sailing ships at left and right	
	Reverse Design	Value in central guilloche	
	Size	105 x 65 mm	
	Signatures	G7, VG14	

MZ60a

MZ60a

			Issued Notes		
MZ60	Start of Print Run	End of Print Run	Good	Fine	EF
a	Unknown	Unknown	$150	$400	$1,000

MZ61	**20 centavos**	1 January 1920	SCWPM 63
	Printer	Litografia Nacional, Lda, Porto	
	Total Printed	1500000	
	Circulation	Withdrawn in stages on 16. 08. 1934, 26. 05. 1937 and 29. 09. 1937	
	Colour	Green	
	Obverse Design	Two cherubs above sailing ships at left and right, value at upper left and right	
	Reverse Design	Value in central guilloche	
	Size	105 x 65 mm	
	Signatures	G7, VG14	

MZ61a

MZ61a

			Issued Notes		
MZ61	Start of Print Run	End of Print Run	Good	Fine	EF
a	Unknown	Unknown	$150	$400	$1,000

MZ62	**50 centavos**	1 January 1920	SCWPM 64
	Printer	Litografia Nacional, Lda, Porto	
	Total Printed	2100000	
	Circulation	Withdrawn in stages on 16. 08. 1934, 26. 05. 1937 and 29. 09. 1937	
	Colour	Blue. Reverse brown	
	Obverse Design	Mercury and ship at left, allegorical female representing industry and male farmer at right	
	Reverse Design	Ship in roundel at centre, value in four corners set in ornate borders	
	Size	120 x 75 mm	
	Signatures	G7, VG14	

MZ62a

MZ62a

			Issued Notes		
MZ62	Start of Print Run	End of Print Run	Good	Fine	EF
a	Unknown	Unknown	$200	$500	$1,200

MZ63 **50 escudos** 1 January 1920 SCWPM 65

Printer Litografia Nacional, Lda, Porto
Total Printed 130,000
Circulation Withdrawn in stages on 16. 08. 1934, 26. 05. 1937 and 29. 09. 1937
Colour Blue on pale green underprint. Reverse brown on yellow-orange underprint
Obverse Design Arms at upper centre, value at lower centre and in each corner
Reverse Design Palm trees and coastline in ornate oval at centre, eagles at left and right, value at lower centre
Size 200 x 125 mm
Signatures G7, VG14

MZ63a

MZ63a

			Issued Notes		
MZ63	Start of Print Run	End of Print Run	Good	Fine	EF
a	Unknown	Unknown	$750	$2,000	Rare

1920 CIRCULATING BEARER CHEQUE ISSUE

MZ64	**1 escudo**	10 July 1920	SCWPM unlisted
	Printer	Tip. Minerva Central Lourenço Marques	
	Total Printed	Unknown	
	Colour	Orange on pale grey-green underprint	
	Obverse Design	Winged maiden holding laurel wreath atop a globe	
	Reverse Design	Uniface	
	Size	185 x 70 mm	
	Signature	President of the General Assembly of the Chamber of Commerce of Lourenço Marques	

MZ64a

MZ64	Start of Print Run	End of Print Run	Good	Fine	EF
a	Unknown	Unknown	Rare	Rare	Rare

MZ65	**2½ escudos**	10 July 1920	SCWPM unlisted
	Printer	Tip. Minerva Central, Lourenço Marques	
	Total Printed	Unknown	
	Colour	Unknown colour on orange underprint	
	Obverse Design	Winged maiden holding laurel wreath atop a globe	
	Reverse Design	Uniface	
	Size	185 x 70 mm	
	Signature	President of the General Assembly of the Chamber of Commerce of Lourenço Marques	

MZ65a

MZ65	Start of Print Run	End of Print Run	Good	Fine	EF
a	Unknown	Unknown	Rare	Rare	Rare

INTRODUCTION TO THE CHAMIÇO ISSUES

By the Decree No. 5809 dated 30 May 1919, which instituted a new banking regime for the overseas colonies, a new issue of notes to replace the Vasco da Gama issues was authorised. This new omnibus series, which circulated in all five of the Portuguese African colonies from 1 August 1922 until 30 November 1950, featured a portrait of the founder and first Governor of the BNU, Francisco de Oliveira Chamiço (1819-88).

This new issue, dated 1 January 1921, consisted of values of 1$00, 2$50, 5$00, 10$00, 20$00, 50$00 and 100$00 escudos. For Mozambique only, a 500$00 escudo note dated 25 August 1932 was printed and this circulated from 25 January 1933. There followed a second issue, dated 1 September 1941, consisting of only 1$00, 2$50, 5$00 and 10$00 escudos.

Reverses of the Chamiço Issues

MZ66
and MZ84

MZ67
and MZ85

MZ68
and MZ86

MZ69
and MZ87

MZ70

MZ71

MZ72

MZ73

1921 CHAMIÇO ISSUE

MZ66	**1 escudo**	1 January 1921	SCWPM 66
	Printer	Bradbury Wilkinson & Co. Ltd.	
	Total Printed	5500000*	
	Circulation	Introduced 01. 08. 1922. Withdrawn 30. 11. 1950	
	Colour	Green on multicoloured underprint	
	Obverse Design	Portrait of Francisco de Oliveira Chamiço at left, steamship seal at right, red overprint MOÇAMBIQUE	
	Reverse Design	Allegorical maiden looking at ships	
	Size	128 x 82 mm	
	Signatures	G7, VG14	

MZ66as

MZ66f

				Issued Notes			Archival Specimens	Specimens
MZ66	Start of Print Run	End of Print Run	Order Date (If Known)	VG	VF	Unc	AU	Unc
	Without Decreto							
a	000001	1600000	25.8.20 and 29.6.20	$25	$60	$200	$200	$200
b	1600001	2760000	3.11.21					
c	2760001	3220000	15.11.21					
d	3220001	5000000	9.8.22					
e	5000001	5500000	6.7.28					
	With Decreto							
f	A000001	A1000000	2.5.32	$25	$60	$200	$250	$200

MZ67	**2½ escudos**	1 January 1921	SCWPM 67
	Printer	Thomas De La Rue & Co. Ltd.	
	Total Printed	2500000*	
	Circulation	Introduced 23. 02. 1924. Withdrawn 30. 11. 1950	
	Colour	Blue on multicoloured underprint	
	Obverse Design	Portrait of Francisco de Oliveira Chamiço at left, steamship seal at right	
	Reverse Design	Allegorical maiden looking at ships	
	Size	136 x 69 mm	
	Signatures	G7, VG14	

MZ67a

				Issued Notes			Specimens
MZ67	Start of Print Run	End of Print Run	Order Date (If Known)	Fine	VF	EF	Unc
	Without Decreto						
a	000001	2500000*		$75	$175	$500	$600

N.B. Contrary to what is stated in SCWPM, P67a (With Decreto) does not exist

MZ68 **5 escudos**	1 January 1921	SCWPM 68
Printer	Bradbury Wilkinson & Co. Ltd.	
Total Printed	2564000	
Circulation	Introduced 01. 08. 1922. Withdrawn 30. 11. 1950	
Colour	Black on multicoloured underprint	
Obverse Design	Portrait of Francisco de Oliveira Chamiço at left, steamship seal at right, red overprint MOÇAMBIQUE	
Reverse Design	Allegorical maiden looking at ships	
Size	154 x 92 mm	
Signatures	G7, VG14	

MZ68a

MZ68es

				Issued Notes			Archival Specimens	Specimens
MZ68	Start of Print Run	End of Print Run	Order Date (If Known)	Fine	VF	EF	AU	Unc
	Without Decreto							
a	0000001	1000000	29.6.20 and 25.8.20					
b	1000001	1026000	3.11.21	$70	$175	$500	$400	$350
c	1026001	1624000	15.11.21					
d	1624001	1824000	6.7.28					
	With Decreto							
e	A000001	A740000	16.10.29	$60	$140	$400	$450	$350

MZ69 **10 escudos** 1 January 1921 SCWPM 69

Printer Bradbury Wilkinson & Co. Ltd.

Total Printed 1494000

Circulation Introduced 01. 08. 1922. Withdrawn 30. 11. 1950

Colour Brown on multicoloured underprint

Obverse Design Portrait of Francisco de Oliveira Chamiço at left, steamship seal at right, red overprint MOÇAMBIQUE

Reverse Design Allegorical maiden looking at ships

Size 160 x 105 mm

Signatures G7, VG14

MZ69a

MZ69fs

				Issued Notes			Archival Specimens	Specimens
MZ69	Start of Print Run	End of Print Run	Order Date (If Known)	Fine	VF	EF	AU	Unc
	Without Decreto							
a	000001	180000	29.6.20 and 25.8.20					
b	180001	380000	3.11.21					
c	380001	794000	15.11.21	$175	$300	$850	$450	$400
d	794001	994000	3.11.24					
e	994001	1194000	6.7.28					
	With Decreto							
f	A000001	A200000	16.10.29	$140	$260	$700	$500	$400
g	A200001	A300000	2.9.32					

MZ70 **20 escudos** 1 January 1921 SCWPM 70

Printer	Bradbury Wilkinson & Co. Ltd.
Total Printed	1253000
Circulation	Introduced 01. 08. 1922. Withdrawn 30. 11. 1950
Colour	Blue on multicoloured underprint
Obverse Design	Portrait of Francisco de Oliveira Chamiço at left, steamship seal at right, red overprint MOÇAMBIQUE
Reverse Design	Allegorical maiden looking at ships
Size	170 x 115 mm
Signatures	G7, VG14

MZ70b

MZ70fs

				Issued Notes			Archival Specimens	Specimens
MZ70	Start of Print Run	End of Print Run	Order Date (If Known)	Fine	VF	EF	AU	Unc
	Without Decreto							
a	000001	100000	29.6.20 and 25.8.20	$400	$750	Rare	$500	$450
b	100001	400000	3.11.21					
c	400001	538000	15.11.21					
d	538001	788000	3.11.24					
e	788001	888000	6.7.28					
	With Decreto							
f	A000001	A365000	16.10.29	$300	$550	Rare	$600	$550
ph	Black and white obverse and reverse archival photographs, dated 1 January 1937, serial number A000000, signatures G7, VG14, smaller size note 151 x 90 mm, ink date 3. 12. 36 in lower right corner							Two Pairs Known

MZ70ph

MZ70ph

MZ71	**50 escudos**	1 January 1921 — SCWPM 71
	Printer	Bradbury Wilkinson & Co. Ltd.
	Total Printed	463000
	Circulation	Introduced 01. 08. 1922. Withdrawn 30. 11. 1950
	Colour	Brownish-red on multicoloured underprint
	Obverse Design	Portrait of Francisco de Oliveira Chamiço at left, steamship seal at right, red overprint MOÇAMBIQUE
	Reverse Design	Allegorical maiden looking at ships
	Size	185 x 120 mm
	Signatures	G7, VG14

MZ71b

MZ71s

				Issued Notes			Archival Specimens	Specimens
MZ71	Start of Print Run	End of Print Run	Order Date (If Known)	VG	Fine	VF	AU	Unc
	Without Decreto							
a	000001	080000	29.6.20 and 25.8.20					
b	080001	234000	3.11.21	$300	$700	$2,000	$750	$750
c	234001	303000	15.11.21					
d	303001	383000	3.11.24					
	With Decreto							
e	A000001	A080000	16.10.29	$250	$600	$1500	$850	$750

MZ72	**100 escudos**	1 January 1921	SCWPM 72
	Printer	Bradbury Wilkinson & Co. Ltd.	
	Total Printed	305000	
	Circulation	Introduced 01. 08. 1922. Withdrawn 30. 11. 1950	
	Colour	Slate-purple on multicoloured underprint	
	Obverse Design	Portrait of Francisco de Oliveira Chamiço at left, steamship seal at right, red overprint MOÇAMBIQUE	
	Reverse Design	Allegorical maiden looking at ships	
	Size	193 x 126 mm	
	Signatures	G7, VG14	

MZ72cs

MZ72ds

MZ72	Start of Print Run	End of Print Run	Order Date (If Known)	Issued Notes VG	Issued Notes Fine	Issued Notes VF	Archival Specimens AU	Specimens Unc
	Without Decreto							
a	000001	060000	29.6.20 and 25.8.20					
b	060001	173000	3.11.21	$1,000	$2,750	Rare	$850	$850
c	173001	233000	3.11.24					
	With Decreto							
d	A000001	A042000	16.10.29	$800	$2,000	Rare	$950	$850
e	A042001	A072000	2.9.32					

1932 CHAMIÇO ISSUE

MZ73	**500 escudos**	25 August 1932	SCWPM 73
	Printer	Bradbury Wilkinson & Co. Ltd.	
	Total Printed	20000	
	Circulation	Introduced 25. 01. 1933. Withdrawn 30. 11. 1950	
	Colour	Deep olive-green on multicoloured underprint	
	Obverse Design	Portrait of Francisco de Oliveira Chamiço at left, steamship seal at right, red overprint MOÇAMBIQUE	
	Reverse Design	Allegorical maiden looking at ships	
	Size	193 x 126 mm	
	Signatures	PCA8a as an Administrador, A21	

MZ73as

				Issued Notes			Archival Specimens	Specimens
MZ73	Start of Print Run	End of Print Run	Order Date (If Known)	Fine	VF	EF	EF	EF
a	A000001	A020000	2.9.32	---	---	---	$6,000	$4,500
ph	Black and white obverse and reverse archival photographs dated 22. 6. 32, note undated, blank signatures of Governor and Vice Governor, serial number 000,000							One Pair Known

N.B. This entire issue was redeemed. Accordingly, no issued notes are thought to exist.

MZ73ph

MZ73ph

1935 PROVISIONAL ISSUE

MZ74	**100 Escudos**	ND (1935) - old date 1 March 1909	SCWPM 72A
	Printer	Bradbury Wilkinson & Co. Ltd.	
	Overprint	"CEM ESCUDOS / MOEDA CORRENTE NA COLONIA", "100 ESCUDOS" and "Decreto n.° 17.154" in black on MZ45	
	Total Overprints	Unknown	
	Circulation	Introduced 16. 09. 1935. Withdrawn 30. 11. 1950	
	Colour	Black and blue on yellow underprint	
	Obverse Design	Value at lower centre and in guilloche at left, arms at top centre, steamship seal at right	
	Reverse Design	Brown, value in words in ornate guilloche	
	Size	136 x 75 mm	
	Signatures	G4, VG10, with facsimile signature of a manager	
	Ship Seal	Type 3	

MZ74a

MZ74a

MZ74	Start of Print Run	End of Print Run	Order Date (If Known)	Fine	VF	EF
a	Unknown	Unknown		$800	$1,750	Rare

MZ75	**1000 Escudos**	ND (1935) - old date 1 March 1909	SCWPM 72B
	Printer	Bradbury Wilkinson & Co. Ltd.	
	Overprint	"MIL ESCUDOS / MOEDA CORRENTE NA COLONIA" and "1000 ESCUDOS" in black on MZ50	
	Total Overprints	Unknown	
	Circulation	Introduced 16. 09. 1935. Withdrawn 30. 11. 1950	
	Colour	Brown, purple, orange and pale green. Reverse violet, purple and pale green	
	Obverse Design	Value in words in guilloche at left and in figures at upper and lower right, arms at right	
	Reverse Design	Arms at centre in ornate pattern, value in figures on either side and in words at lower centre	
	Size	160 x 100 mm	
	Signatures	G4, VG10, with facsimile signature of a manager	
	Ship seal	Type 3	

MZ75a

MZ75a

MZ75	Start of Print Run	End of Print Run	Order Date (If Known)	Fine	VF	EF
a	Unknown	Unknown		$700	$1,500	Rare

1936 ND PROVISIONAL ISSUE

MZ76	**50 escudos**	ND (1936) - old date 1 January 1921.	SCWPM unlisted
	Printer	Bradbury Wilkinson & Co. Ltd.	
	Overprint	"MOÇAMBIQUE" in red text on black background on Angola AN56 (SCWPM 60)	
	Total Overprints	Unknown	
	Circulation	Introduced 24. 03. 1936. Withdrawn 30. 11. 1950	
	Colour	Brownish-red on multicoloured underprint	
	Obverse Design	Portrait of Francisco de Oliveira Chamiço at left, steamship seal at right	
	Reverse Design	Allegorical maiden looking at ships	
	Size	185 x 120 mm	
	Signatures	G7, VG14	

MZ76a

MZ76a

Issued Notes

MZ76	Start of Print Run	End of Print Run	VG	Fine	VF
a	Unknown	Unknown	Rare	Rare	Rare

INTRODUCTION TO THE ENNES ISSUES

António José Ennes (1848-1901) was a Portuguese politician and writer, who was the Governor of Mozambique from 1891 to 1896. In that capacity he oversaw the conduct of a war, that was regarded as successful, against the Empire of Gaza, in the southern part of the colony. His portrait appears across six separate issues between 1937 and 1947.

Reverses of the Ennes Issues

MZ95

MZ96

MZ92 and MZ97

MZ93 and MZ98

MZ77, MZ88 and MZ99

MZ78, MZ89
and MZ100

MZ79
and MZ80

MZ94, MZ101
and MZ104

MZ31, MZ90, MZ102 and MZ105

MZ82 and MZ91

MZ103 and MZ106

1937-38 FIRST ENNES ISSUE

MZ77	**20 escudos**	6 April 1937	SCWPM 74
	Printer	Bradbury Wilkinson & Co. Ltd.	
	Total Printed	1000000	
	Circulation	Introduced 28. 10. 1937. Withdrawn 31. 12. 1960	
	Colour	Blue on pink and buff underprint. Reverse blue on pale green and buff underprint	
	Obverse Design	Portrait of António Ennes at left, steamship seal at right.	
	Reverse Design	Allegorical maiden looking at ships	
	Size	130 x 81 mm	
	Signatures	PCA8, A19, A21, A24, A25 and A26	

MZ77s1

				Issued Notes			Specimens
MZ77	Start of Print Run	End of Print Run	Order Date (If Known)	Fine	VF	EF	AU
a	MA000001	MA100000	19.4.37				
b	MB000001	MB100000	19.4.37				
c	MC000001	MC100000	19.4.37				
d	MD000001	MD100000	19.4.37				
e	ME000001	ME100000	19.4.37				
f	MF000001	MF100000	19.4.37	$50	$120	$250	$250
g	MG000001	MG100000	19.4.37				
h	MH000001	MH100000	19.4.37				
i	MI000001	MI100000	19.4.37				
j	MJ000001	MJ100000	19.4.37				
s1	Printer's archival specimen with serial number run MA 000,001 to MJ.100,000. Believed only ten printed, two for each of the five signatures						Rare
s2	Specimen with serial numbers MA.000,000 at upper right and MJ.000,000 at lower left, administrador signatures A19, A21, A24, A25, A26						Rare - $450
ct1	Colour trial proof with obverse in violet and blue on yellow underprint and reverse in issued colours, 000,000 serial numbers, hand-signed by PCA8a and A25						Rare
ct2	Colour trial proof with reverse in blue on violet and blue-green underprint and obverse in issued colours, 000,000 serial numbers						Rare
ph1	Black and white obverse and reverse archival photographs dated 15. 4. 37, note dated 06. 04. 1937, with portrait in round frame and 20 in figures under value in words, signatures PCA8a and A21, serial number 000000						One Pair Known
ph2	Black and white obverse and reverse archival photographs dated 15. 4. 37, note dated 06. 04. 1937, as issued note, but with signatures PCA8a and A21, serial number 000000						One Pair Known

N.B. All five of the above mentioned Administrador signatures were used for a selection of notes in each of the above print runs and for each type of specimen

MZ77ct1

MZ77ct1

MZ77ct2

MZ77ph1

MZ77ph1

MZ77ph2

MZ77ph2

MZ78	**50 escudos**	11 January 1938	SCWPM 75
	Printer	Bradbury Wilkinson & Co. Ltd.	
	Total Printed	400000	
	Circulation	Introduced 17. 09. 1938. Withdrawn 31. 12. 1960	
	Colour	Olive-grey on multi coloured underprint	
	Obverse Design	Portrait of António Ennes at left, steamship seal at right.	
	Reverse Design	Allegorical maiden looking at ships	
	Size	164 x 84 mm	
	Signatures	PCA8, A19, A21, A25 and A26	

MZ78a

				Issued Notes			Specimens
MZ78	Start of Print Run	End of Print Run	Order Date (If Known)	Fine	VF	EF	AU
a	000001	400000	19.1.38	$200	$500	$1,250	$400
dp1	Obverse and reverse die proofs in issued colour olive-grey						$350 (pair)
dp2	Obverse and reverse die proofs in colours other than issued colour						$400 (pair)
ph	Black and white obverse and reverse archival photographs, note dated --- 1938, as issued note, but with different steamship seal at right, serial number 000000						One Pair Known
s1	Printer's archival specimen with serial number run 000,001 to 400,000. Believed only eight printed, two for each of the four signatures						Rare - $600

MZ78dp1

MZ78dp1

MZ78ph

MZ79	**100 escudos**	11 January 1938	SCWPM 76
	Printer	Bradbury Wilkinson & Co. Ltd.	
	Total Printed	300000	
	Circulation	Introduced 17. 09. 1938. Withdrawn 31. 12. 1960	
	Colour	Red-purple on multicoloured underprint	
	Obverse Design	Portrait of António Ennes at left, steamship seal at right.	
	Reverse Design	Allegorical maiden looking at ships	
	Size	170 x 97 mm	
	Signatures	PCA8, A19, A21, A25 and A26	

MZ79a

				Issued Notes			Specimens
MZ79	Start of Print Run	End of Print Run	Order Date (If Known)	Fine	VF	EF	AU
a	000001	300000	19.1.38	$450	$1,200	Rare	$500
dp1	Obverse and reverse die proofs in issued colour red-purple						$400 (pair)
dp2	Obverse and reverse die proofs in colours other than issued colour						$450 (pair)
ph	Black and white obverse and reverse photographs, note dated --- 1938, as issued note, but with Administrador signature block in different position at lower left, serial number 000000						One Pair Known
s1	Printer's archival specimen with serial number run 000,001 to 300,000. Believed only eight printed, two for each of the four signatures						Rare - $700

1941 SECOND ENNES ISSUE

MZ80	**100 escudos**	27 March 1941	SCWPM 77
	Printer	Bradbury Wilkinson & Co. Ltd.	
	Total Printed	500000 (200000 circulated)	
	Circulation	Introduced 09. 01. 1942. Withdrawn 31. 12. 1960	
	Colour	Red-purple on multicoloured underprint	
	Obverse Design	Portrait of António Ennes at left, steamship seal at right.	
	Reverse Design	Allegorical maiden looking at ships	
	Size	170 x 97 mm	

MZ80j

					Issued Notes			Archival Specimens	Specimens (sp)
MZ80	Start of Print Run	End of Print Run	Order Date (If Known)	Signatures	Fine	VF	EF	AU	AU
a	300001	320000	28.3.41	PCA8, A27					
b	320001	340000	28.3.41	PCA8, A26					
c	340001	360000	28.3.41	PCA8, A25					
d	360001	380000	28.3.41	PCA8, A19					
e	380001	400000	28.3.41	PCA8, A29	$650	$1,500	Rare	$450	$450
f	400001	420000	28.3.41	PCA8, A25					
g	420001	440000	28.3.41	PCA8, A26					
h	440001	460000	28.3.41	PCA8, A27					
i	460001	480000	28.3.41	PCA8, A29					
j	480001	500000	28.3.41	PCA8, A19					
k	500001	520000	4.7.42	PCA8, A29					
l	520001	540000	4.7.42	PCA8, A27					
m	540001	560000	4.7.42	PCA8, A25					
n	560001	580000	4.7.42	PCA8, A26					
o	580001	600000	4.7.42	PCA8, A19	---	---	---	$550	---
p	600001	640000	29.7.42	PCA8, A27					
q	640001	680000	29.7.42	PCA8, A26					
r	680001	720000	29.7.42	PCA8, A29					
s	720001	760000	29.7.42	PCA8, A19					
t	760001	800000	29.7.42	PCA8, A25					

N.B. All notes numbered from 500001-800000 were lost on a ship sunk by the Germans in 1942 and replaced with the 1943 issue in orange, see MZ94 below

MZ81 **500 escudos** 27 March 1941 SCWPM 78

Printer	Bradbury Wilkinson & Co. Ltd.
Total Printed	40000
Circulation	Introduced 09. 01. 1942. Withdrawn 31. 12. 1960
Colour	Purple on multicoloured underprint
Obverse Design	Portrait of António Ennes at left, steamship seal at right.
Reverse Design	Allegorical maiden looking at ships
Size	175 x 100 mm

MZ81g

					Issued Notes			Archival Specimens	Specimens
MZ81	Start of Print Run	End of Print Run	Order Date (If Known)	Signatures	Fine	VF	EF	AU	AU
a	00001	04000	28.3.41	PCA8, A25					
b	04001	08000	28.3.41	PCA8, A27					
c	08001	12000	28.3.41	PCA8, A26					
d	12001	16000	28.3.41	PCA8, A19					
e	16001	20000	28.3.41	PCA8, A29	$1,500	Rare	Rare	$750	$750
f	20001	24000	28.3.41	PCA8, A26					
g	24001	28000	28.3.41	PCA8, A19					
h	28001	32000	28.3.41	PCA8, A27					
i	32001	36000	28.3.41	PCA8, A29					
j	36001	40000	28.3.41	PCA8, A25					
dp1	Obverse and reverse die proofs in issued colour purple								$550 (pair)
dp2	Obverse and reverse die proofs in colours other than issued colour								$600 (pair)
ph1	Black and white obverse and reverse archival photographs, undated and unsigned, as issued, photo dated 3. 3. 41, serial number 000000								One Pair Known

MZ81dp1

MZ81dp1

MZ82	1000 escudos	27 March 1941	SCWPM 79
	Printer	Bradbury Wilkinson & Co. Ltd.	
	Total Printed	50000	
	Circulation	Introduced 09. 01. 1942. Withdrawn 31. 12. 1960	
	Colour	Brown on multicoloured underprint	
	Obverse Design	Portrait of António Ennes at left, steamship seal at right.	
	Reverse Design	Allegorical young woman looking out at ships from various eras	
	Size	182 x 103 mm	

MZ82as

					Issued Notes			Archival Specimens	Specimens
MZ82	Start of Print Run	End of Print Run	Order Date (If Known)	Signatures	Fine	VF	EF	AU	AU
a	00001	05000	19.4.41	PCA8, A29					
b	05001	10000	19.4.41	PCA8, A26					
c	10001	15000	19.4.41	PCA8, A19					
d	15001	20000	19.4.41	PCA8, A27					
e	20001	25000	19.4.41	PCA8, A25	$2,000	Rare	Rare	$700	$700
f	25001	30000	19.4.41	PCA8, A19					
g	30001	35000	19.4.41	PCA8, A27					
h	35001	40000	19.4.41	PCA8, A25					
i	40001	45000	19.4.41	PCA8, A29					
j	45001	50000	19.4.41	PCA8, A26					
dp1	Obverse and reverse die proofs in issued colour brown								$800 (pair)
dp2	Obverse and reverse die proofs in colours other than issued colour								$900 (pair)
ph1	Black and white obverse and reverse archival photographs, undated and unsigned, obverse as issued, serial number 000000, photo dated 4. 3. 41, reverse seated maiden as reverse of 500 escudos MZ81 above								One Pair Known
ph2	Black and white reverse archival photograph with same vignette as issued note								One Copy Known

MZ82dp1

MZ82dp1

MZ82ph1

1941 EMERGENCY ISSUE

MZ83	**50 centavos**	1 September 1941	SCWPM 80
	Printer	Imprensa Nacional de Moçambque, Lourenço Marques	
	Total Printed	2000000 (100000 for each series letter)	
	Circulation	Introduced 09. 03. 1942. Withdrawn in two stages 10. 02. 1951 and 04. 10. 1952	
	Colour	Green. Reverse purple	
	Obverse Design	Coat of arms of colony at left, value at lower left	
	Reverse Design	Arms of Portugal set in leaves	
	Size	85 x 51 mm	
	Signatures	Inspector and Gerente	
	Series Letters	A, B, C, D, E, F, G, H, I, J, K, L, M, N, O, P, R, S, T & U	

MZ83a

MZ83a

			Issued Notes		
MZ83	Start of Print Run (for each series letter)	End of Print Run (for each series letter)	VG	VF	Unc
a	00001	100000	$10	$50	$150

1941 CHAMIÇO ISSUE

MZ84	**1 escudo**	1 September 1941	SCWPM 81
	Printer	Bradbury Wilkinson & Co. Ltd.	
	Total Printed	2000000*	
	Circulation	Introduced 1942*. Withdrawn 30. 11. 1950	
	Colour	Green on multicoloured underprint	
	Obverse Design	Portrait of Francisco de Oliveira Chamiço at left, steamship seal at right, red overprint MOÇAMBIQUE	
	Reverse Design	Allegorical maiden looking at ships	
	Size	128 x 82 mm	

MZ84f

					Issued Notes			Archival Specimens	Specimens (sp)
MZ84	Start of print run	End of print run	Order Date (If Known)	Signatures	VG	VF	Unc	AU	AU
a	B000001	B100000	22.8.41	PCA8, A27					
b	B100001	B200000	22.8.41	PCA8, A25					
c	B200001	B300000	22.8.41	PCA8, A19					
d	B300001	B400000	22.8.41	PCA8, A29					
e	B400001	B500000	22.8.41	PCA8, A26					
f	B500001	B600000	22.8.41	PCA8, A25					
g	B600001	B700000	22.8.41	PCA8, A26					
h	B700001	B800000	22.8.41	PCA8, A29					
i	B800001	B900000	22.8.41	PCA8, A19					
j	B900001	B1000000	22.8.41	PCA8, A27	$10	$30	$120	$175	$150
k	B1000001	B1100000	22.8.41	PCA8, A29					
l	B1100001	B1200000	22.8.41	PCA8, A26					
m	B1200001	B1300000	22.8.41	PCA8, A19					
n	B1300001	B1400000	22.8.41	PCA8, A27					
o	B1400001	B1500000	22.8.41	PCA8, A29					
p	B1500001	B1600000	22.8.41	PCA8, A27					
q	B1600001	B1700000	22.8.41	PCA8, A25					
r	B1700001	B1800000	22.8.41	PCA8, A19					
s	B1800001	B1900000	22.8.41	PCA8, A26					
t	B1900001*	B2000000*	22.8.41*	PCA8, A25*					

MZ85 **2½ escudos** 1 September.1941 SCWPM 82

Printer	Thomas De La Rue & Co. Ltd.
Total Printed	2400000
Circulation	Introduced 1942*. Withdrawn 30. 11. 1950
Colour	Blue on multicoloured underprint
Obverse Design	Portrait of Francisco de Oliveira Chamiço at left, steamship seal at right
Reverse Design	Allegorical maiden looking at ships
Size	136 x 69 mm

MZ85b

					Issued Notes			Specimens (sp)
MZ85	Start of Print Run	End of Print Run	Order Date (If Known)	Signatures	VG	VF	Unc	Unc
a	A000001	A120000	22.8.41	PCA8, A29				
b	A120001	A240000	22.8.41	PCA8, A27				
c	A240001	A360000	22.8.41	PCA8, A19				
d	A360001	A480000	22.8.41	PCA8, A26				
e	A480001	A600000	22.8.41	PCA8, A25				
f	A600001	A720000	22.8.41	PCA8, A19				
g	A720001	A840000	22.8.41	PCA8, A26				
h	A840001	A960000	22.8.41	PCA8, A29				
i	A960001	A1080000	22.8.41	PCA8, A27				
j	A1080001	A1200000	22.8.41	PCA8, A27	$30	$120	$750	$400
k	A1200001	A1320000	22.8.41	PCA8, A29				
l	A1320001	A1440000	22.8.41	PCA8, A25				
m	A1440001	A1560000	22.8.41	PCA8, A19				
n	A1560001	A1680000	22.8.41	PCA8, A26				
o	A1680001	A1800000	22.8.41	PCA8, A29				
p	A1800001	A1920000	22.8.41	PCA8, A26				
q	A1920001	A2040000	22.8.41	PCA8, A25				
r	A2040001	A2160000	22.8.41	PCA8, A19				
s	A2160001	A2280000	22.8.41	PCA8, A27				
t	A2280001	A2400000	22.8.41	PCA8, A25				

MZ86	5 escudos	1 September 1941	SCWPM 83
	Printer	Bradbury Wilkinson & Co. Ltd.	
	Total Printed	2000000	
	Circulation	Introduced 1942*. Withdrawn 30. 11. 1950	
	Colour	Black on multicoloured underprint	
	Obverse Design	Portrait of Francisco de Oliveira Chamiço at left, steamship seal at right, red overprint MOÇAMBIQUE	
	Reverse Design	Allegorical maiden looking at ships	
	Size	154 x 92 mm	

MZ86f

					Issued Notes			Archival Specimens	Specimens (sp)
MZ86	Start of Print Run	End of Print Run	Order Date (If Known)	Signatures	Fine	VF	EF	AU	AU
a	B000001	B100000	22.8.41	PCA8, A25					
b	B150001	B250000	22.8.41	PCA8, A27					
c	B300001	B400000	22.8.41	PCA8, A26					
d	B450001	B550000	22.8.41	PCA8, A29					
e	B600001	B750000	22.8.41	PCA8, A19					
f	B750001	B850000	22.8.41	PCA8, A29					
g	B900001	B1000000	22.8.41	PCA8, A25					
h	B1050001	B1150000	22.8.41	PCA8, A19					
i	B1200001	B1300000	22.8.41	PCA8, A26					
j	B1350001	B1450000	22.8.41	PCA8, A27	$40	$65	$200	$275	$225
k	B1500001	B1600000	22.8.41	PCA8, A26					
l	B1650001	B1750000	22.8.41	PCA8, A19					
m	B1800001	B1900000	22.8.41	PCA8, A29					
n	B1950001	B2050000	22.8.41	PCA8, A27					
o	B2100001	B2200000	22.8.41	PCA8, A25					
p	B2250001	B2350000	22.8.41	PCA8, A29					
q	B2400001	B2500000	22.8.41	PCA8, A27					
r	B2550001	B2650000	22.8.41	PCA8, A25					
s	B2700001	B2800000	22.8.41	PCA8, A19					
t	B2850001	B2950000	22.8.41	PCA8, A26					

N.B. All the print runs have 50000 serial number gaps between them, with no notes issued for those serial numbers.

MZ87 **10 escudos** 1 September 1941 SCWPM 84

Printer	Bradbury Wilkinson & Co. Ltd.
Total Printed	1000000
Circulation	Introduced 1942*. Withdrawn 30. 11. 1950
Colour	Brown on multicoloured underprint
Obverse Design	Portrait of Francisco de Oliveira Chamiço at left, steamship seal at right, red overprint MOÇAMBIQUE
Reverse Design	Allegorical maiden looking at ships
Size	160 x 105 mm

MZ87q

					Issued Notes			Archival Specimens	Specimens (sp)
MZ87	Start of Print Run	End of Print Run	Order Date (If Known)	Signatures	Fine	VF	EF	AU	AU
a	B100001	B150000	22.8.41	PCA8, A27	$60	$120	$300	$325	$275
b	B250001	B300000	22.8.41	PCA8, A29					
c	B400001	B450000	22.8.41	PCA8, A25					
d	B550001	B600000	22.8.41	PCA8, A26					
e	B700001	B750000	22.8.41	PCA8, A19					
f	B850001	B900000	22.8.41	PCA8, A25					
g	B1000001	B1050000	22.8.41	PCA8, A29					
h	B1150001	B1200000	22.8.41	PCA8, A26					
i	B1300001	B1350000	22.8.41	PCA8, A19					
j	B1450001	B1500000	22.8.41	PCA8, A27					
k	B1600001	B1650000	22.8.41	PCA8, A29					
l	B1750001	B1800000	22.8.41	PCA8, A27					
m	B1900001	B1950000	22.8.41	PCA8, A26					
n	B2050001	B2100000	22.8.41	PCA8, A19					
o	B2200001	B2250000	22.8.41	PCA8, A25					
p	B2350001	B2400000	22.8.41	PCA8, A26					
q	B2500001	B2550000	22.8.41	PCA8, A29					
r	B2650001	B2700000	22.8.41	PCA8, A25					
s	B2800001	B2850000	22.8.41	PCA8, A19					
t	B2950001	B3000000	22.8.41	PCA8, A27					

N.B. All the print runs have 100000 serial number gaps between them, with no notes issued for those serial numbers

1941 THIRD ENNES ISSUE

MZ88	**20 escudos**	1 November 1941	SCWPM 85
	Printer	Bradbury Wilkinson & Co. Ltd.	
	Total Printed	1950000	
	Circulation	Introduced 1942*. Withdrawn 31. 12. 1960	
	Colour	Blue on pink and buff underprint. Reverse blue on pale green and buff underprint	
	Obverse Design	Portrait of António Ennes at left, steamship seal at right.	
	Reverse Design	Allegorical maiden looking at ships	
	Size	130 x 81 mm	

MZ88g

					Issued Notes			Archival Specimens	Specimens
MZ88	Start of Print Run	End of Print Run	Order Date (If Known)	Signatures	Fine	VF	EF	EF	AU
a	1000001	1040000	21.10.41	PCA8, A25	$35	$80	$175	$200	$150
b	1040001	1080000	21.10.41	PCA8, A26					
c	1080001	1120000	21.10.41	PCA8, A19					
d	1120001	1160000	21.10.41	PCA8, A27					
e	1160001	1200000	21.10.41	PCA8, A29					
f	1200001	1550000	11.2.43	PCA8, A29					
g	1550001	1900000	11.2.43	PCA8, A19					
h	1900001	2250000	11.2.43	PCA8, A26					
i	2250001	2600000	11.2.43	PCA8, A25					
j	2600001	2950000	11.2.43	PCA8, A27					

MZ89	**50 escudos**	1 November 1941	SCWPM 86
	Printer	Bradbury Wilkinson & Co. Ltd.	
	Total Printed	1017000	
	Circulation	Introduced 1942*. Withdrawn 31. 12. 1960	
	Colour	Olive-grey on multicoloured underprint	
	Obverse Design	Portrait of António Ennes at left, steamship seal at right.	
	Reverse Design	Allegorical maiden looking at ships	
	Size	164 x 84 mm	

MZ89c

					Issued Notes			Archival Specimens	Specimens
MZ89	Start of Print Run	End of Print Run	Order Date (If Known)	Signatures	Fine	VF	EF	AU	AU
a	400001	440000	29.10.41	PCA8, A19					
b	440001	480000	29.10.41	PCA8, A26					
c	480001	520000	29.10.41	PCA8, A29					
d	520001	560000	29.10.41	PCA8, A27					
e	560001	600000	29.10.41	PCA8, A25					
f	600001	624000	29.10.41	PCA8, A26					
g	624001	648000	29.10.41	PCA8, A29					
h	648001	672000	29.10.41	PCA8, A27	$65	$200	$400	$300	$225
i	672001	696000	29.10.41	PCA8, A19					
j	696001	720000	29.10.41	PCA8, A25					
k	720001	860000	9.2.43	PCA8, A19					
l	860001	1000000	9.2.43	PCA8, A26					
m	1000001	1140000	9.2.43	PCA8, A27					
n	1140001	1280000	9.2.43	PCA8, A25					
o	1280001	1420000†	9.2.43	PCA8, A29					

† Although the last printer's archival spec men for this date ran to 1420000, only notes numbered up to 1417000 were issued. See MZ100 below

MZ90 **500 escudos** 1 November 1941 SCWPM 87

Printer Bradbury Wilkinson & Co. Ltd.

Total Printed 160000

Circulation Introduced 1942*. Withdrawn 31. 12. 1960

Colour Purple on multicoloured underprint

Obverse Design Portrait of António Ennes at left, steamship seal at right.

Reverse Design Allegorical maiden looking at ships

Size 175 x 100 mm

MZ90b

					Issued Notes			Archival Specimens	Specimens
MZ90	Start of Print Run	End of Print Run	Order Date (If Known)	Signatures	Fine	VF	EF	AU	AU
a	40001	52000	29.10.41	PCA8, A25					
b	52001	64000	29.10.41	PCA8, A27					
c	64001	76000	29.10.41	PCA8, A29					
d	76001	88000	29.10.41	PCA8, A19					
e	88001	100000	29.10.41	PCA8, A26	$1,200	$2,500	Rare	$650	$600
f	100001	120000	11.2.43	PCA8, A27					
g	120001	140000	11.2.43	PCA8, A26					
h	140001	160000	11.2.43	PCA8, A19					
i	160001	180000	11.2.43	PCA8, A25					
j	180001	200000	11.2.43	PCA8, A29					

MZ91	**1000 escudos**	1 November 1941 SCWPM 88
	Printer	Bradbury Wilkinson & Co. Ltd.
	Total Printed	80000
	Circulation	Introduced 1942*. Withdrawn 31. 12. 1960
	Colour	Brown on multicoloured underprint
	Obverse Design	Portrait of António Ennes at left, steamship seal at right.
	Reverse Design	Allegorical young woman looking out at ships from various eras
	Size	182 x 103 mm

MZ91js

					Issued Notes			Archival Specimens	Specimens
MZ91	Start of Print Run	End of Print Run	Order Date (If Known)	Signatures	Fine	VF	EF	AU	AU
a	50001	60000	28.10.41	PCA8, A26	$1,800	Rare	Rare	$750	$650
b	60001	70000	28.10.41	PCA8, A25					
c	70001	80000	28.10.41	PCA8, A29					
d	80001	90000	28.10.41	PCA8, A27					
e	90001	100000	28.10.41	PCA8, A19					
f	100001	106000	28.10.41	PCA8, A25					
g	106001	112000	9.2.43	PCA8, A27					
h	112001	118000	9.2.43	PCA8, A19					
i	118001	124000	11.2.43	PCA8, A29					
j	124001	130000	11.2.43	PCA8, A26					

1943 FOURTH ENNES ISSUE

MZ92	**5 escudos**	15 April 1943	SCWPM 89
	Printer	Bradbury Wilkinson & Co. Ltd.	
	Total Printed	750000	
	Circulation	Introduced 07. 09. 1944. Withdrawn 31. 12. 1960	
	Colour	Green on buff underprint	
	Obverse Design	Portrait of António Ennes at left, steamship seal at right.	
	Reverse Design	Allegorical maiden looking at ships	
	Size	126 x 75 mm	

MZ92e

MZ92	Start of Print Run	End of Print Run	Order Date (If Known)	Signatures	Issued Notes VG	Issued Notes VF	Issued Notes Unc	Archival Specimens AU	Specimens AU
a	000001	150000	22.4.43	PCA8, A27					
b	160001	310000	22.4.43	PCA8, A26					
c	320001	470000	22.4.43	PCA8, A29	$20	$50	$180	$250	$150
d	480001	630000	22.4.43	PCA8, A25					
e	640001	790000	22.4.43	PCA8, A19					
ct	Specimen colour trial in brown, no serial numbers, no signatures, overprinted SPECIMEN in red diagonally, two punch holes								Unc - $350
N.B.	All the print runs have 10000 serial number gaps between them, with no notes issued for those serial numbers								

MZ92ct

MZ92ct

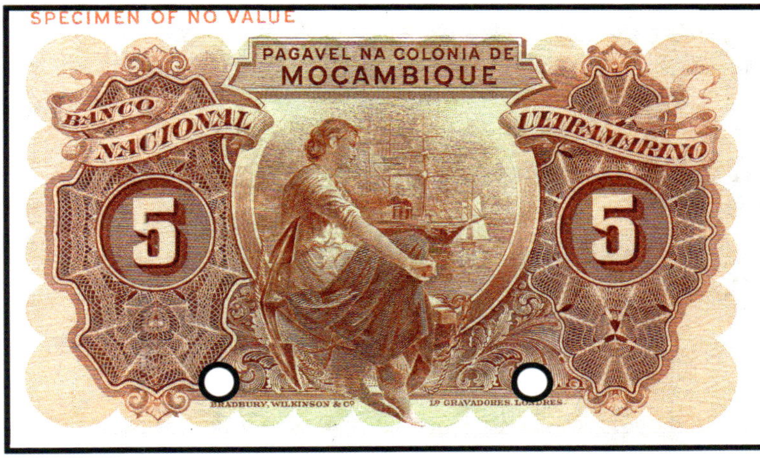

MZ93 **10 escudos** 15 April 1943 SCWPM 90

Printer Bradbury Wilkinson & Co. Ltd.

Total Printed 375000

Circulation Introduced 07. 09. 1944. Withdrawn 31. 12. 1960

Colour Brown on pink and pale green underprint

Obverse Design Portrait of António Ennes at left, steamship seal at right.

Reverse Design Allegorical maiden looking at ships

Size 126 x 75 mm

MZ93b

					Issued Notes			Archival Specimens	Specimens
MZ93	Start of Print Run	End of Print Run	Order Date (If Known)	Signatures	Fine	VF	EF	AU	AU
a	000001	075000	22.4.43	PCA8, A26					
b	080001	155000	22.4.43	PCA8, A29					
c	160001	235000	22.4.43	PCA8, A27	$40	$100	$250	$300	$200
d	240001	315000	22.4.43	PCA8, A19					
e	320001	395000	22.4.43	PCA8, A25					
ct	Specimen colour trial in olive-green, reverse purple on pink underprint, no serial numbers, no signatures, overprinted SPECIMEN in red horizontally, two punch holes								Unc - $450
N.B.	All the print runs have 5000 serial number gaps between them, with no notes issued for those serial numbers								

MZ93ct

MZ93ct

MZ94	**100 escudos**	27 January 1943	SCWPM 91
	Printer	Bradbury Wilkinson & Co. Ltd.	
	Total Printed	800000	
	Circulation	Introduced 1943*. Withdrawn 31. 12. 1960	
	Colour	Orange on multicoloured underprint	
	Obverse Design	Portrait of António Ennes at left, steamship seal at right.	
	Reverse Design	Allegorical maiden looking at ships	
	Size	170 x 97 mm	

MZ94c

					Issued Notes			Archival Specimens	Specimens
MZ94	Start of Print Run	End of Print Run	Order Date (If Known)	Signatures	Fine	VF	EF	AU	AU
a	000001	060000	8.2.43	PCA8, A26	$400	$1,000	$2,200	$450	$400
b	060001	120000	8.2.43	PCA8, A29					
c	120001	180000	8.2.43	PCA8, A27					
d	180001	240000	8.2.43	PCA8, A25					
e	240001	300000	8.2.43	PCA8, A19					
f	300001	400000	29.8.43	PCA8, A29					
g	400001	500000	29.8.43	PCA8, A27					
h	500001	600000	29.8.43	PCA8, A19					
i	600001	700000	29.8.43	PCA8, A26					
j	700001	800000	29.8.43	PCA8, A25					
dp	Obverse and reverse die proofs in issued colour orange								$550 (pair)
sp	Specimen proof in issued colours, signatures PCA8 and A19, serial number 000,000, with manuscript signatures of A25 and A27 on reverse					Rare			

MZ94dp

MZ94dp

1944-45 FIFTH ENNES ISSUE

MZ95	**1 escudo**	23 May 1944	SCWPM 92
	Printer	Bradbury Wilkinson & Co. Ltd.	
	Total Printed	4000000	
	Circulation	Introduced 13. 06. 1945. Withdrawn in two stages on 10. 02. 1951 and 04. 10. 1952	
	Colour	Black on olive and multicoloured underprint	
	Obverse Design	Portrait of António Ennes at left, steamship seal at right.	
	Reverse Design	Arms and value set in ornate pattern	
	Size	105 x 60 mm	
	Signatures	PCA8, A27	

MZ95s

				Issued Notes			Specimens (sp)
MZ95	Start of Print Run	End of Print Run	Order Date (If Known)	VG	VF	Unc	Unc
a	A.0250001	E.1250000	24.5.44				
b	E.1250001	E.2250000	24.5.44	$10	$35	$120	$250
c	I. 2250001	I 3250000	24.5.44				
d	0.3250001	0.4250000	24.5.44				
p	Reverse omnibus proof in issued colours endorsed in black type "Ultramarino 1$00 back."						AU - $100
ph	Back and white obverse and reverse archival photographs, dated 11 January 1943, serial number 000,000, signatures PCA8 and A26						One Pair Known
s	Printer's archival specimen with serial number run A.0,250,001 to 0.4,250,000. Two copies known						Rare
N.B.	Only prefixes A, E, I and O were issued. The O prefix is stylised (rectangular)						

MZ95ph

MZ96	**2½ escudos**	23 May 1944	SCWPM 93
	Printer	Bradbury Wilkinson & Co. Ltd.	
	Total Printed	4000000	
	Circulation	Introduced 13. 06. 1945. Withdrawn in two stages on 10. 02. 1951 and 04. 10. 1952	
	Colour	Blue on multicoloured underprint	
	Obverse Design	Portrait of António Ennes at left, steamship seal at right.	
	Reverse Design	Arms and value set in ornate pattern	
	Size	120 x 60 mm	
	Signatures	PCA8, A27	

MZ96a

				Issued Notes			Specimens (sp)
MZ96	Start of Print Run	End of Print Run	Order Date (If Known)	VG	VF	Unc	Unc
a	E.0120001	E.1120000	24.5.44	$12	$45	$160	$250
b	I. 1120001	I.2120000	24.5.44				
c	0.2120001	0.3120000	24.5.44				
d	U.3120001	U.4120000	24.5.44				
p	Reverse omnibus proof in issued colours endorsed in black type "Ultramarino 2$50 back."						AU - $100
ph	Back and white obverse and reverse archival photographs dated 3. 3. 41, note dated 11 January 1943, serial number 000,000, signatures PCA8 and A26						One Pair Known
s	Printer's archival specimen with serial number run E.0,120,001 to U.4,120,000. Two copies known						Rare
N.B.	Only prefixes E, I, O and U were issued. The O and U prefixes are stylised (rectanguar)						

MZ96ph

MZ97 **5 escudos** 29 November 1945 SCWPM 94

Printer	Bradbury Wilkinson & Co. Ltd.
Total Printed	2250000
Circulation	Introduced 1946*. Withdrawn 31. 12. 1960
Colour	Green on buff underprint
Obverse Design	Portrait of António Ennes at left, steamship seal at right.
Reverse Design	Allegorical maiden looking at ships
Size	126 x 75 mm

MZ97g

					Issued Notes			Archival Specimens	Specimens
MZ97	Start of Print Run	End of Print Run	Order Date (If Known)	Signatures	VG	VF	Unc	AU	AU
a	800001	1120000	6.12.45	PCA8, A30					
b	1130001	1450000	6.12.45	PCA8, A25					
c	1460001	1780000	6.12.45	PCA8, A19					
d	1790001	2110000	6.12.45	PCA8, A27	$15	$45	$180	$220	$150
e	2120001	2440000	6.12.45	PCA8, A26					
f	2450001	2775000	6.12.45	PCA8, A29					
g	2785000	3110000	6.12.45	PCA8, A18					
dp	Obverse and reverse die proof in issued colours								$375 (pair)
N.B.	All the print runs have 10000 serial number gaps between them, with no notes issued for those serial numbers								

MZ98 **10 escudos** 29 November 1945 SCWPM 95

Printer Bradbury Wilkinson & Co. Ltd.
Total Printed 3125000
Circulation Introduced 1946*. Withdrawn 31. 12. 1960
Colour Brown on pink and pale green underprint
Obverse Design Portrait of António Ennes at left, steamship seal at right.
Reverse Design Allegorical maiden looking at ships
Size 126 x 75 mm

MZ98m

					Issued Notes			Archival Specimens	Specimens
MZ98	Start of Print Run	End of Print Run	Order Date (If Known)	Signatures	VG	VF	Unc	AU	AU
a	400001	565000	6.12.45	PCA8, A29					
b	570001	730000	6.12.45	PCA8, A18					
c	735001	895000	6.12.45	PCA8, A25					
d	900001	1060000	6.12.45	PCA8, A26					
e	1065001	1225000	6.12.45	PCA8, A30					
f	1230001	1390000	6.12.45	PCA8, A27					
g	1395001	1555000	6.12.45	PCA8, A19	$20	$75	$250	$220	$180
h	1560001	1855000	13.10.49	PCA8, A18					
i	1860001	2160000	13.10.49	PCA8, A19					
j	2165001	2525000	13.10.49	PCA8, A25					
k	2530001	2745000	13.10.49	PCA8, A26					
l	2750001	3145000	13.10.49	PCA8, A30					
m	3150001	3585000	13.10.49	PCA8, A29					
dp	Obverse and reverse die proof in issued colours								$375 (pair)

N.B. All the print runs have 5000 serial number gaps between them, with no notes issued for those serial numbers

MZ99	**20 escudos**	29 November 1945	SCWPM 96
	Printer	Bradbury Wilkinson & Co. Ltd.	
	Total Printed	1750000	
	Circulation	Introduced 1946*. Withdrawn 31. 12. 1960	
	Colour	Blue on pink and buff underprint. Reverse blue on pale green and buff underprint	
	Obverse Design	Portrait of António Ennes at left, steamship seal at right.	
	Reverse Design	Allegorical maiden looking at ships	
	Size	130 x 81 mm	

MZ99g

					Issued Notes			Archival Specimens	Specimens
MZ99	Start of Print Run	End of Print Run	Order Date (If Known)	Signatures	Fine	VF	EF	AU	AU
a	2950001	3070000	6.12.45	PCA8, A26					
b	3070001	3170000	6.12.45	PCA8, A27					
c	3170001	3270000	6.12.45	PCA8, A25					
d	3270001	3380000	6.12.45	PCA8, A30					
e	3380001	3480000	6.12.45	PCA8, A19					
f	3480001	3580000	6.12.45	PCA8, A18					
g	3580001	3700000	6.12.45	PCA8, A29	$35	$80	$175	$250	$200
h	3700001	3892000	13.10-49	PCA8, A30					
i	3892001	4250000	13.10.49	PCA8, A18					
j	4250001	4382000	13.10.49	PCA8, A29					
k	4382001	4560000	13.10.49	PCA8, A19					
l	4560001	4672000	13.10.49	PCA8, A26					
m	4672001	4700000	13.10.49	PCA8, A25					

MZ100	**50 escudos**	29 November 1945	SCWPM 96A
	Printer	Bradbury Wilkinson & Co. Ltd.	
	Total Printed	400000	
	Circulation	Introduced 1946*. Withdrawn 31. 12. 1960	
	Colour	Olive-grey on multicoloured underprint	
	Obverse Design	Portrait of António Ennes at left, steamship seal at right.	
	Reverse Design	Allegorical maiden looking at ships	
	Size	164 x 84 mm	

MZ100c

					Issued Notes			Archival Specimens	Specimens
MZ100	Start of Print Run	End of Print Run	Order Date (If Known)	Signatures	Fine	VF	EF	AU	AU
a	1417001	1467000	6.12.45	PCA8, A19					
b	1467001	1527000	6.12.45	PCA8, A30					
c	1527001	1587000	6.12.45	PCA8, A29					
d	1587001	1650000	6.12.45	PCA8, A25	$65	$150	$300	$275	$200
e	1650001	1700000	6.12.45	PCA8, A27					
f	1700001	1750000	6.12.45	PCA8, A18					
g	1750001	1817000	6.12.45	PCA8, A26					

MZ101	**100 escudos**	29 November 1945 — SCWPM 97
	Printer	Bradbury Wilkinson & Co. Ltd.
	Total Printed	500000
	Circulation	Introduced 1946*. Withdrawn 31. 12. 1960
	Colour	Orange on multicoloured underprint
	Obverse Design	Portrait of António Ennes at left, steamship seal at right.
	Reverse Design	Allegorical maiden looking at ships
	Size	170 x 97 mm

MZ101c

					Issued Notes			Archival Specimens	Specimens
MZ101	Start of Print Run	End of Print Run	Order Date (If Known)	Signatures	Fine	VF	EF	AU	AU
a	800001	880000	6.12.45	PCA8, A25					
b	880001	950000	6.12.45	PCA8, A29					
c	950001	1010000	6.12.45	PCA8, A26					
d	1010001	1060000	6.12.45	PCA8, A18	$200	$500	$1,500	$400	$350
e	1060001	1150000	6.12.45	PCA8, A27					
f	1150001	1230000	6.12.45	PCA8, A30					
g	1230001	1300000	6.12.45	PCA8, A19					

MZ102	**500 escudos**	29 November 1945	SCWPM 98
	Printer	Bradbury Wilkinson & Co. Ltd.	
	Total Printed	60000	
	Circulation	Introduced 1946*. Withdrawn 31. 12. 1960	
	Colour	Purple on multicoloured underprint	
	Obverse Design	Portrait of António Ennes at left, steamship seal at right.	
	Reverse Design	Allegorical maiden looking at ships	
	Size	175 x 100 mm	

MZ102as

					Issued Notes			Archival Specimens	Specimens
MZ102	Start of Print Run	End of Print Run	Order Date (If Known)	Signatures	Fine	VF	EF	AU	AU
a	200001	210000	6.12.45	PCA8, A18					
b	210001	220000	6.12.45	PCA8, A19					
c	220001	230000	6.12.45	PCA8, A26					
d	230001	235000	6.12.45	PCA8, A29	$1,000	$2,200	Rare	$650	$600
e	235001	245000	6.12.45	PCA8, A27					
f	245001	255000	6.12.45	PCA8, A30					
g	255001	260000	6.12.45	PCA8, A25					

MZ103	**1000 escudos**	29 November 1945	SCWPM 99a
	Printer	Bradbury Wilkinson & Co. Ltd.	
	Total Printed	100000	
	Circulation	Introduced 1946*. Withdrawn 31. 12. 1960	
	Colour	Blue on multicoloured underprint	
	Obverse Design	Portrait of António Ennes at left, steamship seal at right.	
	Reverse Design	Allegorical young woman looking out at ships from various eras	
	Size	182 x 103mm	

MZ103c

					Issued Notes			Archival Specimens	Specimens
MZ103	Start of Print Run	End of Print Run	Order Date (If Known)	Signatures	Fine	VF	EF	EF	AU
a	130001	142000	6.12.45	PCA8, A27					
b	142001	154000	6.12.45	PCA8, A18					
c	154001	168000	6.12.45	PCA8, A29					
d	168001	182000	6.12.45	PCA8, A26	$800	$2,000	Rare	$650	$600
e	182001	198000	6.12.45	PCA8, A25					
f	198001	214000	6.12.45	PCA8, A19					
g	214001	230000	6.12.45	PCA8, A30					
dp	Obverse and reverse die proof in issued colours								AU - $700 (pair)

1947 SIXTH ENNES ISSUE

MZ104 **100 escudos** 27 March 1947 SCWPM 100

Printer	Bradbury Wilkinson & Co. Ltd.
Total Printed	200000
Circulation	Introduced 1947*. Withdrawn 31. 12. 1960
Colour	Orange on multicoloured underprint
Obverse Design	Portrait of António Ennes at left, steamship seal at right.
Reverse Design	Allegorical maiden looking at ships
Size	170 x 97 mm

MZ104a

					Issued Notes			Archival Specimens	Specimens
MZ104	Start of Print Run	End of Print Run	Order Date (If Known)	Signatures	Fine	VF	EF	AU	AU
a	1300001	1328000	31.3.47	PCA8, A29					
b	1328001	1357000	31.3.47	PCA8, A18					
c	1357001	1385000	31.3.47	PCA8, A26					
d	1385001	1415000	31.3.47	PCA8, A30	Rare	Rare	Rare	$1,000	$1,000
e	1415001	1443000	31.3.47	PCA8, A19					
f	1443001	1471000	31.3.47	PCA8, A28					
g	1471001	1500000	31.3.47	PCA8, A25					

N.B. Fewer than 10 issued copies of MZ104 are known

MZ105 **500 escudos** 27 March 1947 SCWPM 101

Printer	Bradbury Wilkinson & Co. Ltd.
Total Printed	180000
Circulation	Introduced 1947*. Withdrawn 31. 12. 1960
Colour	Purple on multicoloured underprint
Obverse Design	Portrait of António Ennes at left, steamship seal at right.
Reverse Design	Allegorical maiden looking at ships
Size	175 x 100 mm

MZ105g

					Issued Notes			Archival Specimens	Specimens
MZ105	Start of Print Run	End of Print Run	Order Date (If Known)	Signatures	Fine	VF	EF	AU	AU
a	260001	285000	31.3.47	PCA8, A26					
b	285001	310000	31.3.47	PCA8, A25					
c	310001	336000	31.3.47	PCA8, A30					
d	336001	362000	31.3.47	PCA8, A19	$700	$1,800	Rare	$650	$600
e	362001	387000	31.3.47	PCA8, A18					
f	387001	413000	31.3.47	PCA8, A28					
g	413001	440000	31.3.47	PCA8, A29					

MZ106 **1000 escudos** 27 March 1947 SCWPM 99b

Printer Bradbury Wilkinson & Co. Ltd.

Total Printed 389500

Circulation Introduced 1947. Withdrawn 31. 12. 1960

Colour Blue on multicoloured underprint

Obverse Design Portrait of António Ennes at left, steamship seal at right.

Reverse Design Allegorical young woman looking out at ships from various eras

Size 182 x 103 mm

MZ106j

					Issued Notes			Archival Specimens	Specimens (sp)
MZ106	Start of Print Run	End of Print Run	Order Date (If Known)	Signatures	Fine	VF	EF	AU	AU
a	230001	243000	8.4.47	PCA8, A18					
b	243001	256000	8.4.47	PCA8, A26					
c	256001	270000	8.4.47	PCA8, A19					
d	270001	282000	8.4.47	PCA8, A29					
e	282001	295000	8.4.47	PCA8, A25					
f	295001	307000	8.4.47	PCA8, A30					
g	307001	319500	8.4.47	PCA8, A28					
h	319501	335000	2.10.47	PCA8, A18					
i	335001	345000	2.10.47	PCA8, A26					
j	345001	360000	2.10.47	PCA8, A29					
k	360001	375000	2.10.47	PCA8, A25	$350	$750	$1,800	$450	$400
l	375001	390000	2.10.47	PCA8, A28					
m	390001	405000	2.10.47	PCA8, A30					
n	405001	419500	2.10.47	PCA8, A19					
o	419501	440000	13.10.49	PCA8, A18					
p	440001	459000	13.10.49	PCA8, A28					
q	459001	470000	13.10.49	PCA8, A26					
r	470001	499000	13.10.49	PCA8, A29					
s	499001	530000	13.10.49	PCA8, A19					
t	530001	569000	13.10.49	PCA8, A25					
u	569001	619500	13.10.49	PCA8, A30					

INTRODUCTION TO THE HEROES OF OCCUPATION ISSUES

This series features four so-called "Heroes of Occupation" as follows:-

1. **Eduardo Augusto Ferreiro da Costa (Eduardo Costa) (1865-1907)** was born in Lisbon and attended the Colégio Militar between 1875-79. He rose to be a major in the Portuguese army, prior to his appointment as Acting Governor of Angola from 1903-04 and Governor General of Angola from 1906-07. In 1932 he was awarded posthumously with the Grand Cross of the Order of the Colonial Empire.

2. **Aires de Ornelas e Vasconcelos (Aires de Ornelas) (1866-1930)** was born into a distinguished Madeiran family and as a military man was involved in the conquest and pacification of Portugal's colonial African empire. From 1896-98 he was Governor General of Mozambique and later Minister of the Navy and Overseas Government. He published several works on Portugal's campaigns in Africa and also on Portugal's colonial administration.

3. **Alfredo Augusto Caldas Xavier (Caldas Xavier) (1852-96)** was a colonial administrator, military engineer and explorer, who with Ennes, Xavier and Costa was involved in the subjugation of Mozambique in the early 1890s.

4. **Joaquim Augusto Mousinho de Albuquerque (Mousinho de Albuquerque) (1855-1902)** was born in Batalha and was a cavalry officer, who with António Ennes played a decisive role in the military campaigns, which secured Portuguese control of Mozambique. For more than 50 years he was to become a model of almost unattainable heroism, an image vigorously promoted under the Estado Novo, the Portuguese Second Republic (1933-74).

1950-53 HEROES OF OCCUPATION ISSUE

MZ107	**50 escudos**	16 February 1950	SCWPM 102
	Printer	Thomas De La Rue & Co. Ltd.	
	Total Printed	8000000	
	Circulation	Introduced 29. 11. 1950	
	Colour	Black on multicoloured underprint. Reverse green on orange and lilac underprint	
	Obverse Design	Portrait of Eduardo Costa at right	
	Reverse Design	Doorway in the fortress of São Sebastião on the Island of Mozambique, value at left	
	Watermark	Coat of Arms of Portuguese Mozambique	
	Size	162 x 80 mm	

MZ107sp

MZ107sp

					Issued Notes			Specimens (sp)
MZ107	Start of Print Run	End of Print Run	Order Date (If Known)	Signatures	VG	VF	Unc	AU
a	000001	142850	31.7.50	VPCA9, A31				
b	142851	285900	31.7.50	VPCA9, A19				
c	285901	429900	31.7.50	VPCA9, A25				
d	429901	572720	31.7.50	VPCA9, A26				
e	572721	715380	31.7.50	VPCA9, A29				
f	715381	858400	31.7.50	VPCA9, A30				
g	858401	1000000	31.7.50	VPCA9, A28				
h	1000001	1143000	20.10.52	VPCA9, A29				
i	1143001	1280000	20.10.52	VPCA9, A31				
j	1280001	1330000	20.10.52	VPCA9, A25				
k	1330001	1470000	20.10.52	VPCA9, A26				
l	1470001	1610000	20.10.52	VPCA9, A19				
m	1610001	1810000	20.10.52	VPCA9, A30				
n	1810001	2000000	20.10.52	VPCA9, A28	$40	$220	$600	$150
o	2000001	2428000	6.4.53	VPCA9, A30				
p	2428001	2856000	6.4.53	VPCA9, A19				
q	2856001	3285000	6.4.53	VPCA9, A31				
r	3285001	3800000	6.4.53	VPCA9, A25				
s	3800001	4230000	6.4.53	VPCA9, A29				
t	4230001	4656000	6.4.53	VPCA9, A25				
u	4656001	5000000	6.4.53	VPCA9, A28				
v	5000001	5500000	18.11.53	VPCA9, A30				
w	5500001	6000000	18.11.53	VPCA9, A19				
x	6000001	6400000	18.11.53	VPCA9, A25				
y	6400001	6900000	18.11.53	VPCA9, A28				
z	6900001	7500000	18.11.53	VPCA9, A26				
a1	7500001	8000000	18.11.53	VPCA9, A31				
ph	Black and white obverse and reverse archival photographs dated 22. 12. 49, note dated 16 November 1950, serial number 000 000, signatures G8 and A27							One Pair Known

MZ107ph

MZ107ph

MZ108 **100 escudos** 16 February 1950 SCWPM 103

Printer	Thomas De La Rue & Co. Ltd.
Total Printed	5000000
Circulation	Introduced 28. 02. 1951
Colour	Orange on multicoloured underprint
Obverse Design	Portrait of Aires de Ornelas at right
Reverse Design	Gateway in the fortress of São Sebastião on the Island of Mozambique at centre, value at left
Watermark	Coat of Arms of Portuguese Mozambique
Size	165 x 85 mm

MZ108b

MZ108b

					Issued Notes			Specimens (sp)
MZ108	Start of Print Run	End of Print Run	Order Date (If Known)	Signatures	VG	VF	Unc	AU
a	000001	160000	21.11.50	VPCA9, A19				
b	160001	326000	21.11.50	VPCA9, A30				
c	326001	500000	21.11.50	VPCA9, A29				
d	500001	670000	21.11.50	VPCA9, A28				
e	670001	835000	21.11.50	VPCA9, A26				
f	835001	1000000	21.11.50	VPCA9, A31				
g	1000001	1285000	6.4.53	VPCA9, A19				
h	1285001	1570000	6.4.53	VPCA9, A30				
i	1570001	1850000	6.4.53	VPCA9, A25				
j	1850001	2145000	6.4.53	VPCA9, A28	$70	$300	$800	$325
k	2145001	2430000	6.4.53	VPCA9, A31				
l	2430001	2715000	6.4.53	VPCA9, A26				
m	2715001	3000000	6.4.53	VPCA9, A29				
n	3000001	3400000	18.11.53	VPCA9, A19				
o	3400001	3700000	18.11.53	VPCA9, A25				
p	3700001	4100000	18.11.53	VPCA9, A28				
q	4100001	4500000	18.11.53	VPCA9, A30				
r	4500001	4800000	18.11.53	VPCA9, A31				
s	4800001	5000000	18.11.53	VPCA9, A26				
aw	Obverse and reverse artwork on cardboard, note dated 16 November 1950, differences in design from issued note, serial number 000 000, signatures G8 and A27							Unique

MZ108aw

MZ108aw

MZ109 **500 escudos** 31 July 1953 SCWPM 104

Printer Bradbury Wilkinson & Co. Ltd.
Total Printed 700000
Circulation Introduced 12. 07. 1954
Colour Purple on multicoloured underprint
Obverse Design Portrait of Caldas Xavier at right
Reverse Design Arms of Mozambique at centre, ship seal at left
Watermark Mousinho de Albuquerque
Size 170 x 89 mm

MZ109c

MZ109c

					Issued Notes			Archival Specimens	Specimens
MZ109	Start of Print Run	End of Print Run	Order Date (If Known)	Signatures	VG	VF	Unc	VF	AU
a	000001	042800	8.5.53	G9, A30					
b	042801	095700	8.5.53	G9, A19					
c	095701	135000	8.5.53	G9, A33					
d	135001	170000	8.5.53	G9, A32					
e	170001	212800	8.5.53	G9, A34					
f	212801	266000	8.5.53	G9, A35					
g	266001	300000	8.5.53	G9, A36	$40	$250	$800	$250	$300
h	300001	360000	31.12.58	G9, A34					
i	360001	450000	31.12.58	G9, A19					
j	450001	520000	31.12.58	G9, A19					
k	520001	580000	31.12.58	G9, A36					
l	580001	650000	31.12.58	G9, A35					
m	650001	700000	31.12.58	G9, A36					
ct	Specimen colour trial in grey-green and multicoloured, no date, serial number 000000, no signatures, overprinted SPECIMEN in red horizontally, two punch holes								Unc - $180
ph1	Black and white obverse and reverse archival photographs dated 21. 3. 53, note dated 16 December 1953, Decreto No. 17154, serial number 000,000, signatures G9 and A29, reverse with different steamship seal from issued note								One Pair Known
ph2	Black and white reverse archival photograph dated 21. 3. 53, with different arms and steamship seal from issued note and additional bank legend above arms								One Copy Known

MZ109ct

MZ109ct

MZ109ph1

MZ109ph1

MZ109ph2

MZ110 **1000 escudos** 31 July 1953 SCWPM 105

Printer Bradbury Wilkinson & Co. Ltd.
Total Printed 1500000
Circulation Introduced 12. 07. 1954
Colour Blue on pink and multicoloured underprint
Obverse Design Portrait of Mousinho de Albuquerque at right
Reverse Design Arms of Mozambique at centre, ship seal at left
Watermark Mousinho de Albuquerque
Size 175 x 96 mm

MZ110m

MZ110m

MZ110	Start of Print Run	End of Print Run	Order Date (If Known)	Signatures	Issued Notes VG	VF	Unc	Archival Specimens AU	Specimens AU
a	000001	030000	8.5.53	G9, A30					
b	030001	058000	8.5.53	G9, A33					
c	058001	075500	8.5.53	G9, A32					
d	075501	104000	8.5.53	G9, A19					
e	104001	132000	8.5.53	G9, A35					
f	132001	150000	8.5.53	G9, A36					
g	150001	200000	8.5.53	G9, A34	$15	$100	$375	$250	$200
h	200001	380000	1.1.59	G9, A19					
i	380001	560000	1.1.59	G9, A36					
j	560001	750000	1.1.59	G9, A19					
k	750001	935000	1.1.59	G9, A36					
l	935001	1112000	1.1.59	G9, A34					
m	1112001	1500000	1.1.59	G9, A35					
ct	Specimen colour trial in brown and multicoloured, no date, serial number 000000, no signatures, overprinted SPECIMEN in red horizontally, two punch holes								Unc - $200
dp	Obverse and reverse die proof in issued colours								AU - $400 (pair)
ph	Black and white obverse and reverse archival photographs dated 21. 3. 53, note dated 16 December 1953, Decreto No. 17154, serial number 000,000, signatures G9 and A29, obverse with different design from issued note, reverse with no bank seal								One Pair Known

MZ110ct

MZ110ct

MZ110ph

MZ110ph

1958 HEROES OF OCCUPATION ISSUE

MZ111 **50 escudos** 24 July 1958 SCWPM 106

Printer Thomas De La Rue & Co. Ltd.
Total printed 10800000
Circulation Introduced 13. 07. 1959
Colour Black on multicoloured underprint. Reverse green on orange and lilac underprint
Obverse Design Portrait of Eduardo Costa at right
Reverse Design Gateway in the fortress of São Sebastião on the Island of Mozambique, ship seal at upper left, value at lower left
Watermark Coat of Arms of Portuguese Mozambique
Size 162 x 80 mm

MZ111d

MZ111d

MZ111	Start of Print Run	End of Print Run	Order Date (If Known)	Signatures	Issued Notes VG	Issued Notes VF	Issued Notes Unc	Specimens Unc
a	B0000001	B1600000	30.7.58	G9, A19	$7	$20	$65	$125
b	B1600001	B3500000	30.7.58	G9, A36				
c	B3500001	B5600000	30.7.58	G9, A34				
d	B5600001	B7000000	30.7.58	G9, A35				
e	B7000001	B8400000	30.7.58	G9, A37				
f	B8400001	B9800000	30.7.58	G9, A38				
g	B9800001	B10200000	30.1.70	G9, A35				
h	B10200001	B10500000	30.1.70	G9, A36				
i	B10500001	B10800000	30.1.70	G9, A38				

MZ112	**100 escudos**	24 July 1958	SCWPM 107
	Printer	Thomas De La Rue & Co. Ltd.	
	Total Printed	7000000	
	Circulation	Introduced 13. 07. 1959	
	Colour	Orange on multicoloured underprint	
	Obverse Design	Portrait of Aires de Ornelas at right	
	Reverse Design	Gateway in the fortress of São Sebastião on the Island of Mozambique, ship seal at upper left, value at lower left	
	Watermark	Coat of Arms of Portuguese Mozambique	
	Size	165 x 85 mm	

MZ112f

MZ112f

MZ112	Start of Print Run	End of Print Run	Order Date (If Known)	Signatures	Issued Notes VG	Issued Notes VF	Issued Notes Unc	Specimens Unc
a	B0000001	B1160000	30.7.58	G9, A26				
b	B1160001	B2300000	30.7.58	G9, A35				
c	B2300001	B3500000	30.7.58	G9, A19	$20	$70	$250	$150
d	B3500001	B4600000	30.7.58	G9, A38				
e	B4600001	B5800000	30.7.58	G9, A34				
f	B5800001	B7000000	30.7.58	G9, A37				
dp	Obverse and reverse die proof in issued colours							AU - $400 (pair)

N.B. Contrary to what is stated in SCWPM, P108 does not exist and no 500 escudo note dated 24 July 1958 was ever issued

1961-1967 HEROES OF OCCUPATION ISSUE

MZ113 **100 escudos** 27 March 1961 SCWPM 109a

Printer Bradbury Wilkinson & Co. Ltd.
Total Printed 13000000
Circulation Introduced 24. 04. 1962
Colour Green on multicoloured underprint
Obverse Design Portrait of Aires de Ornelas at right
Reverse Design Large ornate ship seal at left
Watermark Coat of Arms of Portuguese Mozambique
Size 165 x 85 mm

MZ113b

MZ113b

					Issued Notes			Archival Specimens	Specimens
MZ113	Start of Print Run	End of Print Run	Order Date (If Known)	Signatures	VG	VF	Unc	AU	Unc
a	C0000001	C1100000	2.5.61	G9, A19	$5	$15	$50	$175	$150
b	C1100001	C2000000	2.5.61	G9, A39†	$10	$25	$70	$225	$225
c	C2000001	C3500000	2.5.61	G9, A36					
d	C3500001	C4000000	2.5.61	G9, A38					
e	C4000001	C5000000	2.5.61	G9, A37					
f	C5000001	C6000000	2.5.61	G9, A35					
g	C6000001	C7000000	2.5.61	G9, A40					
h	C7000001	C7250000	9.5.67	G9, A35	$5	$15	$50	$175	$150
i	C7250001	C7500000	9.5.67	G9, A38					
j	C7500001	C7750000	9.5.67	G9, A36					
k	C7750001	C8000000	9.5.67	G9, A37					
l	C8000001	C10000000	5.2.70	G9, A35					
m	C10000001	C11500000	5.2.70	G9, A38					
n	C11500001	C13000000	5.2.70	G9, A36					

ct1	Specimen colour trial in purple and multicoloured, no date, serial number C0000000, no signatures, overprinted SPECIMEN in red horizontally, two punch holes	$180
ct2	Specimen colour trial in purple and multicoloured, dated 27 March 1961, serial number C0000000, signatures G9 and A36, overprinted SPECIMEN in red horizontally, two punch holes	$250
ph	Black and white obverse and reverse archival photographs dated 16. 3. 61, note dated 20 February 1961, serial number 000000, signatures G8 and A27	One Pair Known
†	A39 - these are the only notes ever signed by Gabriel Mauricio Teixeira and as such are likely to command a premium	

MZ113ct2

MZ113ct2

MZ113ph

MZ113ph

MZ114 **100 escudos** 27 March 1961 SCWPM 109b

Printer Canadian Banknote Company
Total Printed 10000000
Circulation Introduced 1975*
Colour Green on multicoloured underprint
Obverse Design Portrait of Aires de Ornelas at right
Reverse Design Large ornate ship seal at left
Watermark None
Size 165 x 85 mm

MZ114a

					Issued Notes			Specimens
MZ114	Start of Print Run	End of Print Run	Order Date (If Known)	Signatures	VG	VF	Unc	Unc
a	C13000001	C16000000	13.11.74	G9, A35				
b	C16000001	C19000000	13.11.74	G9, A38	$4	$8	$40	$125
c	C19000001	C23000000	13.11.74	G9, A36				

MZ115 **500 escudos** 22 March 1967 SCWPM 110

Printer Bradbury Wilkinson & Co. Ltd.
Total Printed 700000
Circulation Introduced 1967*
Colour Purple on multicoloured underprint
Obverse Design Portrait of Caldas Xavier at right
Reverse Design Arms of Mozambique at centre, ship seal at left
Watermark Mousinho de Albuquerque
Size 170 x 89 mm

MZ115g

MZ115g

					Issued Notes			Archival Specimens	Specimens
MZ115	Start of Print Run	End of Print Run	Order Date (If Known)	Signatures	VG	VF	Unc	EF	Unc
a	700001	800000	10.5.67	G9, A38					
b	800001	900000	10.5.67	G9, A36					
c	900001	1000000	10.5.67	G9, A37					
d	1000001	1100000	10.5.67	G9, A41	$15	$45	$250	$250	$150
e	1100001	1200000	10.5.67	G9, A42					
f	1200001	1300000	10.5.67	G9, A44					
g	1300001	1400000	10.5.67	G9, A43					
ct	Specimen colour trial in grey-green and multicoloured, dated 22 March 1967, serial number 0000000, overprinted SPECIMEN in red horizontally, two punch holes			G9, All as above					$150

MZ115ct

MZ115ct

1970 AZEVEDO COUTINHO ISSUE

João António de Azevedo Coutinho Fragoso de Sequeira (João de Azevedo Coutinho) (1865-1944) was a Portuguese politician and colonial administrator who rose to be a rear admiral in the Portuguese Navy. He took part in the campaign to pacify Portugal's African colonies and acted as Deputy Governor General of Mozambique from 1905-06. A dedicated monarchist, he supported the deposed King Manuel II (1889-1932), during his exile in England, in the period immediately following the establishment of the first Portuguese Republic in 1910.

MZ116	**50 escudos**	27 October 1970	SCWPM 111
	Printer	Thomas De La Rue & Co. Ltd.	
	Total printed	6000000	
	Circulation	Introduced 30. 11. 1972	
	Colour	Black on green and purple underprint. Reverse green on pale orange and lilac underprint	
	Obverse Design	Portrait of João de Azevedo Coutinho at centre left	
	Reverse Design	Ornate ship seal	
	Watermark	Coat of Arms of Portuguese Mozambique	
	Size	160 x 80 mm	

MZ116s

MZ116s

MZ116	Start of Print Run	End of Print Run	Order Date (If Known)	Signatures	Issued Notes VG	Issued Notes VF	Issued Notes Unc	Specimens Unc
a	000001	450000	18.5.70	G9, A38	$3	$10	$30	$100
b	450001	900000	18.5.70	G9, A36				
c	900001	1350000	18.5.70	G9, A44				
d	1350001	1800000	18.5.70	G9, A45				
e	1800001	2200000	18.5.70	G9, A43				
f	2200001	2600000	18.5.70	G9, A41				
g	2600001	3000000	18.5.70	G9, A42				
h	3000001	3450000	13.5.72	G9, A38				
i	3450001	3900000	13.5.72	G9, A36				
j	3900001	4350000	13.5.72	G9, A44				
k	4350001	4800000	13.5.72	G9, A45				
l	4800001	5200000	13.5.72	G9, A43				
m	5200001	5600000	13.5.72	G9, A41				
n	5600001	6000000	13.5.72	G9, A42				

1972 D. AFONSO V ISSUE

Afonso V (1432-81) was a King of Portugal known as "O Africano" (The African), because he was the first Portuguese king to rule over "The Algarves" (plural) as a result of his conquest of territories in North Africa. These lands, part of present-day Morocco, were incorporated into the then separate kingdom of the Algarve. Afonso also supported Prince Henry the Navigator in his journeys of exploration, but this sponsorship ceased after Prince Henry's death in 1460. After concluding his African campaigns, Afonso in 1475 went into battle against Castille, but the result was inconclusive and disillusioned he abdicated in favour of his son João II in November 1477. Retiring to a monastery in Sintra, he died there in 1481.

MZ117	**1000 escudos**	16 May 1972	SCWPM 112
	Printer	Casa da Moeda, Lisbon	
	Total Printed	2,050,000	
	Circulation	Introduced 17. 10. 1972. Withdrawn 10. 05. 1980	
	Colour	Grey-blue on salmon and multicoloured underprint	
	Obverse Design	Portrait of D. Afonso V at right	
	Reverse Design	Maiden standing and looking at ships through the ages	
	Watermark	D. Afonso V	
	Size	175 x 95 mm	
	Serial number varieties	3mm tall serial no with no prefix; 3mm tall serial no with prefix; 3.5mm tall serial no with no prefix; 3.5mm tall serial no with prefix	
	Signatures	VG27 and A36, A38, A41, A42, A43, A44, A45	

MZ117a1

MZ117f1

MZ117f1

BANCO NACIONAL ULTRAMARINO
PAGAVEL EM MOÇAMBIQUE
1000
BANCO NACIONAL ULTRAMARINO
LISBOA-1864
MIL
ESCUDOS
1000
1000
1000

					Issued Notes			Specimens
MZ117	Start of Print Run	End of Print Run	Order Date (If Known)	Signatures	VG	VF	Unc	Unc
a1	000001	015000	Ist order for 100,000 notes in May 1972	VG27, A38	$8	$25	$90	$225
a2	015001	030000		VG27, A36				
a3	030001	045000		VG27, A44				
a4	045001	060000		VG27, A45				
a5	060001	070000		VG27, A43				
a6	070001	085000		VG27, A41				
a7	085001	100000		VG27, A42				
b1	100001	140000	2nd order for 300,000 notes in June 1972	VG27, A38				
b2	140001	180000		VG27, A36				
b3	180001	220000		VG27, A44				
b4	220001	260000		VG27, A45				
b5	260001	300000		VG27, A43				
b6	300001	350000		VG27, A41				
b7	350001	400000		VG27, A42				
c1	400001	410000	3rd order for 100,000 notes in December 1972	VG27, A38				
c2	410001	425000		VG27, A36				
c3	425001	440000		VG27, A44				
c4	440001	455000		VG27, A45				
c5	455001	470000		VG27, A43				
c6	470001	485000		VG27, A41				
c7	485001	500000		VG27, A42				
d1	500001	570000	4th order for 500,000 notes in February 1973	VG27, A38				
d2	570001	640000		VG27, A36				
d3	640001	710000		VG27, A44				
d4	710001	780000		VG27, A45				
d5	780001	850000		VG27, A43				
d6	850001	920000		VG27, A41				
d7	920001	1000000		VG27, A42				
e1	1000001	1050000	5th order for 50,000 notes in October 1974	VG27, unknown				
f1	COV 00001	COV 79167	6th order for 1,000,000 notes in October 1974	VG27, A36				
f2	DPX 00001	DPX 79167		VG27, A36				
f3	EQZ 00001	EQZ 79167		VG27, A44				
f4	FRA 00001	FRA 79167		VG27, A44				
f5	GSB 00001	GSB 79167		VG27, A45				
f6	HTC 00001	HTC 79167		VG27, A45				
f7	IUD 00001	IUD 79167		VG27, A43				
f8	JVE 00001	JVE 79167		VG27, A43				
f9	LXF 00001	LXF 79167		VG27, A41				
f10	MZG 00001	MZG 79167		VG27, A41				
f11	NAH 00001	NAH 79167		VG27, A42				
f12	OBI 00001	OBI 79163		VG27, A42				

N.B.1 It has not been possible to trace the administrador signatures on the 50,000 notes contained in the 5th order

N.B.2 The Espécime specimens are known with six zeros and seven zeros

1972 GAGO COUTINHO ISSUE

Carlos Viegas Gago Coutinho (Gago Coutinho) (1869-1959) was a Portuguese geographer, historian, cartographer, naval officer and pioneer aviator. Accompanied by Sacadura Cabral (1881-1924), he made the first aerial crossing of the South Atlantic to mark the centennial of Brazilian independance in 1922. Flying in stages, using three different Fairey III biplanes, they covered the 5,209 miles (8,383 km) from Lisbon to Rio de Janeiro between 30 March and 17 June. The flight proved to be a milestone in transatlantic aviation with its use of the technological innovation of a false horizon.

MZ118	**100 escudos**	23 May 1972	SCWPM 113
	Printer	Thomas De La Rue & Co. Ltd.	
	Total Printed	5000000	
	Circulation	Introduced 14. 02. 1974	
	Colour	Blue on multicoloured underprint	
	Obverse Design	Busts of Gago Coutinho and Sacadura Cabral at left	
	Reverse Design	Gago Coutinho looking through a sextant	
	Watermark	Gago Coutinho	
	Size	150 x 80 mm	

MZ118a

MZ118a

MZ118	Start of Print Run	End of Print Run	Order Date (If Known)	Signatures	Issued Notes VG	Issued Notes VF	Issued Notes Unc	Specimens Unc
a	0000001	2500000	22.8.73	VG27, A44	$7	$20	$75	$100
b	2500001	5000000	22.8.73	VG27, A45				
aw	Obverse artwork on cardboard, note dated 27 October 1970, differences in design and colour from issued note, serial number A0000000, signatures G9 and A35							Unique

MZ118aw

MZ119 **500 escudos** 23 May 1972 SCWPM 114

Printer	Thomas De La Rue & Co. Ltd.
Total Printed	1400000
Circulation	Introduced 18. 07. 1974
Colour	Reddish purple and black on multicoloured underprint
Obverse Design	Portrait of Gago Coutinho at left
Reverse Design	Sacadura Cabral at left, seaplane “Lusitania” at centre
Watermark	Gago Coutinho
Size	160 x 85 mm

MZ119b

MZ119b

					Issued Notes			Specimens
MZ119	Start of Print Run	End of Print Run	Order Date (If Known)	Signatures	VG	VF	Unc	Unc
a	0000001	0200000	10.4.73	VG27, A38				
b	0200001	0400000	10.4.73	VG27, A36				
c	0400001	0600000	10.4.73	VG27, A44				
d	0600001	0800000	10.4.73	VG27, A45	$10	$35	$100	$125
e	0800001	1000000	10.4.73	VG27, A43				
f	1000001	1200000	10.4.73	VG27, A41				
g	1200001	1400000	10.4.73	VG27, A42				
aw	Reverse artwork on cardboard, slight differences in design and colour from issued note							Unique

MZ119aw

MZ120	**1000 escudos**	23 May 1972	SCWPM 115
	Printer	Thomas De La Rue & Co. Ltd.	
	Total Printed	1500000	
	Circulation	Introduced 01. 03. 1974	
	Colour	Green on multicoloured underprint	
	Obverse Design	Portrait of Gago Coutinho at left	
	Reverse Design	Gago Coutinho and Sacadura Cabral in cockpit of a seaplane in roundel at left	
	Watermark	Gago Coutinho	
	Size	170 x 85 mm	

MZ120a

MZ120a

					Issued Notes			Specimens
MZ120	Start of Print Run	End of Print Run	Order Date (If Known)	Signatures	VG	VF	Unc	Unc
a	0000001	0750000	22.8.73	VG27, A44	$10	$35	$100	$125
b	0750001	1500000	22.8.73	VG27, A45				

Portuguese Guinea

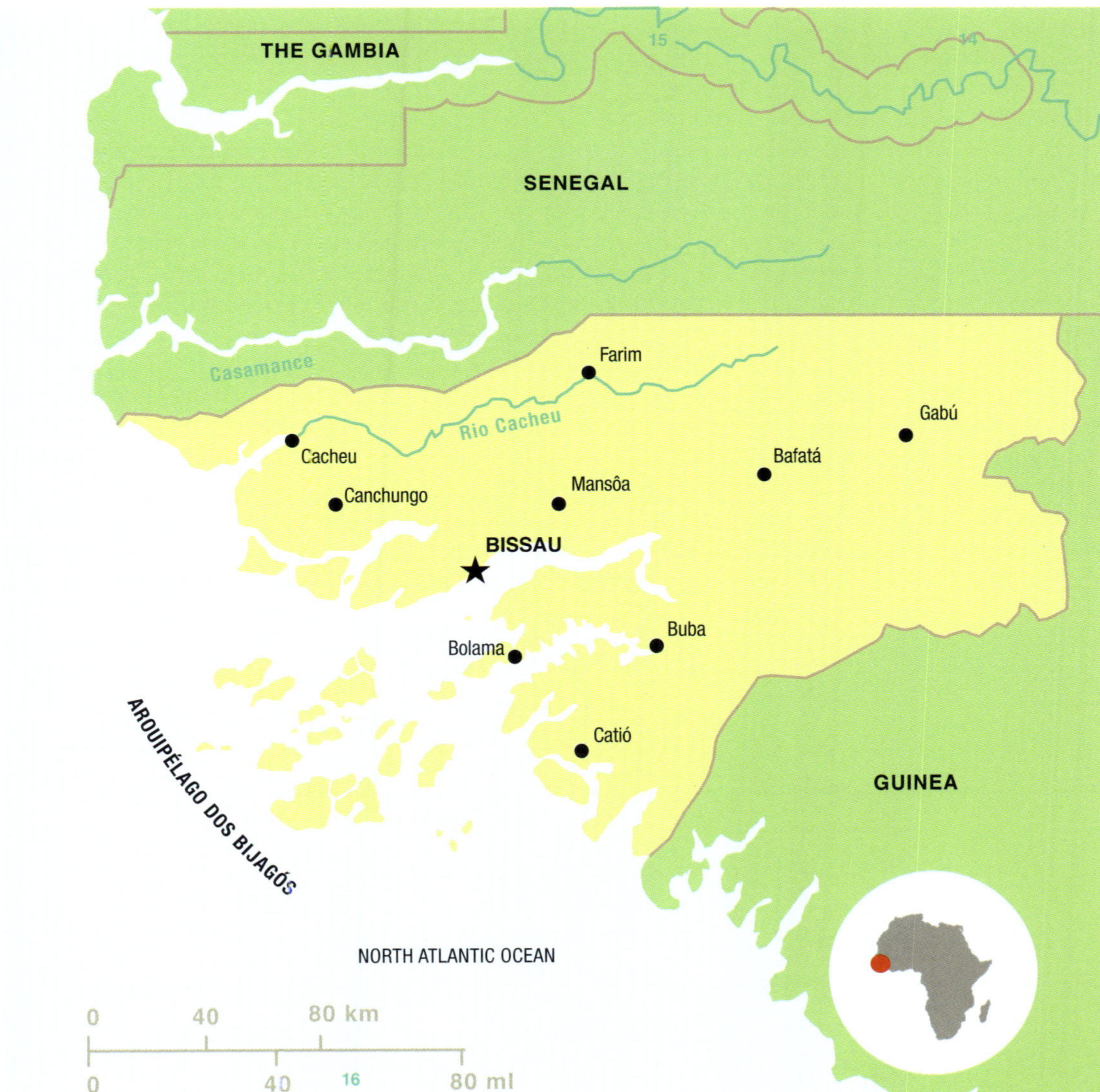

INTRODUCTION

Portuguese contacts with that part of the West African coast now known as Guinea-Bissau began during the 1440s. In 1443, Dom Pedro (1392-1449) granted his younger brother Prince Henry the Navigator (1394-1460) the monopoly of navigation, war and trade for the lands to the south of Cape Bojador in present-day Mauretania. Later this monopoly would be enforced by the papal bulls Dum Diversas (1452) and Romanus Pontifex (1455), granting Portugal the trade monopoly for the newly discovered countries and laying the foundation for the Portuguese empire. During two expeditions in 1445 and 1446, Álvaro Fernandes is said by the historian João de Barros to have reached what is now present-day Sierra Leone, but this is disputed by later historians, who believe he only sailed as far as the northern coast of present-day Guinea-Bissau. However, actual settlement of the area did not take place until later in the 15th century and was closely linked with colonisation of the Cape Verde archipelago.

Enslaved labour from Guinea was first used to establish plantations of cotton and indigo in Cape Verde, much of the cloth being sent back to the African mainland for the purchase of enslaved people destined for the Americas. The transatlantic slave trade was assisted by local lançados, who acted as intermediaries between the Guinean rulers and the visiting slave ships. In the 16th century internal warfare in the colony greatly increased the number of prisoners of war available for export as slaves. In addition to the trade in enslaved people, internal commerce focused on salt, kola nuts and other foodstuffs, whilst ivory, wax, hides and dyewood were exported, mainly to Portugal, Britain, Holland and France.

During the next three centuries, when the slave trade was the main activity of the colony, Portugal experienced little opposition to its territorial claims, although the British in The Gambia and the French in Senegal were always a potential threat. In 1687, a Portuguese settlement was established at Bissau in an attempt to frustrate French commercial competition. The relatively weak position of the Portuguese in Upper Guinea was strengthened by the Marquis of Pombal (1699-1782), who promoted the supply of enslaved peoples from this area to provinces in northern Brazil, with 25000 being transported from "the Rivers of Guinea" between 1757-77.

The BNU's Bolama branch. Address: North, with Rua Coelho Latino; South, with the Avenida da República; East, with Avenida Coelho.

The Portuguese occupation of Guinea was later disputed by both the British and the French. Negotiations led to exclusion of the British by 1870 and settlement of the boundaries with the French between 1886-1905. Complete occupation of the interior was achieved through the "pacification" campaigns led by João Teixeira Pinto (1876-1917) between 1913-15 and he appears on the BNU series of notes issued between 1937-64 (see PG31-PG54). There followed a period of a predominantly peaceful Portuguese administration until the rise of African independence movements after World War II.

In 1961 nationalist attacks led by Amílcar Cabral (1924-73) were made on Portuguese administrative and military facilities and an armed struggle ensued based in Conakry, the capital of the French-speaking Republic of Guinea. Its aim was the liberation of Cape Verde and Portuguese Guinea and by 1971 the nationalist forces had occupied much of the interior, although they were unable to take the coastal towns and river ports. In 1973 Guinea-Bissau declared its independence from Portugal and this was acknowledged by the colonial power in 1974 with the withdrawal of all its forces.

The BNU did not operate in the colony until the opening of its first branch in Bolama in 1902. This meant that unlike the four other Portuguese African colonies, no paper money was issued until the Vasco da Gama omnibus series in 1909. However a striking series of banknotes featuring African fauna was prepared in 1907, but the artwork was destroyed and only unique sepia photographs of the designs have survived (see PGA1-PGA6). Thereafter the Vasco da Gama, Cedula and Chamiço omnibus issues were all overprinted "BOLAMA" for use in the colony.

1909 DESIGNS FOR AN UNISSUED AFRICAN WILDLIFE SERIES

PGA1	**1 escudo**	1 March 1909
	Format	Obverse and reverse sepia archival photographs, dated 1 June 1920, of an unissued design with counterfoil and 000000 serial number
	Obverse Design	Two maribou storks at left, flower at centre, value in guilloches in each corner
	Reverse Design	The Banco Nacional Ultramarino branch building in Bolama set in decorated circle at left, value in guilloche at right
	Signatures	G4, VG6 — One Pair Known

PGA1

PGA1

PGA2	**2½ escudos**	1 March 1909
	Format	Obverse and reverse sepia archival photographs, dated 1 May 1920, of an unissued design with counterfoil and 000000 serial number
	Obverse Design	African spurred tortoise at left, value repeated in four guilloches
	Reverse Design	Value in guilloche at lower left, the Banco Nacional Ultramarino branch building in Bolama at right
	Signatures	G4, VG6 — One Pair Known

PGA2

PGA2

PGA3	**5 escudos**	1 March 1909
	Format	Obverse and reverse sepia archival photographs, dated 31 May 1920 and 12 May 1920 respectively, of an unissued design with counterfoil and 000000 serial number
	Obverse Design	West African chimpanzee and tree at left, value in guilloches in each corner
	Reverse Design	The Banco Nacional Ultramarino branch building in Bolama at lower left, value set in guilloche with two fish heads at right, value in guilloches in each corner
	Signatures	G4, VG6

One Pair Known

PGA3

PGA3

PGA4	**10 escudos**	1 March 1909
	Format	Obverse and reverse sepia archival photographs, dated 29 May 1920, of an unissued design with counterfoil and 000000 serial number
	Obverse Design	Grey pelican on tree stump at left, value in guilloches in each corner, coat of arms at right
	Reverse Design	The Banco Nacional Ultramarino branch building in Bolama set in a decorated oval at centre, value set in guilloches at left and right
	Signatures	G4, VG6

One Pair Known

PGA4

PGA4

PGA5	**20 escudos**	1 March 1909
	Format	Obverse and reverse sepia archival photographs, dated 31 May 1920, of an unissued design with counterfoil and 000,000 serial number
	Obverse Design	Two giraffes at centre set in two pillars, value in guilloche at left, coat of arms at right
	Reverse Design	The Banco Nacional Ultramarino branch building in Bolama set in a decorated rectangle at centre, value set in guilloches at left and right
	Signatures	G4, VG6

One Pair Known

PGA5

PGA5

PGA6	**50 escudos**	1 March 1909
	Format	Obverse and reverse sepia archival photographs, dated 31 May 1920, of an unissued design with counterfoil and 000000 serial number
	Obverse Design	African elephant set in columns at centre, value in guilloches at lower left and in top right and left corners
	Reverse Design	The Banco Nacional Ultramarino branch building in Bolama set in a decorated rectangular frame at left, value set in ornate guilloche at right
	Signatures	G4, VG6

One Pair Known

PGA6

PGA6

1909 VASCO DE GAMA ISSUE

By the Law of 27 April 1901, a new legal framework for banking activity in the Portuguese Colonial Empire was established. The new legislation divided banking operations into two groups; the issuance of paper money and the grant of loans secured by real estate. Although the banknote issue was open to competitive tendering, each colony could only have one bank and the BNU was the only bidder for Portuguese Guinea and the other four African colonies. Under this new contract, the BNU prepared a new issue of notes, which were known as the Vasco da Gama Issue.

The notes issued under the new contract for Portuguese Guinea were all dated 1 March 1909 with denominations of 1$000, 2$500, 5$000, 10$000, 20$000 and 50$000 reis, all being signed by the Governor Antonio Teixeira de Sousa (G4) and various Vice Governors (VG6, VG9 and VG10) and with a manuscript or facsimile signature of a manager. Two different types of steamship seal were used: the earlier issues used Type 1 and the later issues used Type 3.

See also "A Summary of the Main Banknote Issues of the Banco Nacional Ultramarino" on page 7 and "A Brief History of the Rise of the Portuguese Empire" on page 11 for further information on Vasco da Gama.

Steamship seal Type 1

Steamship seal Type 3

Reverses of the Vasco da Gama Issue

PG1 and PG2

PG3 and PG4

PG5 and PG6

PG7 and PG8

PG9 and PG10

PG11 and PG12

PG1	**1000 reis**	1 March 1909	SCWPM 1
	Printer	Bradbury Wilkinson & Co. Ltd.	
	Total Printed	620000	
	Circulation	Withdrawn 27. 07. 1922	
	Colour	Black on green and yellow underprint	
	Obverse Design	Value in guilloches, crowned arms at upper right, overprint BOLAMA	
	Reverse Design	Allegorical maiden looking at ships	
	Size	138 x 80 mm	
	Ship Seal	Type 1	

PG1f

					Issued Notes			Archival Specimens
PG1	Start of Print Run	End of Print Run	Order Date (If Known)	Signatures	VG	Fine	VF	AU
a	00001	03333*		G4, VG9*	Rare	Rare	Rare	$1,100
b	03334*	06667*		G4, VG6*	$250	$450	$700	$750
c	06668	10000		G4, VG10				
d	10001	15000	25.1.16	G4, VG6				
e	15001	20000	25.1.16	G4, VG10				
f	20001	45000	8.12.16	G4, VG6				
g	45001	70000	8.12.16	G4, VG10				
h	70001	95000	16.7.17	G4 VG6				
i	95001	120000	16.7.17*	G4, VG10				
j	120001	125000	14.11.17*	G4, VG6*				
k	125001	130000	14.11.17	G4, VG10				
l	130001	250000	18.2.18	G4, VG6				
m	250001	370000	18.2.18	G4, VG10				
n	370001	495000	30.12.18	G4, VG6				
o	495001	620000	30.12.18	G4, VG10				

PG2	**1000 reis**	1 March 1909	SCWPM 1A
	Printer	Bradbury Wilkinson & Co. Ltd.	
	Total Printed	200000	
	Circulation	Withdrawn 27. 07. 1922	
	Colour	Black on green and yellow underprint	
	Obverse Design	Value in guilloches, crowned arms at upper right, overprint BOLAMA	
	Reverse Design	Allegorical maiden looking at ships	
	Size	138 x 80 mm	
	Ship Seal	Type 3	

PG2c

PG2	Start of Print Run	End of Print Run	Order Date (If Known)	Signatures	Issued Notes VG	Issued Notes Fine	Issued Notes VF	Archival Specimens AU
a	620001	670000	28.1.20	G4, VG6				
b	670001	720000	28.1.20	G4, VG10	$250	$450	$700	$850
c	720001	770000	18.5.20	G4, VG6				
d	770001	820000	18.5.20	G4, VG10				

PG3	**2500 reis**	1 March 1909	SCWPM 2
	Printer	Bradbury Wilkinson & Co. Ltd.	
	Total Printed	750000	
	Circulation	Withdrawn 27. 07. 1922	
	Colour	Black on green and yellow underprint. Reverse blue	
	Obverse Design	Vasco da Gama and his passage round the Cape, overprint BOLAMA	
	Reverse Design	Allegorical maiden looking at ships	
	Size	148 x 94 mm	
	Ship Seal	Type 1	

PG3h

PG3	Start of Print Run	End of Print Run	Order Date (If Known)	Signatures	Issued Notes VG	Issued Notes Fine	Issued Notes VF	Archival Specimens AU
a	00001	06667*		G4, VG9*	Rare	Rare	Rare	$1,250
b	06668	13334		G4, VG6				
c	13335	20000*		G4, VG10*				
d	20001	22500	25.1.16	G4, VG6				
e	22501	25000	25.1.16	G4, VG10	$700	$1,200	Rare	$1,000
f	25001	35000	18.1.17	G4, VG6				
g	35001	45000	18.1.17	G4, VG10				
h	45001	60000	14.11.17	G4, VG6				
i	60001	75000	14.11.17	G4, VG10				

PG4	**2500 reis**	1 March 1909	SCWPM 2A
	Printer	Bradbury Wilkinson & Co. Ltd.	
	Total Printed	90000	
	Circulation	Withdrawn 27. 07. 1922	
	Colour	Black on green and yellow underprint. Reverse blue	
	Obverse Design	Vasco da Gama and his passage round the Cape, overprint BOLAMA	
	Reverse Design	Allegorical maiden looking at ships	
	Size	148 x 94 mm	
	Ship Seal	Type 3	

PG4ds

PG4	Start of Print Run	End of Print Run	Order Date (If Known)	Signatures	Issued Notes VG	Issued Notes Fine	Issued Notes VF	Archival Specimens AU
a	75001	95000	28.1.20*	G4, VG6	$650	$1,100	Rare	$1,250
b	95001	115000	28.1.20	G4, VG10				
c	115001	140000	18.5.20	G4, VG6				
d	140001	165000	18.5.20	G4, VG10				

PG5	**5 mil reis**	1 March 1909	SCWPM 3
	Printer	Bradbury Wilkinson & Co. Ltd.	
	Total Printed	90000	
	Circulation	Withdrawn 27. 07. 1922	
	Colour	Black on blue and multicoloured underprint. Reverse green	
	Obverse Design	Vasco da Gama and his passage round The Cape, overprint BOLAMA	
	Reverse Design	Allegorical maiden looking at ships	
	Size	160 x 100 mm	
	Ship Seal	Type 1	

PG5is

					Issued Notes			Archival Specimens
PG5	Start of Print Run	End of Print Run	Order Date (If Known)	Signatures	VG	Fine	VF	AU
a	00001	10000*		G4, VG9*	Rare	Rare	Rare	$1,250
b	10001	20000	18.1.17	G4, VG6	$900	$1,400	Rare	$850
c	20001	30000	18.1.17	G4, VG10				
d	30001	32500	18.1.17	G4, VG6				
e	32501	35000	18.1.17	G4, VG10				
f	35001	37500*	14.11.17*	G4, VG6*				
g	37501	40000	14.11.17	G4, VG10				
h	40001	65000	30.12.18	G4, VG6				
i	65001	90000	30.12.18	G4, VG10				

PG6	**5 mil reis**	1 March 1909	SCWPM 3A
	Printer	Bradbury Wilkinson & Co. Ltd.	
	Total Printed	90000	
	Circulation	Withdrawn 27. 07. 1922	
	Colour	Black on blue and multicoloured underprint. Reverse green	
	Obverse Design	Vasco da Gama and his passage round The Cape, overprint BOLAMA	
	Reverse Design	Allegorical maiden looking at ships	
	Size	160 x 100 mm	
	Ship Seal	Type 3	

PG6es

PG6	Start of Print Run	End of Print Run	Order Date (If Known)	Signatures	Issued Notes VG	Fine	VF	Archival Specimens AU
a	90001	105000	28.1.20	G4, VG6				
b	105001	120000	28.1.20	G4, VG10				
c	120001	135000	18.5.20	G4, VG6	$800	$1,250	Rare	$950
d	135001	150000	18.5.20	G4, VG10				
e	150001	180000	10.1.22	G4, VG6				

PG7	**10 mil reis**	1 March 1909	SCWPM 4
	Printer	Bradbury Wilkinson & Co. Ltd.	
	Total Printed	24500	
	Circulation	Withdrawn 27. 07. 1922	
	Colour	Black on yellow and multicoloured underprint. Reverse brown	
	Obverse Design	Vasco da Gama and his passage round The Cape, overprint BOLAMA	
	Reverse Design	Allegorical maiden looking at ships	
	Size	175 x 105 mm	
	Ship Seal	Type 1	

PG7c

PG7	Start of Print Run	End of Print Run	Order Date (If Known)	Signatures	Issued Notes VG	Issued Notes Fine	Issued Notes VF	Archival Specimens AU
a	0001	2500*		G4, Unknown	Rare	Rare	Rare	$1,400
b	2501	4167	July 1912	G4, VG9	$3,500	Rare	Rare	$1,400
c	4168	5834		G4, VG6	$2,800	Rare	Rare	$1,000
d	5835	7500		G4, VG10				
e	7501	8166	Oct 1913	G4, VG9	$3,500	Rare	Rare	$1,400
f	8167	8832		G4, VG6	$2,800	Rare	Rare	$1,000
g	8833	9500		G4, VG10				
h	9501	12000	25.1.16	G4 VG6				
i	12001	14500	25.1.16	G4, VG10				
j	14501	17000	16.7.17	G4, VG6				
k	17001	19500	16.7.17	G4, VG10				
l	19501	22000	14.11.17	G4, VG6				
m	22001	24500	14.11.17	G4, VG10				

PG8	**10 mil reis**	1 March 1909	SCWPM 4A
	Printer	Bradbury Wilkinson & Co. Ltd.	
	Total Printed	30000	
	Circulation	Withdrawn 27. 07. 1922	
	Colour	Black on yellow and multicoloured underprint. Reverse brown	
	Obverse Design	Vasco da Gama and his passage round The Cape, overprint BOLAMA	
	Reverse Design	Allegorical maiden looking at ships	
	Size	175 x 105 mm	
	Ship Seal	Type 3	

PG8ds

PG8	Start of Print Run	End of Print Run	Order Date (If Known)	Signatures	Issued Notes			Archival Specimens
					VG	Fine	VF	EF
a	24501	34500	28.1.20	G4, VG6	$2,500	Rare	Rare	$1,400
b	34501	44500	28.1.20	G4, VG10				
c	44501	49500	18.5.20	G4, VG6				
d	49501	54500	18.5.20	G4, VG10				

PG9	**20 mil reis**	1 March 1909	SCWPM 5
	Printer	Bradbury Wilkinson & Co. Ltd.	
	Total Printed	27000	
	Circulation	Withdrawn 27. 07. 1922	
	Colour	Black on blue and yellow underprint. Reverse brown-red and orange	
	Obverse Design	Portrait of Vasco de Gama and his embarkation, overprint BOLAMA	
	Reverse Design	Allegorical maiden looking at ships	
	Size	180 x 112 mm	
	Ship Seal	Type 1	

PG9fs

PG9	Start of Print Run	End of Print Run	Order Date (If Known)	Signatures	Issued Notes VG	Issued Notes Fine	Issued Notes VF	Archival Specimens AU
a	0001	0417		G4, VG9	Rare	Rare	Rare	$1,800
b	0418	0834		G4, VG6*	Rare	Rare	Rare	$1,100
c	0835	1250		G4, VG10				
d	1251	2917		G4, VG9	Rare	Rare	Rare	$1,500
e	2918	4584	July 1912	G4, VG6	Rare	Rare	Rare	$1,100
f	4585	6250	July 1912	G4, VG10				
g	6251	7583	October 1913	G4, VG9	Rare	Rare	Rare	$1,500
h	7584	8916		G4 VG6	Rare	Rare	Rare	$1,100
i	8917	10250*		G4, VG10				
j	10251	12750	25.1.16*	G4, VG6				
k	12751	15250	25.1.16	G4, VG10				
l	15251	17125	16.7.17	G4, VG6				
m	17126	19000	16.7.17	G4, VG10				
n	19001	20500	14.11.17	G4, VG6				
o	20501	22000	14.11.17	G4, VG10				
p	22001	24500	3.9.19	G4, VG6				
q	24501	27000	3.9.19	G4, VG10				

PG10	**20 mil reis**	1 March 1909	SCWPM 5A
	Printer	Bradbury Wilkinson & Co. Ltd.	
	Total Printed	30000	
	Circulation	Withdrawn 27. 07. 1922	
	Colour	Black on blue and yellow underprint. Reverse brown-red and orange	
	Obverse Design	Vasco de Gama and his embarkation, overprint BOLAMA	
	Reverse Design	Allegorical maiden looking at ships	
	Size	180 x 112 mm	
	Ship Seal	Type 3	

PG10ds

PG10	Start of Print Run	End of Print Run	Order Date (If Known)	Signatures	Issued Notes VG	Issued Notes Fine	Issued Notes VF	Archival Specimens EF
a	27001	37000	28.1.20	G4, VG6				
b	37001	47000	28.1.20*	G4, VG10	Rare	Rare	Rare	$1,400
c	47001	52000	18.5.20	G4, VG6				
d	52001	57000	18.5.20	G4, VG10				

PG11 **50 mil reis** 1 March 1909 SCWPM 5B

Printer Bradbury Wilkinson & Co. Ltd.
Total Printed 5000
Circulation Withdrawn 27. 07. 1922
Colour Black on yellow, green and multicoloured underprint. Reverse green, blue, yellow and pink
Obverse Design Vasco de Gama and his embarkation, overprint BOLAMA
Reverse Design Allegorical maiden looking at ships
Size 198 x 120 mm
Ship Seal Type 1

PG11b

PG11	Start of Print Run	End of Print Run	Order Date (If Known)	Signatures	Issued Notes VG	Fine	VF	Archival Specimens EF
a	0001	1000	16.7.17	G4, VG6				
b	1001	2000	16.7.17	G4, VG10				
c	2001	2500	14.11.17*	G4, VG6	Rare	Rare	Rare	$1,800
d	2501	3000	14.11.17	G4, VG10				
e	3001	4000	3.9.19	G4, VG6				
f	4001	5000	3.9.19	G4, VG10				

PG11fs

PG12	**50 mil reis**	1 March 1909	SCWPM unlisted
	Printer	Bradbury Wilkinson & Co. Ltd.	
	Total Printed	15000	
	Circulation	Withdrawn 27. 07. 1922	
	Colour	Black on yellow, green and multicoloured underprint. Reverse green, blue, yellow and pink	
	Obverse Design	Vasco de Gama and his embarkation, overprint BOLAMA	
	Reverse Design	Allegorical maiden looking at ships	
	Size	198 x 120 mm	
	Ship Seal	Type 3	

PG12b

					Issued Notes			Archival Specimens
PG12	Start of Print Run	End of Print Run	Order Date (If Known)	Signatures	VG	Fine	VF	EF
a	5001	10000	9.1.20	G4, VG6				
b	10001	15000	9.1.20*	G4, VG10	Rare	Rare	Rare	$2,200
c	15001	17500	28.1.20	G4, VG6				
d	17501	20000	28.1.20*	G4, VG10				

N.B. It is believed only one issued note is known with serial number 13963. It is in the António Cupertino de Miranda Museum in Porto

1909 PROVISIONAL ISSUE

PG13 **2500 reis** No date - old date 1 March 1909 SCWPM unlisted

Printer Bradbury Wilkinson & Co. Ltd.

Overprint Black overprint "PAGAVEL...ces agencias de GUINÉ" in rectangular frame on Cape Verde CV7 (SCWPM 5a)

Total Overprints 40000*

Circulation Withdrawal date unknown

Colour Black on blue and multicoloured underprint. Reverse green

Obverse design Vasco da Gama and his passge round The Cape, overprint S. THIAGO

Reverse Design Allegorical maiden looking at ships

Size 148 x 98 mm

Ship Seal Type 1

				Issued Notes		
PG13	Start of Print Run	End of Print Run	Signatures	VG	Fine	VF
a	240001	266667	G4, VG6	Rare	Rare	Rare
b	266668	280000	G4, VG10	Rare	Rare	Rare

PG14 **5 mil reis** No date - old date 1 March 1909 SCWPM 5F

Printer Bradbury Wilkinson & Co. Ltd.

Overprint Black overprint "PAGAVEL...ces agencias de GUINÉ" in rectangular frame on Cape Verde CV10 (SCWPM 6b)

Total Overprints Unknown

Circulation Withdrawal date unknown

Colour Black on blue and multicoloured underprint. Reverse green

Obverse design Vasco da Gama and his passge round The Cape, overprint S. THIAGO

Reverse Design Allegorical maiden looking at ships

Size 160 x 100 mm

Signatures G4, VG6 or VG10

Ship Seal Type 3

			Issued Notes		
PG14	Start of Print Run	End of Print Run	VG	Fine	VF
a	ca 190000 to 240000	Unknown	Rare	Rare	Rare

1914 CEDULA ISSUES

The fractional notes issued by the BNU for the Portuguese African colonies, all dated 5 November 1914, are known as the Cedula Issues and in Portugal as "the London Issue". They were emergency notes printed in London during World War I, as a substitute for metal coinage in short supply. They were issued in denominations of 10cts, 20cts and 50cts for all five of the African colonies. Each colony had its own overprint, with Bolama used for Portuguese Guinea.

It is important to recognise that the issue of these notes, like metallic coins, was a privilege of the state, which was never transferred to the BNU. Accordingly, to be legal tender every issue had to be the subject of specific legislation proposed by the Minister of Colonies and approved by the Council of Ministers and Parliament in Lisbon. Furthermore, the fulfilment of the orders for the notes experienced all the constraints of a world at war. Among the difficulties encountered, which led to serious delays, were the lack of proper materials (appropriate paper and ink), the absence of skilled workers and the disruption of regular maritime transport.

Two types of steamship seal were used for these issues: the earlier issues used Type 2 and the later issues Type 3. The seals were green for the 10cts, red for the 20cts and blue for the 50cts.

Steamship seal Type 2

Steamship seal Type 3

Reverses of the 1914 Cedula Issues

PG15 and PG16

PG17

PG18 and PG19

PG15	**10 centavos**	5 November 1914, first issue	SCWPM 6
	Printer	Bradbury Wilkinson & Co. Ltd.	
	Total Printed	600000	
	Circulation	Withdrawn 09. 03. 1933	
	Colour	Purple on multicoloured underprint. Reverse blue	
	Obverse Design	Value in guilloche at left, arms at right, green steamship seal at lower centre, green overprint BOLAMA	
	Reverse Design	Allegorical maiden looking at ships	
	Size	122 x 72 mm	
	Signatures	G5, VG10	
	Ship seal	Type 2	

PG15b

			Issued Notes			Archival Specimens
PG15	Start of Print Run	End of Print Run	Good	Fine	EF	AU
a	1200001	1350000	$50	$175	$550	$600
b	1450001	1900000				

N.B. An unknown quantity of this issue was overprinted “PAGAVEL EM S. TIAGO” for use in Cape Verde, see CV25 (SCWPM 9A)

PG16	**10 centavos**	5 November 1914, second issue	SCWPM 9
	Printer	Bradbury Wilkinson & Co. Ltd.	
	Total Printed	200000	
	Circulation	Withdrawn 09. 03. 1933	
	Colour	Purple on multicoloured underprint. Reverse blue	
	Obverse Design	Value in guilloche at left, arms at right, green steamship seal at lower centre, green overprint BOLAMA	
	Reverse Design	Allegorical maiden looking at ships	
	Size	122 x 72 mm	
	Signatures	G5, VG10	
	Ship seal	Type 3	

PG16a

			Issued Notes			Archival Specimens
PG16	Start of Print Run	End of Print Run	Good	Fine	EF	AU
a	6620001	6820000	$60	$250	$750	$800

PG17	**20 centavos**	5 November 1914	SCWPM 7
	Printer	Bradbury Wilkinson & Co. Ltd.	
	Total Printed	500000	
	Circulation	Withdrawn 09. 03. 1933	
	Colour	Blue on multicoloured underprint. Reverse purple	
	Obverse Design	Value in guilloche at left, arms at right, red steamship seal at lower centre, red overprint BOLAMA	
	Reverse Design	Allegorical maiden looking at ships	
	Size	122 x 72 mm	
	Signatures	G5, VG10	
	Ship seal	Type 2	

PG17as

PG17	Start of Print Run	End of Print Run	Issued Notes: Good	Issued Notes: Fine	Issued Notes: EF	Archival Specimens: AU
a	2520001	2645000	$65	$275	$850	$600
b	2745001	3120000				

N.B.1 An unknown quantity of this issue was overprinted "PAGAVEL EM S. TIAGO" for use in Cape Verde, see CV26 (SCWPM unlisted)

N.B.2 20 Centavos with ship seal type 3, incorrectly listed as SCWPM 10, does not exist

PG18 **50 centavos** 5 November 1914, first issue SCWPM 8

Printer Bradbury Wilkinson & Co. Ltd.

Total Printed 480000

Circulation Withdrawn 09. 03. 1933

Colour Green on multicoloured underprint. Reverse brown

Obverse Design Value in guilloche at left, arms at right, blue steamship seal at lower centre, blue overprint BOLAMA

Reverse Design Allegorical maiden looking at ships

Size 122 x 72 mm

Signatures G5, VG10

Ship seal Type 2

PG18as

			Issued Notes			Archival Specimens
PG18	Start of Print Run	End of Print Run	Good	Fine	EF	AU
a	1410001	1530000	$70	$300	$900	$700
b	1590001	1950000				

PG19	**50 centavos**	5 November 1914, first issue	SCWPM 11
	Printer	Bradbury Wilkinson & Co. Ltd.	
	Total Printed	200000	
	Circulation	Withdrawn 09. 03. 1933	
	Colour	Green on multicoloured underprint. Reverse brown	
	Obverse Design	Value in guilloche at left, arms at right, blue steamship seal at lower centre, blue overprint BOLAMA	
	Reverse Design	Allegorical maiden looking at ships	
	Size	122 x 72 mm	
	Signatures	G5, VG10	
	Ship seal	Type 3	

PG19a

			Issued Notes			Archival Specimens
PG19	Start of Print Run	End of Print Run	Good	Fine	EF	AU
a	5190001	5390000	$75	$350	$1,000	$850

N.B. All of the 1914 Cedula issues for Portuguese Guinea were withdrawn from circulation and exchanged for coins with the same value under the terms of Decreto No 22.297 issued on 09. 03. 1933

1920 EMERGENCY "PORTO" ISSUE

PG20	**10 centavos**	1 January 1920	SCWPM unlisted
	Printer	Litografia Nacional, Lda, Porto	
	Total Printed	Unknown	
	Circulation	Withdrawn in stages on 16. 08. 1934, 26. 05. 1937 and 29. 09. 1937	
	Colour	Red. Reverse brown-purple	
	Obverse Design	Sailing ships at left and right	
	Reverse Design	Value in central guilloche	
	Size	105 x 65 mm	
	Signatures	G7, VG14	

			Issued Notes		
PG20	Start of Print Run	End of Print Run	Good	Fine	VF
a	Unknown	Unknown	Rare	Rare	Rare

PG21	**20 centavos**	1 January 1920	SCWPM unlisted
	Printer	Litografia Nacional, Lda, Porto	
	Total Printed	Unknown	
	Circulation	Withdrawn in stages on 16. 08. 1934, 26. 05. 1937 and 29. 09. 1937	
	Colour	Green	
	Obverse Design	Two cherubs above sailing ships at left and right, value at upper left and right	
	Reverse Design	Value in central guilloche	
	Size	105 x 65 mm	
	Signatures	G7, VG14	

			Issued Notes		
PG21	Start of Print Run	End of Print Run	Good	Fine	VF
a	Unknown	Unknown	Rare	Rare	Rare

PG22	**50 centavos**	1 January 1920	SCWPM unlisted
	Printer	Litografia Nacional, Lda, Porto	
	Total Printed	Unknown	
	Circulation	Withdrawn in stages on 16. 08. 1934, 26. 05. 1937 and 29. 09. 1937	
	Colour	Blue. Reverse brown	
	Obverse Design	Mercury at left, ships at lower left, allegorical female representing industry, and male farmer at right	
	Reverse Design	Ship in roundel at centre, value in four corners set in ornate borders	
	Size	120 x 75 mm	
	Signatures	G7, VG14	

PG22a

PG22a

			Issued Notes		
PG22	Start of Print Run	End of Print Run	Good	Fine	VF
a	Unknown	Unknown	$1,000	$2,500	$4,500

PG23	**50 escudos**	1 January 1920	SCWPM unlisted
	Printer	Litografia Nacional, Lda. Porto	
	Total Printed	Unknown	
	Colour	Dark blue on pale green underprint. Reverse brown on yellow-orange underprint	
	Obverse Design	Arms at upper centre, value at lower centre and in each corner	
	Reverse Design	Palm trees and coastline in ornate oval at centre, eagles at left and right, value at lower centre	
	Size	200 x 125 mm	
	Signatures	G7, VG14	

			Issued Notes		
PG23	Start of Print Run	End of Print Run	Good	Fine	VF
a	Unknown	Unknown	Rare	Rare	Rare

1921 CHAMIÇO ISSUE

By the Decree No. 5809, dated 30 May 1919, which instituted a new banking regime for the overseas colonies, a new issue of notes to replace the Vasco da Gama issues was authorised. This new omnibus series, which circulated in all five of the Portuguese African colonies from 1 August 1922 until 30 November 1950, featured a portrait of the founder and first Governor of the BNU, Francisco de Oliveira Chamiço (1819-88). This new issue consisted of values of 1$00, 2$50, 5$00, 10$00, 20$00, 50$00 and 100$00 escudos and those issued for Portuguese Guinea were all dated 1 January 1921.

Reverses of the Chamiço Issue

PG24

PG25

PG26

PG27

PG28

PG29

PAGAVEL NAS DEPENDENCIAS DA PROVINCIA DE
GUINÉ
BANCO NACIONAL ULTRAMARINO
50
50
CANCELLED

PG30

PAGAVEL NAS DEPENDENCIAS DA PROVINCIA DE
GUINÉ
BANCO NACIONAL ULTRAMARINO
100
100
CANCELLED

PG24	**1 escudo**	1 January 1921	SCWPM 12
	Printer	Bradbury Wilkinson & Co. Ltd.	
	Total Printed	1600000*	
	Colour	Green on multicoloured underprint	
	Obverse Design	Portrait of Francisco de Oliveira Chamiço at left, steamship seal at right, red overprint GUINÉ	
	Reverse Design	Allegorical maiden looking at ships	
	Size	128 x 82 mm	
	Signatures	G7, VG14	

PG24a

				Issued Notes			Archival Specimens	Specimens
PG24	Start of Print Run	End of Print Run	Order Date (If Known)	VG	Fine	VF	AU	AU
a	000001	200000	25.8.20					
b	200001	280000	3.11.21					
c	280001	370000	15.11.21	$350	$800	$1,500	$250	$200
d	370001	1075000	23.2.23					
e	1075001	1600000*	15.10.24*					
ctp	Uniface obverse and reverse colour trial proofs in brown and multicoloured							$400

PG25	**2½ escudos**	1 January 1921	SCWPM 13
	Printer	Thomas De La Rue & Co. Ltd.	
	Total Printed	1100000*	
	Colour	Blue on multicoloured underprint	
	Obverse Design	Portrait of Francisco de Oliveira Chamiço at left, steamship seal at right	
	Reverse Design	Allegorical maiden looking at ships	
	Size	136 x 69 mm	
	Signatures	G7, VG14	

PG25a

				Issued Notes			Specimens
PG25	Start of Print Run	End of Print Run	Order Date (If Known)	VG	Fine	VF	Unc
a	000001	1100000*		$250	$600	$1,200	$500
ph1	Sepia and white obverse and reverse archival photographs, dated 5. 04. 1923, of undated unissued note with value as 2½ rather than 2$50, serial number 0000000						One Pair Known
ph2	Sepia and white reverse archival photograph, dated 5. 04. 1923, of unissued reverse of note with value as 2½ rather than 2$50, and bank legend instead of allegorical maiden						One Copy Known

PG25s

PG25ph1

PG25ph1

PG25ph2

PG26	**5 escudos**	1 January 1921	SCWPM 14
	Printer	Bradbury Wilkinson & Co. Ltd.	
	Total Printed	600000*	
	Colour	Black on multicoloured underprint	
	Obverse Design	Portrait of Francisco de Oliveira Chamiço at left, steamship seal at right, red overprint GUINÉ	
	Reverse Design	Allegorical maiden looking at ships	
	Size	154 x 92 mm	
	Signatures	G7, VG14	

PG26c

				Issued Notes			Archival Specimens	Specimens
PG26	Start of Print Run	End of Print Run	Order Date (If Known)	VG	Fine	VF	AU	AU
a	000001	080000	25.8.20					
b	080001	880000	3.11.21					
c	088001	205000	15.11.21	$450	$1,000	$1,750	$400	$300
d	205001	400000	22.2.23					
e	400001	600000*	22.2.23*					

PG26s

PG27	**10 escudos**	1 January 1921	SCWPM 15
	Printer	Bradbury Wilkinson & Co. Ltd.	
	Total Printed	300000*	
	Colour	Brown on multicoloured underprint	
	Obverse Design	Portrait of Francisco de Oliveira Chamiço at left, steamship seal at right, red overprint GUINÉ	
	Reverse Design	Allegorical maiden looking at ships	
	Size	160 x 105 mm	
	Signatures	G7, VG14	

PG27b

				Issued Notes			Archival Specimens	Specimens
PG27	Start of Print Run	End of Print Run	Order Date (If Known)	VG	Fine	VF	AU	AU
a	000001	070000	25.8.20					
b	070001	150000	3.11.21	$900	$2,000	Rare	$600	$550
c	150001	231000	15.11.21					
d	231001	300000*						
ctp	Uniface obverse and reverse colour trial proofs in purple and multicoloured							$1,000 (Pair)

PG27ctp

PG28	**20 escudos**	1 January 1921	SCWPM 16
	Printer	Bradbury Wilkinson & Co. Ltd.	
	Total Printed	200000 (20000 notes were overprinted for use in Cape Verde in 1932, see CV50)	
	Colour	Dark blue on multicoloured underprint	
	Obverse Design	Portrait of Francisco de Oliveira Chamiço at left, steamship seal at right, red overprint GUINÉ	
	Reverse Design	Allegorical maiden looking at ships	
	Size	170 x 115 mm	
	Signatures	G7, VG14	

PG28c

PG28	Start of Print Run	End of Print Run	Order Date (If Known)	Issued Notes VG	Fine	VF	Archival Specimens AU	Specimens AU
a	000001	040000	25.8.20					
b	040001	075000	3.11.21	$1250	$2,750	Rare	$800	$700
c	075001	102000	15.11.21					
d	102001	200000	2.10.24					
ctp	Uniface obverse and reverse colour trial proofs in red and multicoloured							$1,500 (Pair)

PG28cs

PG28ctp

PG29	**50 escudos**	1 January 1921	SCWPM 17
	Printer	Bradbury Wilkinson & Co. Ltd.	
	Total Printed	90000 (16000 notes were overprinted for use in Cape Verde in 1932, see CV51)	
	Colour	Brownish-red on multicoloured underprint	
	Obverse Design	Portrait of Francisco de Oliveira Chamiço at left, steamship seal at right, red overprint GUINÉ	
	Reverse Design	Allegorical maiden looking at ships	
	Size	185 x 120 mm	
	Signatures	G7, VG14	

PG29b

PG29	Start of Print Run	End of Print Run	Order Date (If Known)	Issued Notes VG	Issued Notes Fine	Issued Notes VF	Archival Specimens AU	Specimens AU
a	000001	020000	25.8.20	$2,000	$4,500	Rare	$1,000	$850
b	020001	046000	3.11.21					
c	046001	059500	15.11.21					
d	059501	090000	2.10.24					

PG29bs

PG30	**100 escudos**	1 January 1921 — SCWPM 18
	Printer	Bradbury Wilkinson & Co. Ltd.
	Total Printed	50000 (8000 notes were overprinted for use in Cape Verde in 1932, see CV52)
	Colour	Slate-purple on multicoloured underprint
	Obverse Design	Portrait of Francisco de Oliveira Chamiço at left, steamship seal at right, red overprint GUINÉ
	Reverse Design	Allegorical maiden looking at ships
	Size	193 x 126 mm
	Signatures	G7, VG14

PG30cs

				Issued Notes			Archival Specimens	Specimens
PG30	Start of Print Run	End of Print Run	Order Date (If Known)	VG	Fine	VF	AU	AU
a	000001	020000	25.8.20					
b	020001	031000	30.11.21	Rare	Rare	Rare	$1,200	$1,000
c	031001	050000	2.10.24					

INTRODUCTION TO THE TEIXEIRA PINTO ISSUES

João Teixeira Pinto (1876-1917) was a Portuguese military officer, who spent much of his career as an administrator in the Portuguese colonial service. Known as "Capitão Diabo" (The Devil's Chief), he served first in Angola from 1902-11 and then in Portuguese Guinea from 1912-16. Upon the declaration of war against Germany in 1916, he was posted to Mozambique, where he oversaw troop movements and combined with British and Belgian forces in several military incursions into what was then German East Africa. In November 1917, the Portuguese suffered a major defeat at the hands of the Germans with all commanding officers, including Pinto, killed in a battle to defend Fort Ngomano. There is a statue commemorating Teixeira Pinto in Bissau, the capital of what is now Guinea-Bissau.

Reverses of the 1937-47 Teixeira Pinto Issues

PG37

PG35 and PG38

PG31 and PG39

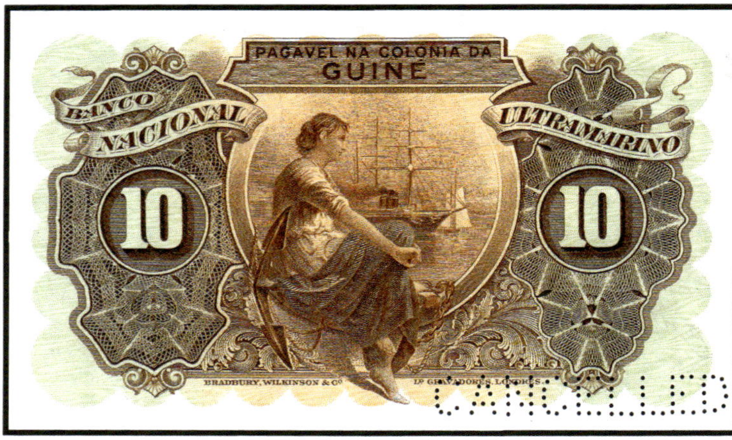

PG32, PG40
and PG43

PG33, PG41
and PG44

PG34, PG42 and PG45

PG46

1937 TEIXEIRA PINTO ISSUE

PG31	**10 escudos**	14 September 1937	SCWPM 21
	Printer	Bradbury Wilkinson & Co. Ltd.	
	Total Printed	1000000	
	Circulation	Unknown	
	Colour	Red-brown on multicoloured underprint	
	Obverse Design	Portrait of João Teixeira Pinto at left, steamship seal at right.	
	Reverse Design	Allegorical maiden looking at ships	
	Size	125 x 75 mm	

PG31d

PG31pp1

PG31pp2

PG31	Start of Print Run	End of Print Run	Signatures	Issued Notes Fine	VF	EF	Specimens (sp) AU
a	GK000001	GK025000	PCA8, A21	$250	$450	$1,000	$500
b	GK025001	GK050000	PCA8, A19				
c	GK050001	GK075000	PCA8, A25				
d	GK075001	GK100000	PCA8, A26				
e	GL100001	GL125000	PCA8, A19				
f	GL125001	GL150000	PCA8, A26				
g	GL150001	GL175000	PCA8, A21				
h	GL175001	GL200000	PCA8, A25				
i	GM200001	GM225000	PCA8, A25				
j	GM225001	GM250000	PCA8, A21				
k	GM250001	GM275000	PCA8, A26				
l	GM275001	GM300000	PCA8, A19				
m	GN300001	GN325000	PCA8, A26				
n	GN325001	GN350000	PCA8, A25				
o	GN350001	GN375000	PCA8, A19				
p	GN375001	GN400000	PCA8, A21				
q	GO400001	GO425000	PCA8, A26				
r	GO425001	GO450000	PCA8, A25				
s	GO450001	GO475000	PCA8, A19				
t	GO475001	GO500000	PCA8, A21				
u	GP500001	GP525000	PCA8, A25				
v	GP525001	GP550000	PCA8, A21				
w	GP550001	GP575000	PCA8, A26				
x	GP575001	GP600000	PCA8, A19				
y	GQ600001	GQ625000	PCA8, A26				
z	GQ625001	GQ650000	PCA8, A19				
aa	GQ650001	GQ675000	PCA8, A21				
bb	GQ675001	GQ700000	PCA8, A25				
cc	GR700001	GR725000	PCA8, A25				
dd	GR725001	GR750000	PCA8, A21				
ee	GR750001	GR775000	PCA8, A19				
ff	GR775001	GR800000	PCA8, A26				
gg	GS800001	GS825000	PCA8, A19				
hh	GS825001	GS850000	PCA8, A26				
ii	GS850001	GS875000	PCA8, A21				
jj	GS875001	GS900000	PCA8, A25				
kk	GT900001	GT925000	PCA8, A26				
ll	GT925001	GT950000	PCA8, A21				
mm	GT950001	GT975000	PCA8, A25				
nn	GT975001	GT1000000	PCA8, A19				
pp1	Uniface reverse specimen proof in issued colours, with manuscript signatures of G8 and A25 on obverse, perforated CANCELLED						Rare
pp2	Specimen proof in issued colours, no signatures, serial number A000,000, with manuscript signature of A25 on obverse, two punch holes						$650
N.B.	No printer's archival specimens for this issue are known						

PG32	**20 escudos**	14 September 1937	SCWPM 22
	Printer	Bradbury Wilkinson & Co. Ltd.	
	Total Printed	500000	
	Circulation	Unknown	
	Colour	Blue on multicoloured underprint	
	Obverse Design	Portrait of João Teixeira Pinto at left, steamship seal at right.	
	Reverse Design	Allegorical maiden looking at ships	
	Size	138 x 80 mm	

PG32m

<table>
<tr><th></th><th></th><th></th><th></th><th colspan="3">Issued Notes</th><th>Specimens (sp)</th></tr>
<tr><th>PG32</th><th>Start of Print Run</th><th>End of Print Run</th><th>Signatures</th><th>Fine</th><th>VF</th><th>EF</th><th>AU</th></tr>
<tr><td>a</td><td>GU00001</td><td>GU25000</td><td>PCA8, A26</td><td rowspan="20">$700</td><td rowspan="20">$1,500</td><td rowspan="20">Rare</td><td rowspan="20">$850</td></tr>
<tr><td>b</td><td>GU25001</td><td>GU50000</td><td>PCA8, A25</td></tr>
<tr><td>c</td><td>GU50001</td><td>GU75000</td><td>PCA8, A19</td></tr>
<tr><td>d</td><td>GU75001</td><td>GU100000</td><td>PCA8, A21</td></tr>
<tr><td>e</td><td>GV100001</td><td>GV125000</td><td>PCA8, A25</td></tr>
<tr><td>f</td><td>GV125001</td><td>GV150000</td><td>PCA8, A21</td></tr>
<tr><td>g</td><td>GV150001</td><td>GV175000</td><td>PCA8, A26</td></tr>
<tr><td>h</td><td>GV175001</td><td>GV200000</td><td>PCA8, A19</td></tr>
<tr><td>i</td><td>GX200001</td><td>GX225000</td><td>PCA8, A19</td></tr>
<tr><td>j</td><td>GX225001</td><td>GX250000</td><td>PCA8, A26</td></tr>
<tr><td>k</td><td>GX250001</td><td>GX275000</td><td>PCA8, A21</td></tr>
<tr><td>l</td><td>GX275001</td><td>GX300000</td><td>PCA8, A25</td></tr>
<tr><td>m</td><td>GY300001</td><td>GY325000</td><td>PCA8, A21</td></tr>
<tr><td>n</td><td>GY325001</td><td>GY350000</td><td>PCA8, A19</td></tr>
<tr><td>o</td><td>GY350001</td><td>GY375000</td><td>PCA8, A25</td></tr>
<tr><td>p</td><td>GY375001</td><td>GY400000</td><td>PCA8, A26</td></tr>
<tr><td>q</td><td>GZ400001</td><td>GZ425000</td><td>PCA8, A21</td></tr>
<tr><td>r</td><td>GZ425001</td><td>GZ450000</td><td>PCA8, A19</td></tr>
<tr><td>s</td><td>GZ450001</td><td>GZ475000</td><td>PCA8, A25</td></tr>
<tr><td>t</td><td>GZ475001</td><td>GZ500000</td><td>PCA8, A26</td></tr>
<tr><td>pp1</td><td colspan="6">Uniface reverse specimen proof in issued colours, with manuscript signatures of G8 and A25 on obverse, perforated CANCELLED</td><td>Rare</td></tr>
<tr><td>pp2</td><td colspan="6">Specimen proof in issued colours, no signatures, serial number 000,000, with manuscript signature of A25 on obverse, two punch holes</td><td>$900</td></tr>
<tr><td>N.B.</td><td colspan="7">No printer's archival specimens for this issue are known</td></tr>
</table>

PG32sp

PG33	**50 escudos**	14 September 1937	SCWPM 23
	Printer	Bradbury Wilkinson & Co. Ltd.	
	Total Printed	100000	
	Circulation	Unknown	
	Colour	Red on multicoloured underprint	
	Obverse Design	Portrait of João Teixeira Pinto at left, steamship seal at right.	
	Reverse Design	Allegorical maiden looking at ships	
	Size	165 x 85 mm	

PG33b

				Issued Notes			Specimens
PG33	Start of Print Run	End of Print Run	Signatures	Fine	VF	EF	AU
a	GA000001	GA010000	PCA8, A25				
b	GA010001	GA020000	PCA8, A19				
c	GA020001	GA030000	PCA8, A21				
d	GA030001	GA040000	PCA8, A26				
e	GB040001	GB050000	PCA8, A21	$750	$1,750	Rare	$1,000
f	GB050001	GB060000	PCA8, A25				
g	GB060001	GB070000	PCA8, A26				
h	GB070001	GB080000	PCA8, A19				
i	GC080001	GC090000	PCA8, A21				
j	GC090001	GC100000	PCA8, A19				
ph	Black and white obverse and reverse photographs, dated 05. 11. 1937, serial number C000,000, note dated -- de -- 1937, no signatures, with printer's imprint on obverse and no printer's imprint on reverse						One Pair Known
p1	Uniface reverse specimen proof in issued colours, with manuscript signatures of G8 and A25 on obverse, perforated CANCELLED						Rare
p2	Specimen proof in issued colours, no signatures, serial number 000,000, with manuscript signature of A25 on obverse, two punch holes						$1,200
N.B.	No printer's archival specimens for this issue are known						

PG33ph

PG33ph

PG33s

PG34	**100 escudos**	14 September 1937	SCWPM 24
	Printer	Bradbury Wilkinson & Co. Ltd.	
	Total Printed	50000	
	Circulation	Unknown	
	Colour	Slate-purple on multicoloured underprint	
	Obverse Design	Portrait of João Teixeira Pinto at left, steamship seal at right.	
	Reverse Design	Allegorical maiden looking at ships	
	Size	171 x 98 mm	

PG34c

				Issued Notes			Specimens
PG34	Start of Print Run	End of Print Run	Signatures	Fine	VF	EF	AU
a	GD000001	GD005000	PCA8, A19				
b	GD005001	GD010000	PCA8, A21				
c	GD010001	GD015001	PCA8, A26				
d	GD015001	GD020000	PCA8, A25				
e	GE020001	GE025000	PCA8, A21	Rare	Rare	Rare	$1,200
f	GE025001	GE030000	PCA8, A25				
g	GE030001	GE035000	PCA8, A19				
h	GE035001	GE040000	PCA8, A26				
i	GF040001	GF045000	PCA8, A19				
j	GF045001	GF050000	PCA8, A25				
ph	Black and white obverse and reverse photographs, dated 05. 11. 1937, serial number D000,000, note dated -- de -- 1937, no signatures, with printer's imprint on obverse and no printer's imprint on reverse						One Pair Known
p1	Uniface reverse specimen proof in issued colours, with manuscript signatures of G8 and A25 on obverse, perforated CANCELLED						Rare
p2	Specimen proof in issued colours, no signatures, serial number 000,000, with manuscript signature of A25 on obverse, two punch holes						$1,400
N.B.	No printer's archival specimens for this issue are known						

PG34ph

PG34ph

PG34s

1944 TEIXEIRA PINTO ISSUE

PG35	**5 escudos**	2 November 1944	SCWPM 25
	Printer	Bradbury Wilkinson & Co. Ltd.	
	Total Printed	1000000	
	Circulation	Unknown	
	Colour	Green on multicoloured underprint	
	Obverse Design	Portrait of João Teixeira Pinto at left, steamship seal at right.	
	Reverse Design	Allegorical maiden looking at ships	
	Size	125 x 75 mm	

PG35e

					Issued Notes			Archival Specimens	Specimens
PG35	Start of Print Run	End of Print Run	Order Date (If Known)	Signatures	Fine	VF	EF	AU	AU
a	000001	150000	5.11.44	PCA8, A27					
b	150001	300000	5.11.44	PCA8, A18					
c	300001	400000	5.11.44	PCA8, A19					
d	400001	500000	5.11.44	PCA8, A25	$180	$375	$800	$250	$200
e	500001	650000	5.11.44	PCA8, A29					
f	650001	825000	5.11.44	PCA8, A26					
g	825001	1000000	5.11.44	PCA8, A30					
dp	Obverse and reverse die proofs, in issued colour deep olive-green								$450 (pair)

PG35dp

PG35dp

1945 TEIXEIRA PINTO ISSUE

PG36 **1 escudo** 2 January 1945 SCWPM unlisted

Printer	Bradbury Wilkinson & Co. Ltd.
Total Printed	Proofs and photographs only
Circulation	Never circulated
Colour	Purple on pale green underprint
Obverse Design	Portrait of João Teixeira Pinto at left, steamship seal at right.
Reverse Design	Arms and value set in ornate pattern
Size	105 x 60 mm
Signatures	PCA8, A27

PG36p

p	Specimen proof with serial number A.0,000,000	Rare
ph	Black and white obverse archival photograph, note dated 23 May 1944, serial number A.0,000,000, signatures PCA8, A27, photograph dated 13 September 1944	One Copy Known

PG36ph

PG37	**2½ escudos**	2 January 1945	SCWPM 26
	Printer	Bradbury Wilkinson & Co. Ltd.	
	Total Printed	1000000	
	Circulation	Withdrawn 31.12.1960	
	Colour	Violet and multicoloured	
	Obverse Design	Portrait of João Teixeira Pinto at left, steamship seal at right.	
	Reverse Design	Arms at top centre, value in figures at lower centre, ornate geometric patterns at left and right	
	Size	120 x 65 mm	
	Signatures	PCA8, A27	

PG37a

PG37	Start of Print Run	End of Print Run	Order Date (If Known)	Issued Notes VG	Issued Notes VF	Issued Notes Unc	Archival Specimens AU	Specimens Unc
a	A.0,000,001	A.1,000,000		$40	$180	$600	$500	$250
dp	Obverse die proof in issued colour violet, reverse multicoloured proof							AU - $450 (pair)
p	Specimen proof in issued colours, serial number A.0,000,000, one punch hole, approval with manuscript signature of A27							$500
ph	Black and white obverse archival photograph, note dated 23 May 1944, serial number A.0,000,000, signatures PCA8, A27, photograph dated 13 September 1944							One Copy Known

PG37dp

PG37dp

PG37p

PG37ph

PG38	**5 escudos**	16 November 1945	SCWPM 27
	Printer	Bradbury Wilkinson & Co. Ltd.	
	Total Printed	400000	
	Circulation	Withdrawn 31. 12. 1960	
	Colour	Green on multicoloured underprint	
	Obverse Design	Portrait of João Teixeira Pinto at left, steamship seal at right.	
	Reverse Design	Allegorical maiden looking at ships	
	Size	125 x 75 mm	

PG38gs

					Issued Notes			Archival Specimens	Specimens
PG38	Start of Print Run	End of Print Run	Order Date (If Known)	Signatures	Fine	VF	AU†	AU	AU
a	1000001	1050000	2.11.45	PCA8, A30					
b	1050001	1110000	2.11.45	PCA8, A19					
c	1110001	1160000	2.11.45	PCA8, A29					
d	1160001	1220000	2.11.45	PCA8, A18	$80	$150	$350	$250	$200
e	1220001	1270000	2.11.45	PCA8, A25					
f	1270001	1330000	2.11.45	PCA8, A27					
g	1330001	1400000	2.11.45	PCA8, A26					

N.B. † An unknown quantity of this issue, all graded AU, came onto the market in ca. 2016

PG39	**10 escudos**	16 November 1945	SCWPM 28
	Printer	Bradbury Wilkinson & Co. Ltd.	
	Total Printed	100000	
	Circulation	Withdrawn 31.12.1960	
	Colour	Red-brown on multicoloured underprint	
	Obverse Design	Portrait of João Teixeira Pinto at left, steamship seal at right.	
	Reverse Design	Allegorical maiden looking at ships	
	Size	125 x 75 mm	

PG39d

					Issued Notes			Archival Specimens	Specimens
PG39	Start of Print Run	End of Print Run	Order Date (If Known)	Signatures	Fine	VF	EF	AU	AU
a	1000001	1025000	21.11.45	PCA8, A18					
b	1025001	1050000	21.11.45	PCA8, A29					
c	1050001	1065000	21.11.45	PCA8, A27					
d	1065001	1080000	21.11.45	PCA8, A25	$300	$700	$1,500	$300	$250
e	1080001	1090000	21.11.45	PCA8, A26					
f	1090001	1095000	21.11.45	PCA8, A30					
g	1095001	1100000	21.11.45	PCA8, A19					

PG39as

PG40	**20 escudos**	16 November 1945	SCWPM 29
	Printer	Bradbury Wilkinson & Co. Ltd.	
	Total Printed	100000	
	Circulation	Withdrawn 31. 12. 1960	
	Colour	Blue on multicoloured underprint	
	Obverse Design	Portrait of João Teixeira Pinto at left, steamship seal at right.	
	Reverse Design	Allegorical maiden looking at ships	
	Size	138 x 80 mm	

PG40as

					Issued Notes			Archival Specimens	Specimens
PG40	Start of Print Run	End of Print Run	Order Date (If Known)	Signatures	Fine	VF	EF	AU	AU
a	500001	525000	21.11.45	PCA8, A29					
b	525001	550000	21.11.45	PCA8, A19					
c	550001	560000	21.11.45	PCA8, A27					
d	560001	570000	21.11.45	PCA8, A26	$350	$750	$1,600	$350	$300
e	570001	580000	21.11.45	PCA8, A18					
f	580001	590000	21.11.45	PCA8, A30					
g	590001	600000	21.11.45	PCA8, A25					

PG41	**50 escudos**	16 November 1945	SCWPM 30
	Printer	Bradbury Wilkinson & Co. Ltd.	
	Total Printed	40000	
	Circulation	Withdrawn 31.12.1960	
	Colour	Red on multicoloured underprint	
	Obverse Design	Portrait of João Teixeira Pinto at left, steamship seal at right.	
	Reverse Design	Allegorical maiden looking at ships	
	Size	165 x 85 mm	

PG41as

					Issued Notes			Archival Specimens	Specimens
PG41	Start of Print Run	End of Print Run	Order Date (If Known)	Signatures	Fine	VF	EF	EF	AU
a	100001	115000	21.11.45	PCA8, A26					
b	115001	130000	21.11.45	PCA8, A25	Rare	Rare	Rare	$600	$500
c	130001	140000	21.11.45	PCA8, A30					

PG42	**100 escudos**	16 November 1945	SCWPM 31
	Printer	Bradbury Wilkinson & Co. Ltd.	
	Total Printed	30000	
	Circulation	Withdrawn 31. 12. 1960	
	Colour	Slate-purple on multicoloured underprint	
	Obverse Design	Portrait of João Teixeira Pinto at left, steamship seal at right.	
	Reverse Design	Allegorical maiden looking at ships	
	Size	171 x 98 mm	

PG42as

					Issued Notes			Archival Specimens	Specimens
PG42	Start of Print Run	End of Print Run	Order Date (If Known)	Signatures	Fine	VF	EF	EF	AU
a	050001	065000	21.11.45	PCA8, A27	Rare	Rare	Rare	$750	$650
b	065001	080000	21.11.45	PCA8, A18					

N.B. 500 escudos dated 16 November 1945, incorrectly listed as SCWPM 32, does not exist

1947 TEIXEIRA PINTO ISSUE

PG43 **20 escudos** 27 March 1947 SCWPM 33

Printer	Bradbury Wilkinson & Co. Ltd.
Total Printed	750000
Circulation	Withdrawn 31. 12. 1960
Colour	Blue on multicoloured underprint
Obverse Design	Portrait of João Teixeira Pinto at left, steamship seal at right.
Reverse Design	Allegorical maiden looking at ships
Size	138 x 80 mm

PG43i

					Issued Notes			Archival Specimens	Specimens
PG43	Start of Print Run	End of Print Run	Order Date (If Known)	Signatures	Fine	VF	EF	AU	AU
a	600001	635000	30.5.47	PCA8, A28	$200	$450	$1,000	$250	$200
b	635001	674500	30.5.47	PCA8, A29					
c	674501	700000	30.5.47	PCA8, A25					
d	700001	735000	30.5.47	PCA8, A30					
e	735001	774500	30.5.47	PCA8, A26					
f	774501	810000	30.5.47	PCA8, A18					
g	810001	850000	30.5.47	PCA8, A19					
h	850001	920000	5.4.48	PCA8, A18					
i	920001	1000000	5.4.48	PCA8, A26					
j	1000001	1070000	5.4.48	PCA8, A30					
k	1070001	1130000	5.4.48	PCA8, A19					
l	1130001	1200000	5.4.48	PCA8, A29					
m	1200001	1270000	5.4.48	PCA8, A28					
n	1270001	1350000	5.4.48	PCA8, A25					

PG43ns

PG44	**50 escudos**	27 March 1947	SCWPM 34
	Printer	Bradbury Wilkinson & Co. Ltd.	
	Total Printed	560000	
	Circulation	Withdrawn 31. 12. 1960	
	Colour	Red on multicoloured underprint	
	Obverse Design	Portrait of João Teixeira Pinto at left, steamship seal at right.	
	Reverse Design	Allegorical maiden looking at ships	
	Size	165 x 85 mm	

PG44m

PG44	Start of Print Run	End of Print Run	Order Date (If Known)	Signatures	Issued Notes Fine	Issued Notes VF	Issued Notes EF	Archival Specimens AU	Specimens AU
a	140001	160000	30.5.47	PCA8, A19	$350	$800	$1,500	$300	$250
b	160001	175000	30.5.47	PCA8, A18					
c	175001	190000	30.5.47	PCA8, A28					
d	190001	200000	30.5.47	PCA8, A29					
e	200001	242000	29.3.48	PCA8, A30					
f	242001	285000	29.3.48	PCA8, A28					
g	285001	326000	29.3.48	PCA8, A25					
h	326001	360000	29.3.48	PCA8, A26					
i	360001	400000	29.3.48	PCA8, A18					
j	400001	450000	29.3.48	PCA8, A29					
k	450001	500000	29.3.48	PCA8, A19					
l	500001	560000	20.7.54	PCA8, A18					
m	560001	630000	20.7.54	PCA8, A30					
n	630001	700000	20.7.54	PCA8, A19					

PG44as

PG45	**100 escudos**	27 March 1947	SCWPM 35
	Printer	Bradbury Wilkinson & Co. Ltd.	
	Total Printed	320000	
	Circulation	Withdrawn 31. 12. 1960	
	Colour	Slate-purple on multicoloured underprint	
	Obverse Design	Portrait of João Teixeira Pinto at left, steamship seal at right.	
	Reverse Design	Allegorical maiden looking at ships	
	Size	171 x 98 mm	

PG45e

PG45	Start of Print Run	End of Print Run	Order Date (If Known)	Signatures	Issued Notes Fine	Issued Notes VF	Issued Notes EF	Archival Specimens EF	Specimens AU
a	080001	085000	30.5.47	PCA8, A30					
b	085001	090000	30.5.47	PCA8, A25					
c	090001	095000	30.5.47	PCA8, A29					
d	095001	100000	30.5.47	PCA8, A26					
e	100001	121500	29.3.48	PCA8, A19					
f	121501	143000	29.3.48	PCA8, A18					
g	143001	165000	29.3.48	PCA8, A28	$650	$1,800	Rare	$350	$300
h	165001	187000	29.3.48	PCA8, A26					
i	187001	200000	29.3.48	PCA8, A29					
j	200001	230000	29.3.48	PCA8, A25					
k	230001	250000	29.3.48	PCA8, A30					
l	250001	300000	27.3.54	PCA8, A19					
m	300001	350000	27.3.54	PCA8, A18					
n	350001	400000	27.3.54	PCA8, A30					

FG45as

PG46	**500 escudos**	27 March 1947	SCWPM 36
	Printer	Bradbury Wilkinson & Co. Ltd.	
	Total Printed	40000	
	Circulation	Withdrawn 31. 12. 1960	
	Colour	Green on multicoloured underprint	
	Obverse Design	Portrait of João Teixeira Pinto at left, steamship seal at right.	
	Reverse Design	Allegorical maiden looking at ships	
	Size	176 x 101 mm	

PG46as

					Issued Notes			Archival Specimens	Specimens
PG46	Start of Print Run	End of Print Run	Order Date (If Known)	Signatures	Fine	VF	EF	EF	AU
a	000001	002800	30.5.47	PCA8, A18					
b	002801	005650	30.5.47	PCA8, A26					
c	005651	008150	30.5.47	PCA8, A19					
d	008151	011150	30.5.47	PCA8, A25					
e	011151	014000	30.5.47	PCA8, A29					
f	014001	016900	30.5.47	PCA8, A30					
g	016901	020000	30.5.47	PCA8, A28	Rare	Rare	Rare	$700	$650
h	020001	022900	29.3.48	PCA8, A18					
i	022901	025000	29.3.48	PCA8, A28					
j	025001	026500	29.3.48	PCA8, A30					
k	026501	028000	29.3.48	PCA8, A29					
l	028001	030000	29.3.48	PCA8, A25					
m	030001	035000	29.3.48	PCA8, A19					
n	035001	040000	29.3.48	PCA8, A26					
dp	Obverse and reverse die proofs in issued colour green								EF - $650 (pair)

1958 TEIXEIRA PINTO ISSUE

Reverses of the 1958-64 Teixeira Pinto Issues

PG47

PG48
and PG49

PG50
and PG51

PG52

PG53

PG54

PG47 **50 escudos**	20 November 1958	SCWPM 37
Printer	Bradbury Wilkinson & Co. Ltd.	
Total Printed	800000	
Circulation	Withdrawn 31. 10. 1965	
Colour	Red on multicoloured underprint	
Obverse Design	Portrait of João Teixeira Pinto at left, ship seal at right.	
Reverse Design	Allegorical maiden looking at ships	
Size	165 x 85 mm	

PG47f

PG47	Start of Print Run	End of Print Run	Order Date (If Known)	Signatures	Issued Notes Fine	Issued Notes VF	Issued Notes EF	Archival Specimens AU	Specimens AU
a	B000001	B130000	10.12.58	G9, A19	$200	$450	$1,000	$300	$250
b	B130001	B260000	10.12.58	G9, A36					
c	B260001	B400000	10.12.58	G9, A35					
d	B400001	B530000	10.12.58	G9, A34					
e	B530001	B660000	10.12.58	G9, A38					
f	B660001	B800000	10.12.58	G9, A37					
ct	Specimen colour trial in blue, pink and multicoloured, reverse blue and green on salmon underprint, no date, black serial number B000000, overprinted SPECIMEN in red horizontally, two punch holes								Unc - $350
dp	Obverse and reverse die proofs in issued colour red								AU - $450 (pair)
p1	Specimen proof dated 20. 11. 1958, red serial number B123456 at lower left, red serial number B789012 at upper right, signatures G9 and A34, one punch hole								Rare
p2	Specimen proof dated 20. 11. 1958, black serial number B123456 at lower left, black serial number B789012 at upper right, signatures G9 and A34 with manuscript signature of A39, one punch hole								Rare

PG47ct

PG47ct

PG47p1

PG47p2

PG48	**100 escudos**	20 November 1958, first issue. **Without security thread.**	SCWPM 38
	Printer	Bradbury Wilkinson & Co. Ltd.	
	Total Printed	500000	
	Circulation	Withdrawn 31. 10. 1965	
	Colour	Slate-purple on multicoloured underprint	
	Obverse Design	Portrait of João Teixeira Pinto at left, ship seal at right.	
	Reverse Design	Allegorical maiden looking at ships	
	Size	171 x 98 mm	

PG48c

					Issued Notes			Archival Specimens	Specimens
PG48	Start of Print Run	End of Print Run	Order Date (If Known)	Signatures	Fine	VF	EF	AU	AU
a	B000001	B080000	10.12.58	G9, A37					
b	B080001	B150000	10.12.58	G9, A19					
c	B150001	B250000	10.12.58	G9, A36	$600	$1,400	Rare	$350	$300
d	B250001	B330000	10.12.58	G9, A38					
e	B330001	B450000	10.12.58	G9, A34					
f	B450001	B500000	10.12.58	G9, A35					
ct	Specimen colour trial in olive-green and multicoloured, no date, no security thread, serial number 00000, no signatures, overprinted SPECIMEN in red horizontally								Unc - $350
dp	Obverse and reverse die proofs in issued colour slate-purple								AU - $500 (pair)
p	Specimen proof dated 20. 11. 1958, red serial number B123456 at lower left, red serial number B789012 at upper right, signatures G9 and A34 with manuscript signature of A39, one punch hole								Rare

PG48ct

PG48ct

PG48p

PG49	**100 escudos**	20 November 1958, second issue. **With security thread.** SCWPM unlisted
	Printer	Bradbury Wilkinson & Co. Ltd.
	Total Printed	100000
	Circulation	Withdrawn 31. 10. 1965
	Colour	Slate-purple on multicoloured underprint
	Obverse Design	Portrait of João Teixeira Pinto at left, ship seal at right.
	Reverse Design	Allegorical maiden looking at ships
	Size	171 x 98 mm

PG49as

					Issued Notes			Archival Specimens	Specimens
PG49	Start of Print Run	End of Print Run	Order Date (If Known)	Signatures	Fine	VF	EF	AU	AU
a	B500001	B525000	10.12.62	G9, A37	$800	$1,800	Rare	$450	$400
b	B525001	B550000	10.12.62	G9, A36					
c	B550001	B575000	10.12.62	G9, A38					
d	B575001	B600000	10.12.62	G9, A35					
ct	Specimen colour trial in olive-green and multicoloured, no date, with security thread, serial number B000000, no signatures, overprinted SPECIMEN in red horizontally, two punch holes								Unc - $450

PG49ct

PG49ct

PG50 **500 escudos** 20 November 1958, first issue. **Without security thread.** SCWPM 39

Printer Bradbury Wilkinson & Co. Ltd.

Total Printed 50000

Circulation Withdrawn 31. 10. 1965

Colour Green on multicoloured underprint

Obverse Design Portrait of João Teixeira Pinto at left, ship seal at right.

Reverse Design Allegorical maiden looking at ships

Size 176 x 101 mm

PG50b

					Issued Notes			Archival Specimens	Specimens
PG50	Start of Print Run	End of Print Run	Order Date (If Known)	Signatures	Fine	VF	EF	EF	AU
a	B000001	B008000	10.12.58	G9, A34					
b	B008001	B020000	10.12.58	G9, A35					
c	B020001	B030000	10.12.58	G9, A19	Rare	Rare	Rare	$600	$500
d	B030001	B038000	10.12.58	G9, A37					
e	B038001	B045000	10.12.58	G9, A36					
f	B045001	B050000	10.12.58	G9, A38					
ct	Specimen colour trial in yellow-brown on pink and green underprint, no date, no security thread, serial number B000000, no signatures, overprinted SPECIMEN in red horizontally, two punch holes								Unc - $400
dp	Obverse and reverse die proofs in issued colour green								AU - $550 (pair)
p	Specimen proof dated 20. 11. 1958, red serial number B123456 at lower left, red serial number B789012 at upper right, signatures G9 and A34 with manuscript signature of A39, one punch hole								Rare

PG50ct

PG50ct

PG50p

PG51	**500 escudos**	20 November 1958, second issue. **With security thread.**	SCWPM unlisted
	Printer	Bradbury Wilkinson & Co. Ltd.	
	Total Printed	40000	
	Circulation	Withdrawn 31. 10. 1965	
	Colour	Green on multicoloured underprint	
	Obverse Design	Portrait of João Teixeira Pinto at left, ship seal at right.	
	Reverse Design	Allegorical maiden looking at ships	
	Size	176 x 101 mm	

PG51as

					Issued Notes			Archival Specimens	Specimens
PG51	Start of Print Run	End of Print Run	Order Date (If Known)	Signatures	Fine	VF	EF	AU	AU
a	B050001	B060000	10.12.62	G9, A36					
b	B060001	B070000	10.12.62	G9, A38	Rare	Rare	Rare	$750	$600
c	B070001	B080000	10.12.62	G9, A35					
d	B080001	B090000	10.12.62	G9, A37					
ct	Specimen colour trial in dark brown on pink and green underprint, no date, with security thread, serial number B000000, no signatures, overprinted SPECIMEN in red horizontally, two punch holes								Unc - $500

PG51ct

PG51ct

1964 TEIXEIRA PINTO ISSUE

PG52	**50 escudos**	30 June 1964	SCWPM 40
	Printer	Bradbury Wilkinson & Co. Ltd.	
	Total Printed	800000	
	Circulation	Unknown	
	Colour	Deep blue-green on pink and multicoloured underprint	
	Obverse Design	Portrait of João Teixeira Pinto at left, ship seal at right.	
	Reverse Design	Allegorical maiden looking at ships	
	Size	165 x 85 mm	

PG52f

					Issued Notes			Archival Specimens	Specimens
PG52	Start of Print Run	End of Print Run	Order Date (If Known)	Signatures	VG	VF	Unc	AU	AU
a	C000001	C130000	22.6.64	G9, A35	$30	$80	$250	$225	$175
b	C130001	C260000	22.6.64	G9, A37					
c	C260001	C400000	22.6.64	G9, A36					
d	C400001	C530000	22.6.64	G9, A38					
e	C530001	C660000	22.6.64	G9, A41					
f	C660001	C800000	22.6.64	G9, A40					
p	Specimen proof in issued colours, dated 30 June 1964, with incorrect "DECRETOS-LEIS Nos 39221-E 44891", red serial number B000000, signatures G9 and A35, one punch hole								Rare
ct	Specimen colour trial in purple and multicoloured, reverse colours as issued note, dated 30 June 1964, red serial number C000000, signatures G9, A35, overprinted SPECIMEN in red horizontally, two punch holes								Unc - $400

PG52ct

PG52ct

PG52p

PG53	**100 escudos**	30 June 1964	SCWPM 41
	Printer	Bradbury Wilkinson & Co. Ltd.
	Total Printed	700000
	Circulation	Unknown
	Colour	Blue on pink and multicoloured underprint
	Obverse Design	Portrait of João Teixeira Pinto at left, ship seal at right.
	Reverse Design	Allegorical maiden looking at ships
	Size	171 x 98 mm

PG53a

					Issued Notes			Archival Specimens	Specimens
PG53	Start of Print Run	End of Print Run	Order Date (If Known)	Signatures	VG	VF	Unc	EF	AU
a	C000001	C120000	22.6.64	G9, A40	$50	$125	$400	$450	$350
b	C120001	C240000	22.6.64	G9, A41					
c	C240001	C360000	22.6.64	G9, A38					
d	C360001	C480000	22.6.64	G9, A36					
e	C480001	C590000	22.6.64	G9, A37					
f	C590001	C700000	22.6.64	G9, A35					
p	Specimen proof in issued colours, no date, serial number B000000, no signatures, one punch hole								Rare
ct	Specimen colour trial in deep olive-green and multicoloured, dated 30 June 1964, serial number C000000, signatures G9, A41, overprinted SPECIMEN in red horizontally, two punch holes								Unc - $450

PG53ct

PG53ct

PG53p

PG54	**500 escudos**	30 June 1964	SCWPM 42
	Printer	Bradbury Wilkinson & Co. Ltd.	
	Total Printed	90000	
	Circulation	Unknown	
	Colour	Brown on multicoloured underprint	
	Obverse Design	Portrait of João Teixeira Pinto at left, ship seal at right.	
	Reverse Design	Allegorical maiden looking at ships	
	Size	176 x 101 mm	

PG54b

					Issued Notes			Archival Specimens	Specimens
PG54	Start of Print Run	End of Print Run	Order Date (If Known)	Signatures	VG	VF	Unc	EF	AU
a	C000001	C015000	22.6.64	G9, A41					
b	C015001	C030000	22.6.64	G9, A40					
c	C030001	C045000	22.6.64	G9, A35	$90	$350	$900	$600	$500
d	C045001	C060000	22.6.64	G9, A37					
e	C060001	C075000	22.6.64	G9, A36					
f	C075001	C090000	22.6.64	G9, A38					
p	Specimen proof in issued colours, dated 30 June 1964, no security thread, black serial number B000000, signatures G9, A35, one punch hole								Rare
ct	Specimen colour trial in red on pale violet and multicoloured underprint, dated 30 June 1964, serial number C000000, signatures G9, A41, overprinted SPECIMEN in black horizontally, two punch holes								Unc - $550

PG54ct

PG54ct

PG54p

1964 BARRETO ISSUE

Honório Pereira Barreto (1813-59) was born in Portuguese Guinea of a Guinean mother and Cape Verdean father. Educated in Lisbon, he became Governor of Portuguese Guinea, a position he held for three separate terms between 1837 and his death in service in 1859. As the province's most famous governor, he was frequently cited by the Portuguese as an example of what the local population might achieve.

PG55	**1000 escudos**	30 April 1964	SCWPM 43
	Printer	Bradbury Wilkinson & Co. Ltd.	
	Total Printed	205000	
	Circulation	Unknown	
	Colour	Red-orange on multicoloured underprint	
	Obverse Design	Portrait of Honório Barreto at right, ship seal at uper centre.	
	Reverse Design	Allegorical young woman looking out at ships from various eras	
	Size	176 x 95 mm	

PG55as

PG55as

					Issued Notes			Archival Specimens	Specimens
PG55	Start of Print Run	End of Print Run	Order Date (If Known)	Signatures	VG	VF	Unc	EF	AU
a	000001	004500	15.9.64	G9, A35					
b	004501	009000	15.9.64	G9, A36					
c	009001	013000	15.9.64	G9, A37					
d	013001	017000	15.9.64	G9, A38					
e	017001	021000	15.9.64	G9, A41					
f	021001	025000	15.9.64	G9, A40					
g	025001	050000	3.6.69	G9, A36	$30	$100	$400	$375	$300
h	050001	075000	3.6.69	G9, A38					
i	075001	105000	3.6.69	G9, A41					
j	105001	130000	25.3.71	G9, A35					
k	130001	155000	25.3.71	G9, A36					
l	155001	180000	25.3.71	G9, A38					
m	180001	205000	25.3.71	G9, A41					
ct	Specimen colour trial in black-brown on multicoloured underprint, dated 30 April 1964, serial number 000000, signatures G9, A35, overprinted SPECIMEN in red horizontally, two punch holes								Unc - $350
dp	Obverse and reverse die proofs in issued colour red-orange								AU - $450 (pair)
ph1	Black and white obverse and reverse archival photographs, undated note, serial number 000000, no signatures, both hand drawn with arms of Portugal at top centre on obverse, reverse photograph dated 19.6.64								One Pair Known
ph2	Black and white obverse and reverse archival photographs, note dated 30.4.1964, serial number 000000, signatures G9, A37, both hand drawn with bank seal at top centre on obverse, photographs dated 16.9.64								One Pair Known
p1	Specimen proof, undated, no serial numbers, no signatures, perforated SPECIMEN								EF - $450
p2	Specimen proof, dated 30. 4. 1964, serial number 123456 at lower left, serial number 789012 at upper right, signatures G9, A35, "AS SUBMITTED, 2. 2. 65" in top right corner								Rare

PG55ct

PG55ct

PG55dp

PG55dp

PG55ph1

PG55ph1

PG55ph2

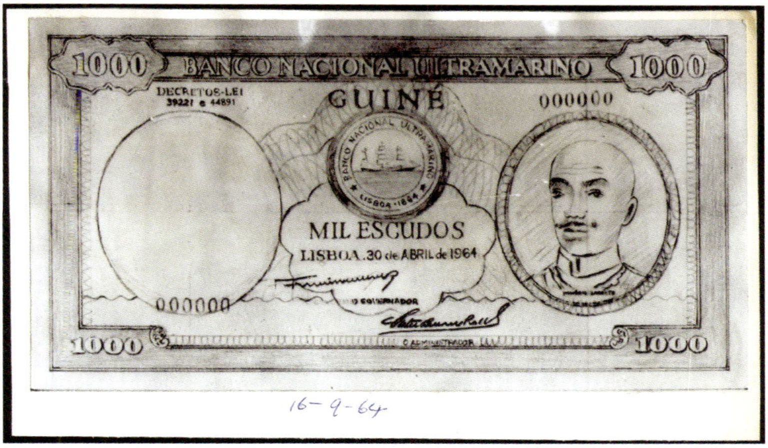

PG55ph2

1971 TRISTÃO ISSUE

Nuno Tristão (d. 1446) was a knight in the household of Prince Henry the Navigator, who sent him on a mission with one of the newly-invented caravels, to discover the coast of Africa south of Cape Barbas. Whether or not he sailed as far south as Guinea is disputed, some historians claiming he went no further than the mouth of the Gambia River. During this voyage he met up with Antão Gonçalves, who had been sent by Prince Henry on a separate mission and after this rendezvous the two men made a raid on a fishing village and captured the first African slaves. Gonçalves then returned with the slaves to Portugal, whilst Tristão continued to sail south along the African coast. In all Tristão made four African voyages, but on his fourth voyage in 1446 he and his men were overpowered by about 80 Africans in 13 canoes, who confronted Tristão in an unknown river somewhere south of the peninsula of Cap Vert and killed him and many of his men with poisoned arrows.

PG56	**50 escudos**	17 December 1971	SCWPM 44
	Printer	Bradbury Wilkinson & Co. Ltd.	
	Total Printed	1000000	
	Circulation	Unknown	
	Colour	Olive-green on multicoloured underprint	
	Obverse Design	Portrait of Nuno Tristão at right.	
	Reverse Design	Allegorical young woman looking out at ships from various eras	
	Size	161 x 80 mm	

PG56as

PG56as

PG56	Start of Print Run	End of Print Run	Order Date (If Known)	Signatures	Issued Notes VG	Issued Notes VF	Issued Notes Unc	Archival Specimens AU	Specimens Unc
a	0C0001	140000	19.2.73	G9, A36					
b	140001	280000	19.2.73	G9, A38					
c	230001	420000	19.2.73	G9, A44					
d	420001	560000	19.2.73	G9, A45	$3	$7	$30	$275	$150
e	560001	700000	19.2.73	G9, A43					
f	700001	840000	19.2.73	G9, A41					
g	840001	1000000	19.2.73	G9, A42					
ct	Specimen colour trial in green on multicoloured underprint, no date, serial number 000000, signatures G9, A44, overprinted SPECIMEN in red horizontally, two punch holes								Unc - $175
dp	Obverse and reverse die proofs in issued colour olive-green								AU - $350 (pair)
p	Specimen proof, undated, no serial numbers, no signatures								AU - $250

PG56ct

PG56ct

PG57	**100 escudos**	17 December 1971	SCWPM 45
	Printer	Bradbury Wilkinson & Co. Ltd.	
	Total Printed	1000000	
	Circulation	Unknown	
	Colour	Blue on multicoloured underprint	
	Obverse Design	Portrait of Nuno Tristão at right.	
	Reverse Design	Allegorical young woman looking out at ships from various eras	
	Size	176 x 90 mm	

PG57as

PG57as

					Issued Notes			Archival Specimens	Specimens
PG57	Start of Print Run	End of Print Run	Order Date (If Known)	Signatures	VG	VF	Unc	AU	Unc
a	000001	140000	19.2.73	G9, A36					
b	140001	280000	19.2.73	G9, A38					
c	280001	420000	19.2.73	G9, A44					
d	420001	560000	19.2.73	G9, A45	$3	$8	$40	$300	$175
e	560001	700000	19.2.73	G9, A43					
f	700001	840000	19.2.73	G9, A41					
g	840001	1000000	19.2.73	G9, A42					
ct	Specimen colour trial in olive-grey on multicoloured underprint, no date, serial number 000000, signatures G9, A42, overprinted SPECIMEN in red horizontally, two punch holes								Unc - $200
p	Obverse and reverse die proofs in issued colour deep blue								AU - $350 (pair)
sp	Specimen proof, undated, no serial numbers, no signatures								AU - $275

PG57ct

PG57ct

PG57dp

22 Deep Blue 2.2.73.

PG57dp

22 Deep Blue 2.2.73.

1971 BARRETO ISSUE

PG58	**500 escudos**	27 July 1971	SCWPM 46
	Printer	Bradbury Wilkinson & Co. Ltd.	
	Total Printed	200000	
	Circulation	Unknown	
	Colour	Purple on multicoloured underprint	
	Obverse Design	Portrait of Honorio Barreto at right.	
	Reverse Design	Allegorical young woman looking out at ships from various eras	
	Size	176 x 90 mm	

PG58as

PG58as

					Issued Notes			Archival Specimens	Specimens
PG58	Start of Print Run	End of Print Run	Order Date (If Known)	Signatures	VG	VF	Unc	EF	Unc
a	000001	020000	3.1.72	G9, A38					
b	020001	050000	3.1.72	G9, A36					
c	050001	080000	3.1.72	G9, A44					
d	080001	110000	3.1.72	G9, A45	$40	$125	$325	$350	$200
e	110001	140000	3.1.72	G9, A43					
f	140001	170000	3.1.72	G9, A41					
g	170001	200000	3.1.72	G9, A42					
ct	Specimen colour trial in brown on multicoloured underprint, no date, serial number 000000, signatures G9, A43, overprinted SPECIMEN in red horizontally, two punch holes								Unc - $300
dp	Obverse and reverse die proofs in issued colour purple								AU - $450 (pair)
p1	Specimen proof in issued colours, dated 27 July 1971, serial number 000000, signatures G9, A35, with "O" in front of Governador and Administrador corrected								EF - Rare
p2	Specimen proof, undated, no serial numbers, no signatures								EF - $300

PG58ct

PG58ct

PG58dp

PG58dp

PG58p1

St Thomas and Prince

INTRODUCTION

The islands of St Thomas and Prince (São Tomé and Príncipe), lying just north of the equator in the Gulf of Guinea off the coasts of Gabon and Equatorial Guinea respectively, were first discovered by the Portuguese in the 1470s. King Afonso V (1432-81) granted the monopoly of Portuguese trade with the African coast to Fernão Gomes, who employed able captains to further explore this coast south of the Gulf of Guinea. This is why King Afonso V appears on the 1946 and 1956-8 banknotes of the colony (see ST42-ST44 and ST49-ST52). One of these captains was João de Santarém, who with Pedro de Escobar discovered the uninhabited islands of São Tomé on 21 December 1471 (the feast of St Thomas) and Príncipe on 17 January 1472. Santarém too appears on the paper money of the colony (see ST53).

After the failure of the first settlement in 1485, the Portuguese began to settle convicts and expelled Jews on the islands from 1493. Later they established sugar plantations there, using enslaved labour from the mainland, and the islands developed as a slave entrepôt. However between 1567-1709, the islands went into decline, experiencing a rising of enslaved peoples in 1595 and suffering several attacks by the French and the Dutch. The transfer of the profitable sugar trade to Brazil during the early 17th century led to a collapse in the economy.

In the late 19th century, cocoa was introduced, which led to an increase in prosperity. However by the early 20th century British and German chocolate manufacturers began to boycott the colony, because the workforce used in the plantations was regarded as virtually enslaved. The islands were designated a Portuguese Overseas Province in 1951 and remained so until independence. After 500 years of Portuguese rule, the independent republic of São Tomé and Príncipe came into being on 12 July 1975 and Manuel Pinto da Costa was inaugurated as the first President.

The BNU opened a branch in São Tomé in 1868, the first paper money which circulated being issues of Angola overprinted "S. THOMÉ" (see ST1 and ST2). Specific issues for the colony then circulated between 1891-1909, followed by the omnibus Vasco da Gama, Cedula and Chamiço series overprinted with the name of the colony. The series featuring King Afonso V circulated between 1946 and independence in 1975 and the notes were overprinted in 1976 with the new name of the independent bank, "Banco Nacional de S. Tomé e Príncipe". These overprinted notes are not the subject of this catalogue.

The BNU São Tomé branch. Address: Rua do General Calheiros with Praça da República. Second installation, 1925 to 1975.

1868-70 ISSUE

ST1	**5000 reis**	1 January 1868 (Other dates may exist)	SCWPM unlisted
	Printer	Chambers & Sons, London	
	Overprint	“PAGAVEL NA AGENCIA DE S. THOMÉ” in blue on Angola AN1 (SCWPM 10)	
	Total Overprints	Unknown	
	Circulation	Unknown	
	Colour	Black	
	Obverse Design	Sailing ship at upper centre, value in numerals in oval at upper right, and in words in panel at lower left	
	Reverse Design	Uniface	
	Watermark	BANCO NACIONAL / ULTRAMARINO	
	Size	178 x 111 mm	
	Signatures	Facsimile signature of G1 and manuscript signatures of two managers	

ST1a

ST1	Start of Print Run	End of Print Run	VG	Fine	VF
a	Unknown	Unknown	Rare	Rare	Rare

ST2	**20000 reis**	9 January 1870 (Other dates may exist)	SCWPM unlisted
	Printer	Chambers & Sons, London	
	Overprint	"PAGAVEL NA AGENCIA DE S. THOMÉ" in blue on Angola AN3 (SCWPM 12)	
	Total Overprints	Unknown	
	Circulation	Unknown	
	Colour	Black	
	Obverse Design	Sailing ship at upper centre, value in numerals in oval at upper right, and in words in panel at lower left	
	Reverse Design	Uniface	
	Watermark	BANCO NACIONAL / ULTRAMARINO	
	Size	178 x 111 mm	
	Signatures	Facsimile signature of G1 and manuscript signatures of two managers	

ST2a

ST2	Start of Print Run	End of Print Run	VG	Fine	VF
a	Unknown	Unknown	Rare	Rare	Rare

1891 ISSUE

ST3	**20000 reis**	2 January 1891	SCWPM unlisted
	Printer	Casa de Moeda, Lisbon*	
	Total Printed	Unknown	
	Circulation	Unknown	
	Colour	Blue. Reverse pink	
	Obverse Design	Sailing ship at upper centre, value in numerals in ovals at upper left and right, and in words in panel at centre	
	Reverse Design	20$000 at centre, entwined letters BNU in each corner, foliate patterned borders	
	Watermark	BANCO NACIONAL / ULTRAMARINO	
	Size	Unknown	
	Signatures	Facsimile signatures of G2 and VG5, manuscript signatures of two managers	

ST3a

ST3a

ST3	Start of Print Run	End of Print Run	VG	Fine	VF
a	Unknown	Unknown	Rare	Rare	Rare

1897 ISSUE

ST4 **1000 reis** 2 January 1897 SCWPM 1

Printer Casa da Moeda, Lisbon
Total Printed Unknown
Circulation Withdrawn 17. 02. 1912
Colour Green
Obverse Design Man with bow and arrows at left, sailing ship at centre, elephant's head, arms at upper left
Reverse Design Portuguese text
Watermark Unknown
Size 125 x 91 mm
Signatures G3, VG6 or VG8 and manuscript signatures of two managers

ST4	Start of Print Run	End of Print Run	VG	Fine	VF
a	Unknown	Unknown	Rare	Rare	Rare

ST5 **2000 reis** 2 January 1897 SCWPM 2

Printer Casa da Moeda, Lisbon
Total Printed Unknown
Circulation Withdrawn 17. 02. 1912
Colour Unknown
Obverse Design Unknown
Reverse Design Unknown
Watermark Unknown
Size Unknown
Signatures G3, VG6 or VG8 and manuscript signatures of two managers

ST5	Start of Print Run	End of Print Run	VG	Fine	VF
a	Unknown	Unknown	Rare	Rare	Rare

ST6	**2500 reis**	2 January 1897				SCWPM 3
	Printer	Casa da Moeda, Lisbon				
	Total Printed	Unknown				
	Circulation	Withdrawn 17. 02. 1912				
	Colour	Grey-blue				
	Obverse Design	Steamship at left, field at centre, woman standing at centre right				
	Reverse Design	Large winged vessel, waves, seadogs and seaweed				
	Watermark	Unknown				
	Size	170 x 125 mm				
	Signatures	G3, VG6 or VG8 and manuscript signatures of two managers				

ST6	Start of Print Run	End of Print Run	VG	Fine	VF
a	Unknown	Unknown	Rare	Rare	Rare

ST7	**5000 reis**	2 January 1897				SCWPM 4
	Printer	Casa da Moeda, Lisbon				
	Total Printed	Unknown				
	Circulation	Withdrawn 17. 02. 1912				
	Colour	Blue. Reverse brown				
	Obverse Design	Bush set in columns at left, seated woman holding caduceus, steamship and flora at right				
	Reverse Design	Bank name and value in floral surround				
	Watermark	Unknown				
	Size	170 x 125 mm				
	Signatures	G3, VG6 or VG8 and manuscript signatures of two managers				

ST7	Start of Print Run	End of Print Run	VG	Fine	VF
a	Unknown	Unknown	Rare	Rare	Rare

ST8	**10000 reis**	2 January 1897	SCWPM 5
	Printer	Casa da Moeda, Lisbon	
	Total Printed	Unknown	
	Circulation	Withdrawn 17. 02. 1912	
	Colour	Purple. Reverse deep salmon-pink	
	Obverse Design	Woman representing agriculture at left, steamship at centre, Mercury at right	
	Reverse Design	Bank name and value in floral surround	
	Watermark	BANCO NACIONAL / ULTRAMARINO	
	Size	170 x 125 mm	
	Signatures	G3, VG6 or VG8 and manuscript signatures of two managers	

ST8a

ST8a

ST8	Start of Print Run	End of Print Run	VG	Fine	VF
a	Unknown	Unknown	Rare	Rare	Rare

ST9	**20000 reis**	2 January 1897	SCWPM 6
	Printer	Casa da Moeda, Lisbon	
	Total Printed	Unknown	
	Circulation	Withdrawn 17. 02. 1912	
	Colour	Blue-green on yellow underprint with brown text. Reverse purple on beige underprint	
	Obverse Design	Arms at top left, steamship in framed vignette at upper centre	
	Reverse Design	Value in words in ornate frame	
	Watermark	BANCO NACIONAL / ULTRAMARINO	
	Size	Unknown	
	Signatures	G3, VG6 or VG8 and manuscript signatures of two managers	

ST9a

ST9a

ST9	Start of Print Run	End of Print Run	VG	Fine	VF
a	Unknown	Unknown	Rare	Rare	Rare

1905 DESIGN FOR AN UNISSUED SERIES

STA1	**2500 reis**	1905 (no date)
	Format	Obverse and reverse sepia archival photographs mounted on card, dated 7. 9. 05, of an unissued design, 00000 serial number
	Obverse Design	Maiden with trident riding a mythical sea creature at left, arms at upper right, value in figures at centre, lower right and in each corner
	Reverse Design	Value in figures set in an ornate guilloche
	Signatures	Unsigned

One Pair Known

STA1

STA1

1909 VASCO DE GAMA ISSUE

By the Law of 27 April 1901, a new legal framework for banking activity in the Portuguese Colonial Empire was established. The new legislation divided banking operations into two groups; the issuance of paper money and the grant of loans secured by real estate. Although the banknote issue was open to competitive tendering, each colony could only have one bank and the BNU was the only bidder for St Thomas and Prince and the other four African colonies. Under this new contract, the BNU prepared a new issue of notes, which were known as the Vasco da Gama Issue.

The notes issued under the new contract for St Thomas & Prince were all dated 1 March 1909 with denominations of 1$000, 2$500, 5$000, 10$000, 20$000 and 50$000 reis, all being signed by the Governor Antonio Teixeira de Sousa (G4) and various Vice Governors (VG6, VG9 and VG10) and with a manuscript or facsimile signature of a manager. Two different types of steamship seal were used: the earlier issues used Type 1 and the later issues used Type 3.

See also "A Summary of the Main Banknote Issues of the Banco Nacional Ultramarino" on page 7 and "A Brief History of the Rise of the Portuguese Empire" on page 11 for further information on Vasco da Gama.

Steamship seal Type 1

Steamship seal Type 3

Reverses of the Vasco da Gama Issue

ST10
and ST11

ST12
and ST13

ST14
and ST15

ST16 and ST17

ST18 and ST19

ST20 and ST21

ST10	**1000 reis**	1 March 1909	SCWPM 7a
	Printer	Bradbury Wilkinson & Co. Ltd.
	Total Printed	45000*
	Circulation	Withdrawn 27. 07. 1922
	Colour	Black on green and yellow underprint
	Obverse Design	Value in guilloches, crowned arms at upper right, overprint S. THOMÉ
	Reverse Design	Allegorical maiden looking at ships
	Size	138 x 80 mm
	Ship Seal	Type 1

ST10d

ST10	Start of Print Run	End of Print Run	Order Date (If Known)	Signatures	Issued Notes VG	Fine	VF	Archival Specimens AU
a	00001	08334		G4, VG9	$1,750	Rare	Rare	$1,250
b	08335	16667		G4, VG6	$1,500	Rare	Rare	$750
c	16668	25000		G4, VG10				
d	25001	35000	15.11.17	G4, VG6				
e	35001	45000	15.11.17	G4, VG10				

N.B. There may be additional print runs for this issue, which should be valued at the same levels as ST10b-ST10e

ST10as

ST11	**1000 reis**	1 March 1909	SCWPM 7b
	Printer	Bradbury Wilkinson & Co. Ltd.	
	Total Printed	Unknown	
	Circulation	Withdrawn 27. 07. 1922	
	Colour	Black on green and yellow underprint	
	Obverse Design	Value in guilloches, crowned arms at upper right, overprint S. THOMÉ	
	Reverse Design	Allegorical maiden looking at ships	
	Size	138 x 80 mm	
	Ship Seal	Type 3	

					Issued Notes			Archival Specimens
ST11	Start of Print Run	End of Print Run	Order Date (If Known)	Signatures	VG	Fine	VF	AU
a	---	---	---	---	---	---	---	---

N.B. Wheras the other colonies in this catalogue issued an equivalent 1000 reis with Type 3 ship seal, there are no sale records and we have seen no examples of this issue. Therefore it remains unconfirmed

ST12	**2500 reis**	1 March 1909	SCWPM 8a
	Printer	Bradbury Wilkinson & Co. Ltd.	
	Total Printed	400000*	
	Circulation	Withdrawn 27. 07. 1922	
	Colour	Black on green and yellow underprint. Reverse blue	
	Obverse Design	Vasco da Gama and his passage round The Cape, overprint S. THOMÉ	
	Reverse Design	Allegorical maiden looking at ships	
	Size	148 x 94 mm	
	Ship Seal	Type 1	

ST12b

					Issued Notes			Archival Specimens
ST12	Start of Print Run	End of Print Run	Order Date (If Known)	Signatures	VG	Fine	VF	AU
a	00001	133334*		G4, VG9	$1,000	$2,000	Rare	$1,750
b	133334*	266667*		G4, VG6	$900	$1,750	Rare	$1,500
c	266668*	400000*		G4, VG10				

N.B. An unknown quantity of notes was overprinted "Pagavel na Filial de Loanda" for use in Angola. See AN45 (SCWPM 25)

ST13	**2500 reis**	1 March 1909	SCWPM 8b
	Printer	Bradbury Wilkinson & Co. Ltd.	
	Total Printed	130500*	
	Circulation	Withdrawn 27. 07. 1922	
	Colour	Black on green and yellow underprint. Reverse blue	
	Obverse Design	Vasco da Gama and his passage round The Cape, overprint S. THOMÉ	
	Reverse Design	Allegorical maiden looking at ships	
	Size	148 x 98 mm	
	Ship Seal	Type 3	

ST13b

					Issued Notes			Archival Specimens
ST13	Start of Print Run	End of Print Run	Order Date (If Known)	Signatures	VG	Fine	VF	AU
a	400001*	480000*		G4, VG6				
b	480001	535000 (560000 deleted)	15.11.21	G4, VG10	$800	$1,500	Rare	$1,500

ST14	**5 mil reis**	1 March 1909	SCWPM 9a
	Printer	Bradbury Wilkinson & Co. Ltd.	
	Total Printed	105000*	
	Circulation	Withdrawn 27. 07. 1922	
	Colour	Black on blue and multicoloured underprint. Reverse green	
	Obverse Design	Vasco da Gama and his passage round The Cape, overprint S. THOMÉ	
	Reverse Design	Allegorical maiden looking at ships	
	Size	160 x 100 mm	
	Ship Seal	Type 1	

ST14c

ST14	Start of Print Run	End of Print Run	Order Date (If Known)	Signatures	Issued Notes VG	Issued Notes Fine	Issued Notes VF	Archival Specimens AU
a	000001	033334		G4, VG9	$1,200	$2,500	Rare	$1,500
b	033335	066667*		G4, VG6				
c	066668*	100000		G4, VG10	$1,000	$2,250	Rare	$1,100
d	100001	102500	15.11.17	G4, VG6				
e	102501	105000	15.11.17	G4, VG10				

N.B. An unknown quantity of notes was overprinted "PAGAVEL NA FILIAL DE BENGUELA" for use in Angola. See AN46 (SCWPM 26)

ST14es

ST15 **5 mil reis** 1 March 1909 SCWPM 9b

Printer	Bradbury Wilkinson & Co. Ltd.
Total Printed	135000*
Circulation	Withdrawn 27. 07. 1922
Colour	Black on blue and multicoloured underprint. Reverse green
Obverse Design	Vasco da Gama and his passage round The Cape, overprint S. THOMÉ
Reverse Design	Allegorical maiden looking at ships
Size	160 x 100 mm
Ship Seal	Type 3

ST15	Start of Print Run	End of Print Run	Order Date (If Known)	Signatures	Issued Notes VG	Issued Notes Fine	Issued Notes VF	Archival Specimens AU
a	105001*	123000*		G4, VG6*				
b	123001*	141000*	29.12.19*	G4, VG10*				
c	141001*	146000*		G4, VG6*				
d	146001*	151000*		G4, VG10*	$1,000	$2,250	Rare	$1,100
e	151001*	180000*	1.11.21*	G4, VG6*				
f	180001*	211000*	1.11.21*	G4, VG10*				
g	211001*	240000*		G4, VG6*				

ST16	**10 mil reis**	1 March 1909	SCWPM 10a
	Printer	Bradbury Wilkinson & Co. Ltd.	
	Total Printed	40000*	
	Circulation	Withdrawn 27. 07. 1922	
	Colour	Black on yellow and multicoloured underprint. Reverse brown	
	Obverse Design	Vasco da Gama and his passage round The Cape, overprint S. THOMÉ	
	Reverse Design	Allegorical maiden looking at ships	
	Size	175 x 105 mm	
	Ship Seal	Type 1	

ST16e

ST16	Start of Print Run	End of Print Run	Order Date (If Known)	Signatures	Issued Notes VG	Issued Notes Fine	Issued Notes VF	Archival Specimens AU
a	00001	08334		G4, VG9	$2,000	Rare	Rare	$1,500
b	08335	16667		G4, VG6				
c	16668	25000*		G4, VG10*				
d	25001	30000	8.12.15	G4, VG6	$1,750	Rare	Rare	$1,250
e	30001	35000		G4, VG10				
f	35001	37500	15.11.17	G4, VG6				
g	37501	40000	15.11.17	G4, VG10				

ST16ds

ST17	**10 mil reis**	1 March 1909	SCWPM 10b
	Printer	Bradbury Wilkinson & Co. Ltd.	
	Total Printed	35000*	
	Circulation	Withdrawn 27. 07. 1922	
	Colour	Black on yellow and multicoloured underprint. Reverse brown	
	Obverse Design	Vasco da Gama and his passage round The Cape, overprint S. THOMÉ	
	Reverse Design	Allegorical maiden looking at ships	
	Size	175 x 105 mm	
	Ship Seal	Type 3	

					Issued Notes			Archival Specimens
ST17	Start of Print Run	End of Print Run	Order Date (If Known)	Signatures	VG	Fine	VF	AU
a	40001*	55000*		G4, VG6*				
b	55001*	70000*		G4, VG10	$1,750	Rare	Rare	$1,500
c	70001	75000 (85000 deleted)	9.11.21	G4, VG6				

ST18	**20 mil reis**	1 March 1909	SCWPM 11a
	Printer	Bradbury Wilkinson & Co. Ltd.	
	Total Printed	18000*	
	Circulation	Withdrawn 27. 07. 1922	
	Colour	Black on blue and yellow underprint. Reverse brown-red and orange	
	Obverse Design	Vasco de Gama and his embarkation, overprint S. THOMÉ	
	Reverse Design	Allegorical maiden looking at ships	
	Size	180 x 112 mm	
	Ship Seal	Type 1	

ST18s

					Issued Notes			Archival Specimens
ST18	Start of Print Run	End of Print Run	Order Date (If Known)	Signatures	VG	Fine	VF	AU
a	00001	03334		G4, VG9	Rare	Rare	Rare	$2,500
b	03335	06667*		G4, VG6*				
c	06668*	10000		G4, VG10*				
d	10001	11500	15.11.17	G4, VG6	Rare	Rare	Rare	$2,000
e	11501	13000	15.11.17	G4, VG10				
f	13001	15501		G4, VG6				
g	15501	18000	28.7.19	G4, VG10				

N.B. There may be additional print runs for this issue, which should be valued at the same levels as ST18b-ST18g

ST19 **20 mil reis** 1 March 1909 SCWPM 11b

Printer	Bradbury Wilkinson & Co. Ltd.
Total Printed	Unknown
Circulation	Withdrawn 27. 07. 1922
Colour	Black on blue and yellow underprint. Reverse brown-red and orange
Obverse Design	Vasco de Gama and his embarkation, overprint S. THOMÉ
Reverse Design	Allegorical maiden looking at ships
Size	180 x 112 mm
Ship Seal	Type 3

					Issued Notes			Archival Specimens
ST19	Start of Print Run	End of Print Run	Order Date (If Known)	Signatures	VG	Fine	VF	AU
a	---	---	---	---	---	---	---	---

N.B. Wheras the other colonies in this catalogue issued an equivalent 20 mil reis with Type 3 ship seal, there are no sale records and we have seen no examples of this issue. Therefore it remains unconfirmed

ST20 **50 mil reis** 1 March 1909 SCWPM 12a

Printer	Bradbury Wilkinson & Co. Ltd.
Total Printed	4000*
Circulation	Withdrawn 27. 07. 1922
Colour	Black on yellow, green and multicoloured underprint. Reverse green, blue, yellow and pink
Obverse Design	Vasco de Gama and his embarkation, overprint S. THOMÉ
Reverse Design	Allegorical maiden looking at ships
Size	198 x 120 mm
Ship Seal	Type 1

ST20s

					Issued Notes			Archival Specimens
ST20	Start of Print Run	End of Print Run	Order Date (If Known)	Signatures	VG	Fine	VF	AU
a	0001	0334	16.7.17	G4, VG9				
b	0335	0667	16.7.17	G4, VG6				
c	0668	1000		G4, VG10*				
d	1001	1500	15.11.17	G4, VG6	Rare	Rare	Rare	$2,500
e	1501	2000	15.11.17	G4, VG10				
f	2001	3000	28.7.19	G4, VG6				
g	3001	4000	28.7.19	G4, VG10				

ST21	**50 mil reis**	1 March 1909						SCWPM 12b
	Printer	Bradbury Wilkinson & Co. Ltd.						
	Total Printed	2000*						
	Circulation	Withdrawn 27. 07. 1922						
	Colour	Black on yellow, green and multicoloured underprint. Reverse green, blue, yellow and pink						
	Obverse Design	Vasco de Gama and his embarkation, overprint S. THOMÉ						
	Reverse Design	Allegorical maiden looking at ships						
	Size	198 x 120 mm						
	Ship Seal	Type 3						

					Issued Notes			Archival Specimens
ST21	Start of Print Run	End of Print Run	Order Date (If Known)	Signatures	VG	Fine	VF	AU
a	4001*	5000		G4, VG6*	Rare	Rare	Rare	$3,500
b	5001	6000	11.10.21	G4, VG10				

1914 CEDULA ISSUES

The fractional notes issued by the BNU for the Portuguese African colonies, all dated 5 November 1914, are known as the Cedula Issues and in Portugal as "the London Issue". They were emergency notes printed in London during World War I, as a substitute for metal coinage in short supply. They were issued in denominations of 10cts, 20cts and 50cts for all five of the African colonies. Each colony had its own overprint, with S. TOMÉ or S. THOMÉ used for Saint Thomas and Prince.

It is important to recoginse that the issue of these notes, like metallic coins, was a privilege of the state, which was never transferred to the BNU. Accordingly, to be legal tender every issue had to be the subject of specific legislation proposed by the Minister of Colonies and approved by the Council of Ministers and Parliament in Lisbon. Furthermore, the fulfilment of the orders for the notes experienced all the constraints of a world at war. Among the difficulties encountered, which led to serious delays, were the lack of proper materials (appropriate paper and ink), the absence of skilled workers and the disruption of regular maritime transport.

Unlike the other four African colonies, only one type of steamship seal was used for the issues of St Thomas and Prince. Contrary to the references in SCWPM, only steamship seal type 2 was used and the seals were green for the 10cts, red for the 20cts and blue for the 50cts.

Steamship seal Type 2

Reverses of the 1914 Cedula issue

ST22
and ST23

ST24
and ST25

ST26
and ST27

ST22	**10 centavos**	5 November 1914, first issue	SCWPM 13
	Printer	Bradbury Wilkinson & Co. Ltd.	
	Total Printed	30000	
	Circulation	Withdrawn 25. 04. 1929	
	Colour	Purple on multicoloured underprint. Reverse blue	
	Obverse Design	Value in guilloche at left, arms at right, green steamship seal at lower centre, black overprint S. TOMÉ (without an 'H')	
	Reverse Design	Allegorical maiden looking at ships	
	Size	122 x 72 mm	
	Signatures	G5, VG10	
	Ship seal	Type 2	

				Issued Notes		Archival Specimens
ST22	Start of Print Run	End of Print Run	Good	Fine	VF	AU
a	0160001	0190000	$225	$550	$1,600	$1,000

ST23	**10 centavos**	5 November 1914, second issue	SCWPM 13
	Printer	Bradbury Wilkinson & Co. Ltd.	
	Total Printed	700000	
	Circulation	Withdrawn 25. 04. 1929	
	Colour	Purple on multicoloured underprint. Reverse blue	
	Obverse Design	Value in guilloche at left, arms at right, green steamship seal at lower centre, green overprint S. THOMÉ	
	Reverse Design	Allegorical maiden looking at ships	
	Size	122 x 72 mm	
	Signatures	G5, VG10	
	Ship seal	Type 2	

ST23a

				Issued Notes		Archival Specimens
ST23	Start of Print Run	End of Print Run	Good	Fine	EF	AU
a	2400001	2700000	$35	$100	$400	$550
b	2800001	3200000				

ST24 **20 centavos** 5 November 1914, first issue SCWPM 14

Printer	Bradbury Wilkinson & Co. Ltd.
Total Printed	60000
Circulation	Withdrawn 25. 04. 1929
Colour	Blue on multicoloured underprint. Reverse purple
Obverse Design	Value in guilloche at left, arms at right, red steamship seal at lower centre, black overprint S. TOMÉ (without an 'H')
Reverse Design	Allegorical maiden looking at ships
Size	122 x 72 mm
Signatures	G5, VG10
Ship seal	Type 2

ST24a

			Issued Notes			Archival Specimens
ST24	Start of Print Run	End of Print Run	Good	Fine	VF	AU
a	0590001	0650000	$200	$500	$1,400	$1,000

ST25 **20 centavos** 5 November 1914, second issue SCWPM 14

Printer	Bradbury Wilkinson & Co. Ltd.
Total Printed	150000
Circulation	Withdrawn 25. 04. 1929
Colour	Blue on multicoloured underprint. Reverse purple
Obverse Design	Value in guilloche at left, arms at right, red steamship seal at lower centre, red overprint S. THOMÉ
Reverse Design	Allegorical maiden looking at ships
Size	122 x 72 mm
Signatures	G5, VG10
Ship seal	Type 2

ST25a

ST25	Start of Print Run	End of Print Run	Good	Fine	VF	AU
			Issued Notes			Archival Specimens
a	3870001	3970000	$60	$250	$600	$600
b	4070001	4120000				

ST26	**50 centavos**	5 November 1914, first issue — SCWPM 15
	Printer	Bradbury Wilkinson & Co. Ltd.
	Total Printed	130000
	Circulation	Withdrawn 25. 04. 1929
	Colour	Green on multicoloured underprint. Reverse brown
	Obverse Design	Value in guilloche at left, arms at right, blue steamship seal at lower centre, black overprint S. TOMÉ (without an 'H')
	Reverse Design	Allegorical maiden looking at ships
	Size	122 x 72 mm
	Signatures	G5, VG10
	Ship seal	Type 2

ST26a

ST26	Start of Print Run	End of Print Run	Good	Fine	VF	AU
			Issued Notes			Archival Specimens
a	0750001	0880000	$70	$350	$1,000	$1,000

ST27	**50 centavos**	5 November 1914, second issue	SCWPM 15
	Printer	Bradbury Wilkinson & Co. Ltd.	
	Total Printed	600000	
	Circulation	Withdrawn 25. 04. 1929	
	Colour	Green on multicoloured underprint. Reverse brown	
	Obverse Design	Value in guilloche at left, arms at right, blue steamship seal at lower centre, blue overprint S. THOMÉ	
	Reverse Design	Allegorical maiden looking at ships	
	Size	122 x 72 mm	
	Signatures	G5, VG10	
	Ship seal	Type 2	

ST27a

			Issued Notes			Archival Specimens
ST27	Start of Print Run	End of Print Run	Good	Fine	VF	AU
a	2750001	3050000	$50	$175	$500	$700
b	3190001	3490000				

N.B.1 An unknown quantity of this issue was overprinted "PAGAVEL NA FILIAL DE LOANDA" in red for use in Angola, see AN41 (SCWPM 47)

N.B.2 An unknown quantity of this issue was overprinted "Loanda" in blue for use in Angola, see AN42 (SCWPM 48)

1918 CEDULA ISSUE

ST28	**5 centavos**	19 April 1918	SCWPM 18A
	Printer	Casa de Moeda, Lisbon	
	Total Printed	Unknown	
	Circulation	Withdrawn 25. 04. 1929*	
	Colour	Black and pale olive-green	
	Obverse Design	Value at left, steamship seal at right	
	Reverse Design	Steamship seal at centre, value on each side, anchor at lower centre	
	Size	99 x 63 mm	
	Signatures	G7 only	

ST28a

ST28a

			Issued Notes		
ST28	Start of Print Run	End of Print Run	Good	Fine	EF
a	Unknown	Unknown	Rare	Rare	Rare

INTRODUCTION TO THE CHAMIÇO ISSUES

By the Decree No. 5809, dated 30 May 1919, which instituted a new banking regime for the overseas colonies, a new issue of notes to replace the Vasco da Gama issues was authorised. This new omnibus series, which circulated in all five of the Portuguese African colonies from 1 August 1922 until 30 November 1950, featured a portrait of the founder and first Governor of the BNU, Francisco de Oliveira Chamiço (1819-88). This new issue consisted of values of 1$00, 2$50, 5$00, 10$00, 20$00, 50$00 and 100$00 escudos and those issued for St Thomas and Prince were dated 1 January 1921 with later issues dated 26 June 1935 and 21 March 1944.

Reverses of the Chamiço Issues

ST29

ST30

ST31
and ST36

ST32
and ST37

ST33, ST38
and ST39

ST34
and ST40

ST35
and ST41

1921 CHAMIÇO ISSUES

ST29	**1 escudo**	1 January 1921	SCWPM 19
	Printer	Bradbury Wilkinson & Co. Ltd.	
	Total Printed	500000*	
	Colour	Green on multicoloured underprint	
	Obverse Design	Portrait of Francisco de Oliveira Chamiço at left, steamship seal at right., red overprint S. TOMÉ e PRINCIPE	
	Reverse Design	Allegorical maiden looking at ships	
	Size	128 x 82 mm	
	Signatures	G7, VG14	

ST29d

				Issued Notes			Archival Specimens	Specimens
ST29	Start of Print Run	End of Print Run	Order Date (If Known)	Fine	VF	EF	AU	AU
a	000001	100000	25.8.20					
b	100001	120000	3.11.21					
c	120001	145000*		$200	$450	$1,000	$500	$350
d	145001*	387500*						
e	387501*	500000*						

ST29s

ST30	**2½ escudos**	1 January 1921	SCWPM 20
	Printer	Thomas De La Rue & Co. Ltd.	
	Total Printed	250000*	
	Colour	Blue on multicoloured underprint	
	Obverse Design	Portrait of Francisco de Oliveira Chamiço at left, steamship seal at right	
	Reverse Design	Allegorical maiden looking at ships	
	Size	136 x 69 mm	
	Signatures	G7, VG14	

ST30a

ST30	Start of Print Run	End of Print Run	Order Date (If Known)	Issued Notes VG	Issued Notes Fine	Issued Notes VF	Specimens Unc
a	0000001	0250000*		$150	$450	$1000	$750

ST30s

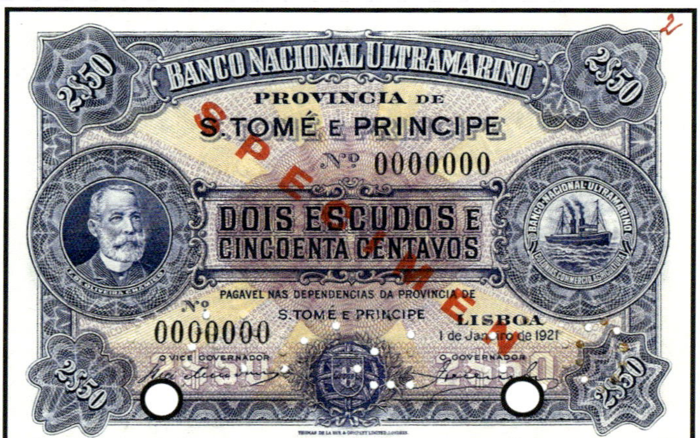

ST31	**5 escudos**	1 January 1921	SCWPM 21
	Printer	Bradbury Wilkinson & Co. Ltd.	
	Total Printed	140000*	
	Colour	Black on multicoloured underprint	
	Obverse Design	Portrait of Francisco de Oliveira Chamiço at left, steamship seal at right, red overprint S. TOMÉ e PRINCIPE	
	Reverse Design	Allegorical maiden looking at ships	
	Size	154 x 92 mm	
	Signatures	G7, VG14	

ST31bs

ST31	Start of Print Run	End of Print Run	Order Date (If Known)	VG	Fine	VF	AU	AU
					Issued Notes		Archival Specimens	Specimens
a	000001	040000	25.8.20	$250	$700	$1,750	$650	$450
b	040001	042000	3.11.21					
c	042001*	068000	15.11.21*					
d	068001	140000	22.2.23					

ST31s

ST32	**10 escudos**	1 January 1921	SCWPM 22
	Printer	Bradbury Wilkinson & Co. Ltd.	
	Total Printed	80000*	
	Colour	Brown on multicoloured underprint	
	Obverse Design	Portrait of Francisco de Oliveira Chamiço at left, steamship seal at right, red overprint S. TOMÉ e PRINCIPE	
	Reverse Design	Allegorical maiden looking at ships	
	Size	160 x 105 mm	
	Signatures	G7, VG14	

ST32c

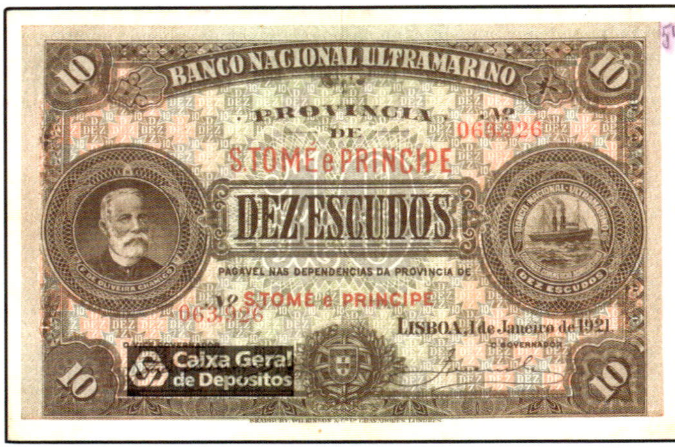

ST32	Start of Print Run	End of Print Run	Order Date (If Known)	VG	Issued Notes Fine	VF	Archival Specimens AU	Specimens AU
a	000001	040000	25.8.20					
b	040001	060000	3.11.21	$400	$1,100	$2,500	$750	$500
c	060001	080000*	15.11.21*					

ST32s

ST33	**20 escudos**	1 January 1921
	Printer	Bradbury Wilkinson & Co. Ltd.
	Total Printed	30000*
	Colour	Dark blue on multicoloured underprint
	Obverse Design	Portrait of Francisco de Oliveira Chamiço at left, steamship seal at right, red overprint S. TOMÉ e PRINCIPE
	Reverse Design	Allegorical maiden looking at ships
	Size	170 x 115 mm
	Signatures	G7, VG14

SCWPM 23

ST33b

				Issued Notes			Archival Specimens	Specimens
ST33	Start of Print Run	End of Print Run	Order Date (If Known)	VG	Fine	VF	AU	AU
a	000001	010000	25.8.20					
b	010001	020000	3.11.21	$600	$1,750	Rare	$800	$550
c	020001*	030000*	15.11.21*					

ST33s

ST34	**50 escudos**	1 January 1921	SCWPM 24
	Printer	Bradbury Wilkinson & Co. Ltd.	
	Total Printed	19000*	
	Colour	Brownish-red on multicoloured underprint	
	Obverse Design	Portrait of Francisco de Oliveira Chamiço at left, steamship seal at right, red overprint S. TOMÉ e PRINCIPE	
	Reverse Design	Allegorical maiden looking at ships	
	Size	185 x 120 mm	
	Signatures	G7, VG14	

ST34s

				Issued Notes			Archival Specimens	Specimens
ST34	Start of Print Run	End of Print Run	Order Date (If Known)	VG	Fine	VF	AU	AU
a	000001	010000	25.8.20					
b	010001	016000	3.11.21	$2,250	$5,000	Rare	$1,000	$650
c	016001	019000	15.11.21					

ST35	**100 escudos**	1 January 1921	SCWPM 25
	Printer	Bradbury Wilkinson & Co. Ltd.	
	Total Printed	7000*	
	Colour	Slate-purple on multicoloured underprint	
	Obverse Design	Portrait of Francisco de Oliveira Chamiço at left, steamship seal at right, red overprint S. TOMÉ e PRINCIPE	
	Reverse Design	Allegorical maiden looking at ships	
	Size	193 x 126 mm	
	Signatures	G7, VG14	

ST35s

				Issued Notes			Archival Specimens	Specimens
ST35	Start of Print Run	End of Print Run	Order Date (If Known)	VG	Fine	VF	AU	AU
a	000001	007000	25.8.20	Rare	Rare	Rare	$1,500	$900

1935 CHAMIÇO ISSUE

ST36 **5 escudos** 26 June 1935 SCWPM 26

Printer	Bradbury Wilkinson & Co. Ltd.
Total Printed	120000
Colour	Black on multicoloured underprint
Obverse Design	Portrait of Francisco de Oliveira Chamiço at left, steamship seal at right, red overprint S. TOMÉ e PRINCIPE
Reverse Design	Allegorical maiden looking at ships
Size	152 x 92 mm
Signatures	PCA8a (short format), A21

ST36a

ST36	Start of Print Run	End of Print Run	Order Date (If Known)	Issued Notes VG	Issued Notes Fine	Issued Notes VF	Archival Specimens AU
a	A000001	A120000	12.7.35	$150	$500	$1,250	$1,250
dp	Black and white obverse die proof, dated 26 June 1935, signatures PC8a and A21						Unc - $400

ST36as

ST36dp

ST37	10 escudos	26 June 1935	SCWPM 27
	Printer	Bradbury Wilkinson & Co. Ltd.	
	Total Printed	50000	
	Colour	Brown on multicoloured underprint	
	Obverse Design	Portrait of Francisco de Oliveira Chamiço at left, steamship seal at right, red overprint S. TOMÉ e PRINCIPE	
	Reverse Design	Allegorical maiden looking at ships	
	Size	160 x 105 mm	
	Signatures	PCA8a (short format), A21	

ST37a

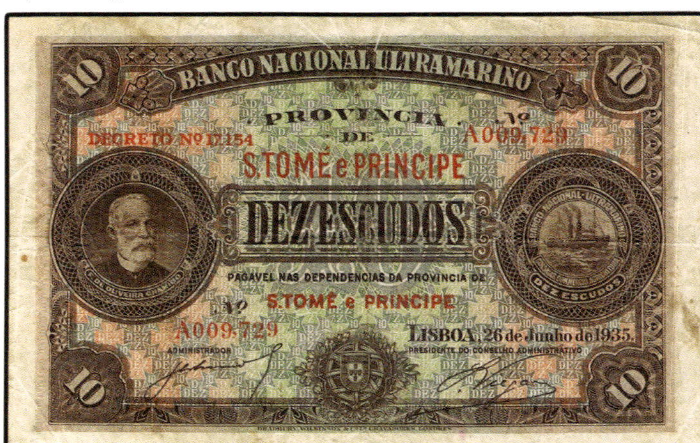

				Issued Notes			Archival Specimens
ST37	Start of Print Run	End of Print Run	Order Date (If Known)	VG	Fine	VF	AU
a	A000001	A050000	12.7.35	$450	$1,250	$2,750	$1,250
dp	Black and white obverse die proof, dated 26 June 1935, signatures PC8a and A21						Unc - $450

ST37as

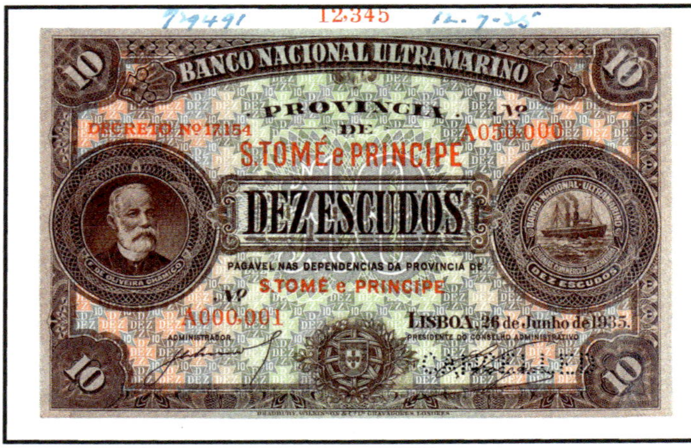

ST37dp

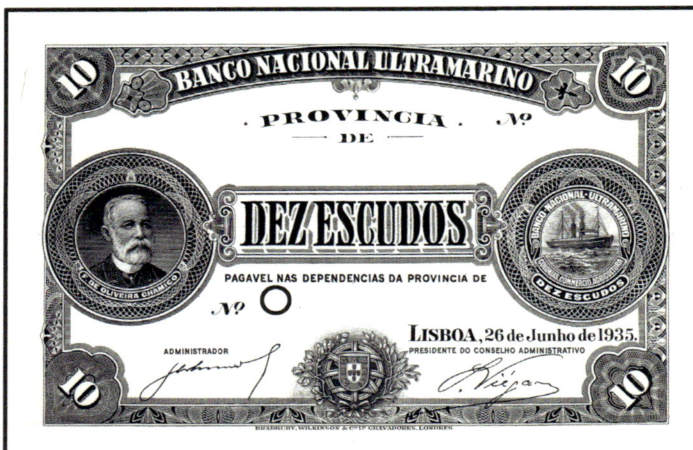

ST38	**20 escudos**	26 June 1935	SCWPM 28
	Printer	Bradbury Wilkinson & Co. Ltd.	
	Total Printed	20000	
	Colour	Dark blue on multicoloured underprint	
	Obverse Design	Portrait of Francisco de Oliveira Chamiço at left, steamship seal at right, red overprint S. TOMÉ e PRINCIPE	
	Reverse Design	Allegorical maiden looking at ships	
	Size	170 x 115 mm	
	Signatures	PCA8a (short format), A21	

ST38as

				Issued Notes			Archival Specimens
ST38	Start of Print Run	End of Print Run	Order Date (If Known)	VG	Fine	VF	AU
a	A000001	A020000	12.7.35	$750	$2,000	Rare	$1,250
dp	Black and white obverse die proof, dated 26 June 1935, signatures PC8a and A21						Unc - $500

ST38dp

1944 CHAMIÇO ISSUE

ST39	**20 escudos**	21 March 1944	SCWPM 29
	Printer	Bradbury Wilkinson & Co. Ltd.	
	Total Printed	45000	
	Colour	Dark blue on multicoloured underprint	
	Obverse Design	Portrait of Francisco de Oliveira Chamiço at left, steamship seal at right, red overprint S. TOMÉ e PRINCIPE	
	Reverse Design	Allegorical maiden looking at ships	
	Size	170 x 115 mm	

ST39e

ST39	Start of Print Run	End of Print Run	Order Date (If Known)	Signatures	Issued Notes VG	Issued Notes Fine	Issued Notes VF	Archival Specimens AU	Specimens AU
a	A20001	A24000	20.3.44	PCA8, A19	$1,000	$2,500	Rare	$600	$600
b	A24001	A28000	20.3.44	PCA8, A27					
c	A28001	A32000	20.3.44	PCA8, A25					
d	A32001	A36000	20.3.44	PCA8, A30					
e	A36001	A40000	20.3.44	PCA8, A26					
f	A40001	A45000	20.3.44	PCA8, A29					

ST39fs

ST40	**50 escudos**	21 March 1944	SCWPM 30
	Printer	Bradbury Wilkinson & Co. Ltd.	
	Total Printed	10000	
	Colour	Brownish-red on multicoloured underprint	
	Obverse Design	Portrait of Francisco de Oliveira Chamiço at left, steamship seal at right, red overprint S. TOMÉ e PRINCIPE	
	Reverse Design	Allegorical maiden looking at ships	
	Size	185 x 120 mm	

ST40b

					Issued Notes			Archival Specimens	Specimens
ST40	Start of Print Run	End of Print Run	Order Date (If Known)	Signatures	VG	Fine	VF	AU	AU
a	A00001	A02500	20.3.44	PCA8, A26	$2,000	Rare	Rare	$650	$650
b	A02501	A04000	20.3.44	PCA8, A29					
c	A04001	A05500	20.3.44	PCA8, A19					
d	A05501	A07000	20.3.44	PCA8, A30					
e	A07001	A08500	20.3.44	PCA8, A25					
f	A08501	A10000	20.3.44	PCA8, A27					

ST40as

ST41 **100 escudos** 21 March 1944 SCWPM 31

Printer Bradbury Wilkinson & Co. Ltd.

Total Printed 10000*

Colour Slate-purple on multicoloured underprint

Obverse Design Portrait of Francisco de Oliveira Chamiço at left, steamship seal at right, red overprint S. TOMÉ e PRINCIPE

Reverse Design Allegorical maiden looking at ships

Size 193 x 126 mm

ST41as

ST41	Start of Print Run	End of Print Run	Order Date (If Known)	Signatures	Issued Notes VG	Issued Notes Fine	Issued Notes VF	Archival Specimens AU	Specimens AU
a	A00001	A01500	20.3.44	PCA8, A29					
b	A01501	A03000	20.3.44	PCA8, A27					
c	A03001	A04500	20.3.44	PCA8, A26	Rare	Rare	Rare	$700	$700
d	A04501	A06500	20.3.44	PCA8, A19					
e	A06501	A08500	20.3.44	PCA8, A30					
f	A08501*	A10000*	20.3.44*	PCA8, A25*					

1946 D. AFONSO V ISSUE

Afonso V (1432-81) was a King of Portugal known as "O Africano" (The African), because he was the first Portuguese king to rule over "The Algarves" (plural) as a result of his conquest of territories in North Africa. These lands, part of present-day Morocco, were incorporated into the then separate kingdom of the Algarve. Afonso also supported Prince Henry the Navigator in his journeys of exploration, but this sponsorship ceased after Prince Henry's death in 1460. After concluding his African campaigns, Afonso in 1475 went into battle against Castille, but the result was inconclusive and disillusioned he abdicated in favour of his son João II in November 1477. Retiring to a monastery in Sintra, he died there in 1481.

Reverses of the 1946 D. Afonso V Issue

ST42

ST43

ST44

ST42	**20 escudos**	12 August 1946	SCWPM 32
	Printer	Bradbury Wilkinson & Co. Ltd.	
	Total Printed	280000	
	Colour	Brown on multicoloured underprint	
	Obverse Design	Portrait of D. Afonso V at right, steamship seal at left, arms at upper centre	
	Reverse Design	Allegorical young woman looking out at ships from various eras	
	Size	150 x 80 mm	

ST42l

ST42	Start of Print Run	End of Print Run	Order Date (If Known)	Signatures	Issued Notes Fine	Issued Notes VF	Issued Notes EF	Archival Specimens AU	Specimens AU
a	000001	030000	15.8.46	PCA8, A18					
b	030001	055000	15.8.46	PCA8, A19					
c	055001	080000	15.8.46	PCA8, A25					
d	080001	095000	15.8.46	PCA8, A29					
e	095001	120000	15.8.46	PCA8, A26					
f	120001	150000	15.8.46	PCA8, A30					
g	150001	155000	29.3.48	PCA8, A25	$60	$125	$300	$250	$200
h	155001	170000	29.3.48	PCA8, A18					
i	170001	180000	29.3.48	PCA8, A29					
j	180001	192000	29.3.48	PCA8, A26					
k	192001	210000	29.3.48	PCA8, A25					
l	210001	230000	29.3.48	PCA8, A19					
m	230001	250000	29.3.48	PCA8, A28					
n	250001	280000	27.4.56	PCA8, A30					
ct	Specimen colour trial in green on multicoloured underprint, no date, no serial number, no signatures, overprinted SPECIMEN in red diagonally, two punch holes								Unc - $600
dp	Obverse and reverse die proof in issued colour brown								EF -$400 (pair)

ST42ct

ST42ct

ST42as

ST43	**50 escudos**	12 August 1946	SCWPM 33
	Printer	Bradbury Wilkinson & Co. Ltd.	
	Total Printed	125000	
	Colour	Slate-violet on multicoloured underprint	
	Obverse Design	Portrait of D. Afonso V at right, steamship seal at left, arms at upper centre	
	Reverse Design	Allegorical young woman looking out at ships from various eras	
	Size	156 x 82 mm	

ST43c

ST43as

ST43	Start of Print Run	End of Print Run	Order Date (If Known)	Signatures	Issued Notes Fine	Issued Notes VF	Issued Notes EF	Archival Specimens AU	Specimens AU
a	000001	020000	15.8.46	PCA8, A30					
b	020001	025000	15.8.46	PCA8, A26					
c	025001	035000	15.8.46	PCA8, A18					
d	035001	040000	15.8.46	PCA8, A29					
e	040001	050000	15.8.46	PCA8, A19					
f	050001	060000	15.8.46	PCA8, A25					
g	060001	065000	29.3.48	PCA8, A26	$90	$200	$450	$300	$250
h	065001	071000	29.3.48	PCA8, A30					
i	071001	077000	29.3.48	PCA8, A29					
j	077001	082000	29.3.48	PCA8, A25					
k	082001	090000	29.3.48	PCA8, A18					
l	090001	095000	29.3.48	PCA8, A28					
m	095001	100000	29.3.48	PCA8, A19					
n	100001	125000	27.4.56	PCA8, A19					
ct	Specimen colour trial in blue on multicoloured underprint, no date, no serial number, no signatures, overprinted SPECIMEN in red diagonally, two punch holes								Unc - $800
dp	Obverse and reverse die proof in issued colour slate-violet								EF - $450 (pair)

ST43ct

ST43ct

ST44	**100 escudos**	12 August 1946	SCWPM 34
	Printer	Bradbury Wilkinson & Co. Ltd.	
	Total Printed	100000*	
	Colour	Purple on multicoloured underprint	
	Obverse Design	Portrait of D. Afonso V at right, steamship seal at left, arms at upper centre	
	Reverse Design	Allegorical young woman looking out at ships from various eras	
	Size	162 x 85 mm	

ST44c

					Issued Notes			Archival Specimens	Specimens
ST44	Start of Print Run	End of Print Run	Order Date (If Known)	Signatures	Fine	VF	EF	EF	AU
a	000001	010000	15.8.46	PCA8, A25					
b	010001	020000	15.8.46	PCA8, A29					
c	020001	025000	15.8.46	PCA8, A26					
d	025001	035000	15.8.46	PCA8, A30					
e	035001	040000	15.8.46	PCA8, A18					
f	040001	050000	15.8.46	PCA8, A19					
g	050001	055000	29.3.48	PCA8, A25					
h	055001	062000	29.3.48	PCA8, A19	$120	$275	$600	$350	$300
i	062001	070000	29.3.48	PCA8, A18					
j	070001	078500 (078000 deleted)	29.3.48	PCA8, A30					
k	078501 (078000 deleted)	085000	29.3.48	PCA8, A26					
l	085001	092000	29.3.48	PCA8, A29					
m	092001	100000	29.3.48	PCA8, A28					
ct	Specimen colour trial in brown on multicoloured underprint, no date, no serial number, no signatures, overprinted SPECIMEN in red diagonally, two punch holes								Unc - $1000
dp	Obverse and reverse die proof in issued colour purple								EF - $500 (pair)
N.B.	Based on confirmed order dates for the $20 and $50 of this issue, it is thought there may have been an additional order in 1956. However, the authors have not seen any notes numbered above 100000 and this is therefore unconfirmed.								

ST44as

1947 CIRCULATING BEARER CHEQUE ISSUE

ST45	**100 escudos**	1947 (various dates)	SCWPM 35A
	Printer	Litografia E. Barrault, Lisboa	
	Total Printed	Unknown	
	Colour	Red on pink underprint	
	Obverse Design	Steamship seal set in two ornate semi-ovals at left. Bank legend at upper centre and as microprint	
	Reverse Design	Uniface	
	Size	165 x 80 mm	
	Signature	Unknown	

ST45c

ST45	Date	Fine	VF	EF
a	10 February 1947			
b	24 February 1947			
c	31 March 1947	$100	$175	$300
d	29 April 1947			
e	2 May 1947			

N.B. Additional dates may exist

ST46	**500 escudos**	1947 (various dates) — SCWPM 35B
	Printer	Litografia E. Barrault, Lisboa
	Total Printed	Unknown
	Colour	Violet
	Obverse Design	Steamship seal set in two ornate semi-ovals at left. Bank legend at upper centre and as microprint
	Reverse Design	Uniface
	Size	165 x 80 mm
	Signature	Unknown

ST46b

ST46e

ST46	Date	Fine	VF	EF
a	10 February 1947	$150	$250	$400
b	27 February 1947			
c	21 March 1947			
c	27 March 1947			
d	28 March 1947			
e	1 April 1947			
N.B.	Additional dates may exist			

ST47 **500 escudos** 30 May 1947 SCWPM 35C

Printer Litografia E. Barrault, Lisboa

Total Printed Unknown

Colour Red on pink underprint

Obverse Design Steamship seal set in two ornate semi-ovals at left. Bank legend at upper centre and as microprint

Reverse Design Uniface

Size 165 x 80 mm

Signature Unknown

ST47	Date	Fine	VF	EF
a	30 May 1947	Rare	Rare	Rare

ST48 **1000 escudos** 3 September 1947 SCWPM unlisted

Printer Litografia E. Barrault, Lisboa

Total Printed Unknown

Colour Red on pink underprint

Obverse Design Steamship seal set in two ornate semi-ovals at left. Bank legend at upper centre and as microprint

Reverse Design Uniface

Size 165 x 80 mm

Signature Unknown

ST48a

ST48	Date	Fine	VF	EF
a	3 September 1947	Rare	Rare	Rare

1956-58 D. AFONSO V ISSUE

Reverses of the 1956-58 D. Afonso V and 1964 Santarém Issues

ST49

ST50

ST51

ST52

BANCO NACIONAL ULTRAMARINO
PAGÁVEL NA PROVÍNCIA DE
S. TOMÉ E PRÍNCIPE
500
500

ST53

BANCO NACIONAL ULTRAMARINO
PAGÁVEL EM
S. TOMÉ E PRÍNCIPE
1000
MIL ESCUDOS

ST49	**20 escudos**	20 November 1958	SCWPM 36
	Printer	Bradbury Wilkinson & Co. Ltd.	
	Total Printed	1350000	
	Colour	Brown on multicoloured underprint	
	Obverse Design	Portrait of D. Afonso V at right, ship seal at left, arms at lower centre	
	Reverse Design	Allegorical young woman looking out at ships from various eras	
	Size	150 x 80 mm	

ST49as

ST49	Start of Print Run	End of Print Run	Order Date (If Known)	Signatures	Issued Notes VG	Issued Notes VF	Issued Notes Unc	Archival Specimens EF	Specimens Unc
a	B000001	B060000	10.12.58	G9, A19					
b	B060001	B120000	10.12.58	G9, A38					
c	B120001	B200000	10.12.58	G9, A36					
d	B200001	B260000	10.12.58	G9, A37					
e	B260001	B320000	10.12.58	G9, A34					
f	B320001	B350000	10.12.58	G9, A35	$7	$20	$60	$150	$125
g	B350001	B500000	6.4.70	G9, A38					
h	B500001	B650000	6.4.70	G9, A36					
i	B650001	B850000	6.4.70	G9, A35					
j	B850001	B1000000	6.4.70*	G9, A38					
k	B1000001	B1150000	6.4.70*	G9, A36					
l	B1150001	B1350000	14.10.74	G9, A35					

ct	Specimen colour trial in green on multicoloured underprint, no date, serial number B000000, no signatures, overprinted SPECIMEN in red horizontally, two punch holes	Unc - $200
dp	Obverse and reverse die proof in issued colour brown	EF - $250 (pair)
ph	Black and white obverse and reverse archival photographs dated 26. 1. 59, note dated 20 November 1958, serial number B000000, signatures G9 and A34, arms set above signatures, larger portrait of D. Afonso V	One Pair Known
N.B.	A large number of notes with serial numbers above B1000000 were overprinted by the Banco Nacional de S. Tomé e Príncipe on independence in 1976. Notes remaining in the vaults and withdrawn notes were overprinted and accordingly overlaps occur	

ST49ct

ST49ct

ST49ph

ST49ph

ST50 **50 escudos** 20 November 1958 SCWPM 37

Printer Bradbury Wilkinson & Co. Ltd.

Total Printed 760000

Colour Slate-violet on multicoloured underprint

Obverse Design Portrait of D. Afonso V at right, ship seal at left, arms at lower centre

Reverse Design Allegorical young woman looking out at ships from various eras

Size 156 x 82 mm

ST50as

					Issued Notes			Archival Specimens	Specimens
ST50	Start of Print Run	End of Print Run	Order Date (If Known)	Signatures	VG	VF	Unc	EF	Unc
a	B000001	B026000	10.12.58	G9, A38	$12	$35	$100	$200	$175
b	B026001	B050000	10.12.58	G9, A35					
c	B050001	B080000	10.12.58	G9, A34					
d	B080001	B110000	10.12.58	G9, A36					
e	B110001	B130000	10.12.58	G9, A37					
f	B130001	B160000	10.12.58	G9, A19					
g	B160001	B230000	6.4.70	G9, A38					
h	B230001	B300000	6.4.70	G9, A36					
i	B300001	B360000	6.4.70	G9, A35					
j	B360001	B500000		G9, A38					
k	B500001	B630000		G9, A36					
l	B630001	B760000		G9, A35					
ct	Specimen colour trial in red on multicoloured underprint, no date, serial number B000000, no signatures, overprinted SPECIMEN in red horizontally, two punch holes								Unc - $250
dp	Obverse and reverse die proof in issued colour slate-violet								EF - $300 (pair)

N.B. A large number of notes with serial numbers above B500000 were overprinted by the Banco Nacional de S. Tomé e Príncipe on independence in 1976. Notes remaining in the vaults and withdrawn notes were overprinted and accordingly overlaps occur

ST50ct

ST50ct

ST51 **100 escudos** 20 November 1958 SCWPM 38

Printer	Bradbury Wilkinson & Co. Ltd.
Total Printed	500000
Colour	Purple on multicoloured underprint
Obverse Design	Portrait of D. Afonso V at right, ship seal at left, arms at lower centre
Reverse Design	Allegorical young woman looking out at ships from various eras
Size	162 x 85 mm

ST51as

					Issued Notes			Archival Specimens	Specimens
ST51	Start of Print Run	End of Print Run	Order Date (If Known)	Signatures	VG	VF	Unc	EF	Unc
a	B000001	B016000	10.12.58	G9, A35					
b	B016001	B030000	10.12.58	G9, A34					
c	B030001	B050000	10.12.58	G9, A19					
d	B050001	B060000	10.12.58	G9, A37					
e	B060001	B080000	10.12.58	G9, A38					
f	B080001	B100000	10.12.58	G9, A36	$20	$60	$140	$250	$175
g	B100001	B170000	6.4.70	G9, A38					
h	B170001	B240000	6.4.70	G9, A36					
i	B240001	B300000	6.4.70*	G9, A35					
j	B300001	B370000	15.2.75	G9, A38					
k	B370001	B440000	15.2.75	G9, A36					
l	B440001	B500000	15.2.75	G9, A35					
ct	Specimen colour trial in brown on multicoloured underprint, no date, serial number B000000, no signatures, overprinted SPECIMEN in red horizontally, two punch holes								Unc - $300
dp	Obverse and reverse die proof in issued colour purple								EF - $350 (pair)
N.B.	A large number of notes with serial numbers above B300000 were overprinted by the Banco Nacional de S. Tomé e Príncipe on independence in 1976. Notes remaining in the vaults and withdrawn notes were overprinted and accordingly overlaps occur								

ST51ct

ST51ct

ST52 **500 escudos** 18 April 1956 SCWPM 39

Printer Bradbury Wilkinson & Co. Ltd.

Total Printed 80000

Colour Blue on multicoloured underprint

Obverse Design Portrait of D. Afonso V at right, ship seal at left, arms at lower right

Reverse Design Allegorical young woman looking out at ships from various eras

Size 165 x 87 mm

ST52k

						Issued Notes		Archival Specimens	Specimens
ST52	Start of Print Run	End of Print Run	Order Date (If Known)	Signatures	VG	VF	Unc	EF	Unc
a	000001	002000	27.4.56	G9, A30					
b	002001	003500	27.4.56	G9, A19					
c	003501	005000	24.4.56	G9, A33					
d	005001	007000	27.4.56	G9, A34					
e	007001	008500	27.4.56	G9, A36					
f	008501	010000	27.4.56	G9, A35					
g	010001	010250	22.4.60	G9, A19					
h	010251	010500	22.4.60	G9, A34	$85	$250	$600	$350	$200
i	010501	010750	22.4.60	G9, A36					
j	010751	020000	22.4.60	G9, A35					
k	020001	027000		G9, A19					
l	027001	034000		G9, A36					
m	034001	040000		G9, A35					
n	040001	060000		G9, A36					
o	060001	080000		G9, A35					
ct	Specimen colour trial in purple on multicoloured underprint, dated 18 April 1956, serial number 000000, signature G9 plus any one of six Administrador signatures above, overprinted SPECIMEN in red horizontally, two punch holes								Unc - $400
dp	Obverse and reverse die proof in issued colour blue								EF - $400 (pair)
ph	Black and white obverse and reverse archival photographs dated 9. 5. 56, note dated 18 April 1956, serial number 000,000, designs as issued note								One Pair Known

N.B.1 The notes with serial numbers above 040000 were part of a special reprint for independence. Unlike the earlier issues, all of them have no comma in the serial number

N.B.2 A large number of notes with serial numbers above 040000 were overprinted by the Banco Nacional de S. Tomé e Príncipe on independence in 1976. Notes remaining in the vaults and withdrawn notes were overprinted and accordingly overlaps occur

ST52as

ST52ct

ST52ct

1964 SANTARÉM ISSUE

João de Santarém (fl. 1470-90) was a Portuguese navigator and explorer, who discovered the Islands of São Tomé on 21 December 1471 (the feast day of St Thomas) and Príncipe on 17 January 1472. Earlier in 1471, together with Pedro Escobar, he also made landfall in the town of Sassandra in the Ivory Coast and after sailing north from Príncipe in 1472 explored the African coast from Ghana up as far as the Niger Delta. From 1484 he was captain of Alcatrazes in Cape Verde.

ST53	**1000 escudos**	11 May 1964	SCWPM 40
	Printer	Bradbury Wilkinson & Co. Ltd.	
	Total Printed	60000	
	Colour	Green on multicoloured underprint	
	Obverse Design	Portrait of João de Santarém at right, ship seal at left, arms at upper centre	
	Reverse Design	Allegorical young woman looking out at ships from various eras	
	Size	176 x 95 mm	

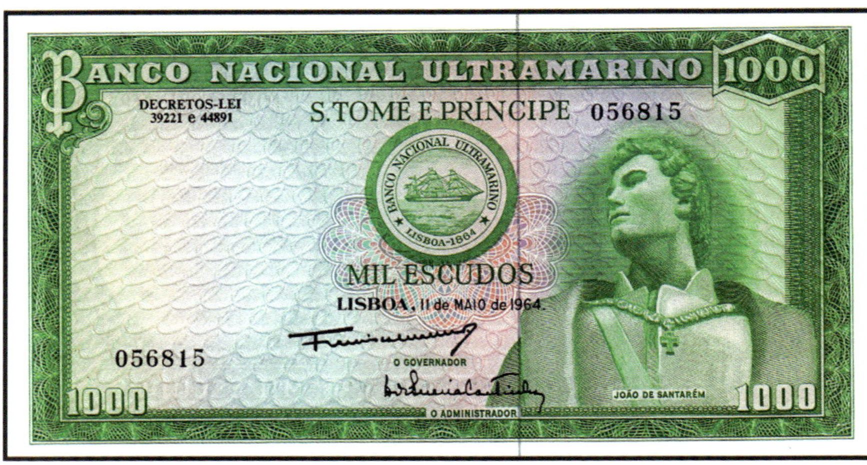

ST53n

ST53as

ST53	Start of Print Run	End of Print Run	Order Date (If Known)	Signatures	Issued Notes VG	Issued Notes VF	Issued Notes Unc	Archival Specimens EF	Specimens Unc
a	000001	003500	31.8.64	G9, A36	$100	$225	$750	$450	$300
b	003501	007000	31.8.64	G9, A40					
c	007001	010500	31.8.64	G9, A38					
d	010501	014000	31.8.64	G9, A37					
e	014001	017000	31.8.64	G9, A35					
f	017001	020000	31.8.64	G9, A41					
g	020001	022500	6.4.70	G9, A38					
h	022501	025000	6.4.70	G9, A36					
i	025001	027500	6.4.70	G9, A35					
j	027501	030000	6.4.70	G9, A41					
k	030001	040000		G9, A38					
l	040001	050000		G9, A36					
m	040001	050001		G9, A35					
n	050001	060000		G9, A35					
ct	Specimen colour trial in purple on multicoloured underprint, dated 11 May 1964, serial number 000000, signature G9 plus any one of six Administrador signatures above, overprinted SPECIMEN in red horizontally, two punch holes								Unc - $400
p	Specimen proof dated 11. 5. 1964, serial number 123456 at lower left and serial number 789012 at upper right, signatures G9, A37, one punch hole								Rare
ph1	Black and white obverse archival photograph dated 14. 8. 64, note dated 11 May 1964, serial number 000000, sketched portrait, slightly different steamship seal at upper centre								One Copy Known
ph2	Black and white obverse and reverse archival photographs dated 22. 6. 64, note undated, serial number 000000, sketched portrait, arms at upper centre, steamship seal at lower left, reverse sketched vignette								One Pair Known

N.B. A large number of notes with serial numbers above 025000 were overprinted by the Banco Nacional de S. Tomé e Princípe on independence in 1976. Notes remaining in the vaults and withdrawn notes were overprinted and accordingly overlaps occur

ST53ct

ST53ct

ST53ph1

ST53ph2

ST53ph2

1974 CIRCULATING BEARER CHEQUE ISSUES

ST54	**100 escudos**	31 March 1974			SCWPM 41
	Printer	Litografia E. Barrault, Lisboa			
	Total Printed	Unknown			
	Colour	Red			
	Obverse Design	Ship seal set in two ornate semi-ovals at left. Bank legend at upper centre and as microprint			
	Reverse Design	Uniface			
	Size	165 x 80 mm			
	Signature	Unknown			

ST54	Start of Print Run	Fine	VF	EF
a	Unknown	Rare	Rare	Rare

ST55	**500 escudos**	28 April 1974			SCWPM 42
	Printer	Litografia E. Barrault, Lisboa			
	Total Printed	Unknown			
	Colour	Red			
	Obverse Design	Ship seal set in two ornate semi-ovals at left. Bank legend at upper centre and as microprint			
	Reverse Design	Uniface			
	Size	165 x 80 mm			
	Signature	Unknown			

ST55	Start of Print Run	Fine	VF	EF
a	Unknown	Rare	Rare	Rare

ST56	**500 escudos**	31 December 1974	SCWPM 43
	Printer	Litografia E. Barrault, Lisboa	
	Total Printed	Unknown	
	Colour	Red	
	Obverse Design	Ship seal set in two ornate semi-ovals at left. Bank legend at upper centre and as microprint	
	Reverse Design	Uniface	
	Size	165 x 80 mm	
	Signature	Unknown	

ST56	Start of Print Run	Fine	VF	EF
a	Unknown	Rare	Rare	Rare

ST57	**1000 escudos**	1974 (various dates)	SCWPM 43a
	Printer	Litografia E. Barrault, Lisboa	
	Total Printed	Unknown	
	Colour	Red	
	Obverse Design	Ship seal set in two ornate semi-ovals at left. Bank legend at upper centre and as microprint	
	Reverse Design	Uniface	
	Size	165 x 80 mm	
	Signature	Unknown	

ST57a

ST57b

ST57b

<table>
<tr><th>ST57</th><th>Date</th><th>Fine</th><th>VF</th><th>EF</th></tr>
<tr><td>a</td><td>23 December 1974</td><td rowspan="2">$150</td><td rowspan="2">$250</td><td rowspan="2">$450</td></tr>
<tr><td>b</td><td>31 December 1974</td></tr>
<tr><td>N.B.</td><td colspan="4">Additional dates may exist</td></tr>
</table>

SIGNATURE TABLES

GOVERNADORES

G1	Francisco de Oliveira Chamiço	1864 – 1888	
G2	Manuel Sarmento Ottolini - Visconde (e Conde) de Ottolini	1888 – 1894	 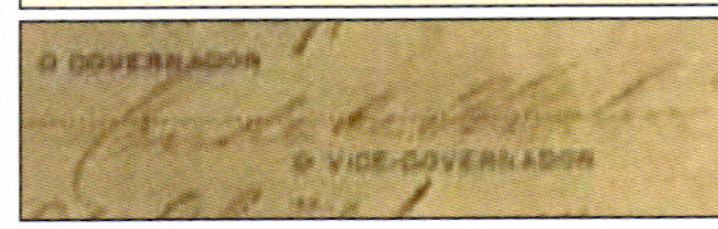
G3	Eduardo Pinto da Silva e Cunha	1894 – 1909	 
G4	António Teixeira de Sousa	1909 – 1910	
G5	Luís Diogo da Silva	1910 – 1917	
G6	Manuel Carlos de Freitas Alzina	1917 – 1918	
G7	João Henrique Ulrich	1918 – 1931	
PCA8 G8† PCA8a	António dos Santos Viegas	1936 - 1949 1931 - 1935	 
G9 VPCA9	Francisco José Vieira Machado	1951 - 1972 1949 - 1950	 

† It is thought that António dos Santos Viegas never signed any issued notes as Governor

N.B. Francis José Vieira Machado signed Mozambique MZ107 and MZ108 as Vice President of the Administrative Council (VPCA9)

VICE-GOVERNADORES

VG1	António Thomaz Pacheco	1864 – 1878	
VG2	Eduardo Jayme Carvalho da Silva	1878 – 1888	
VG3	Manuel Sarmento Ottolini – Visconde de Ottolini	1881 – 1888	
VG4	António Joaquim de Castro Gonçalves	1888 – 1891	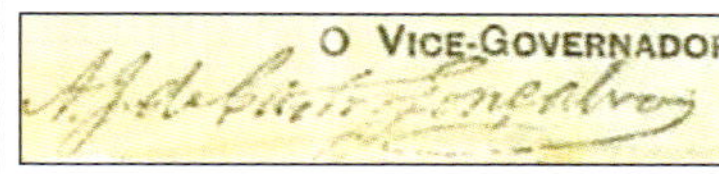
VG5	Luís Adolpho de Oliveira de Sommer	1888 – 1893	
VG6	Luís Diogo da Silva	1891 – 1910	
VG7	Francisco Mantero	1893 – 1894	
VG8	Alfredo Mendes da Silva	1894 – 1911	
VG9	Balthazar Freire Cabral	1905 – 1913	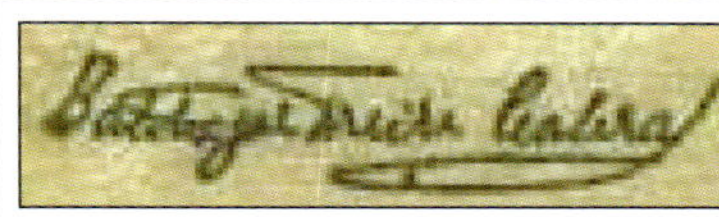
VG10	Manuel Carlos de Freitas Alzina	1905 – 1917	
VG11	João Albino de Sousa Rodrigues	1907 – 1909	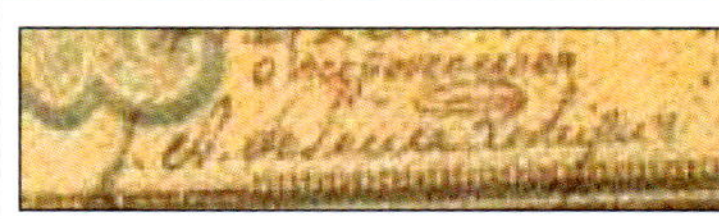
VG12	João Henrique Ulrich	1909 – 1918	
VG13	Bernardo Homem Machado – Conde de Caria	1910 – 1925	
VG14	Henrique José Monteiro de Mendonça	1913 – 1925	

VG15	Arthur Porto de Mello e Faro – Conde de Monte Real	1917 – 1926	
VG16	José da Cunha Rolla Pereira	1918 – 1931	
VG17	Júlio Schmidt	1919 – 1929	
VG18	Francisco Pinto da Cunha Leal	1925 – 1926	
VG19	Francisco Gonçalves Velhinho Correia	1925 – 1926	
VG20	Armando P. C. Agathão Lança	1925 – 1926	
VG21	Ernesto Jardim de Vilhena	1925 – 1928	
VG22	Francisco Pinto Fernandes	1925 – 1929	
VG23	Francisco José Vieira Machado	1926 – 1929	
VG24	Artur Meneses Correia de Sá – Visconde de Merceana	1928 – 1929 1957 – 1966	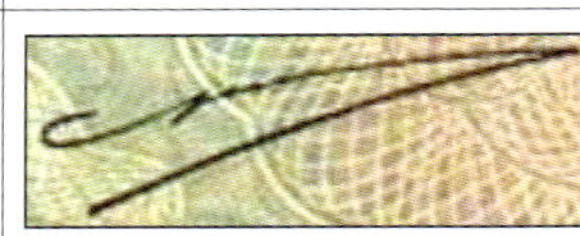
VG25	António Pedroso Pimenta	1951 – 1957	
VG26	António Júlio de Castro Fernandes	1972 – 1973	
VG27	Luís Pereira Coutinho	1974	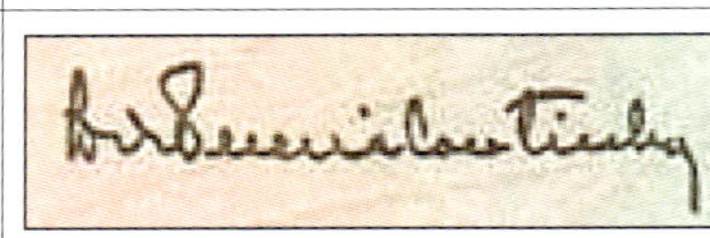

N.B. Francis José Vieira Machado signed Mozambique MZ107 and MZ108 as Vice President of the Administrative Council (see VPCA9 in Governadores Signature Table)

ADMINISTRADORES

A1	António José de Seixas	1864	
A2	Francisco Izidoro Vianna	1864	
A3	Narciso de Freitas Guimarães	1894 – 1909	
A4	António Maria Barreiros Arrobas	1864 – 1965	
A5	João Gomes Roldan	1864 – 1872	
A6	Eduardo Cairns	1864 – 1873	
A7	Luís Jacinto Soares	1864 – 1877	
A10	Augusto Frederico Ferreira	1864 - 1879	
A11	Joaquim Moreira Marques	1878	
A12	João Alfredo Dias	1879	
A13	Emygdio Xavier Pires	1879	
A14	Luís Leite Pereira Jardim	1880	
A15	Nicoll Mac Nicoll	1880	
A16	T. Ribeiro Ermida	1880	
A17	Pedro R. Blanco	1880	
A18	Francisco José Vieira Machado	1929 – 1934 1944 – 1945	
A19	Artur Meneses Correia de Sá – Visconde de Merceana	1929 – 1961	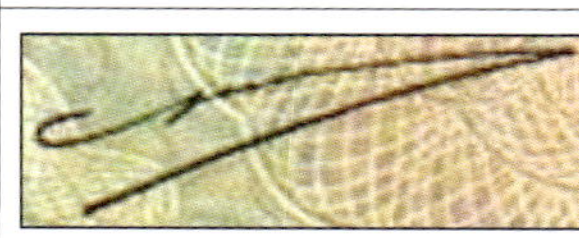
A20	Francisco Pinto Fernandes	1929 – 1931	
A21	Júlio Schmidt	1929 – 1947	
A22	Quirino Avelino de Jesus	1929 – 1935	
A23	João José Sinel de Cordes	1929 – 1930	

A24	Jayme da Fonseca Monteiro	1930 – 1937	
A25	João Baptista de Araújo	1931 – 1950	
A26	José Gabriel Pinto Coelho	1931 – 1951	
A27	Manuel Rodrigues Júnior	1931 – 1932 1940 – 1946	
A28	Francisco Pinto Castelo Branco	1938 – 1951	
A29	António Augusto Correia de Aguiar	1940 – 1951	
A30	António Pedroso Pimenta	1943 – 1953	
A31	Marcello José das Neves Alves Caetano	1948 – 1951	
A32	Pedro Teotónio Pereira	1951 – 1953	
A33	Teófilo Duarte	1951 – 1958	
A34	José de Azeredo Perdigão	1951 – 1960	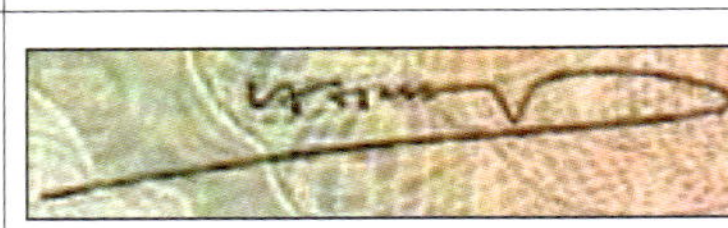
A35	Luís Pereira Coutinho	1951 – 1974	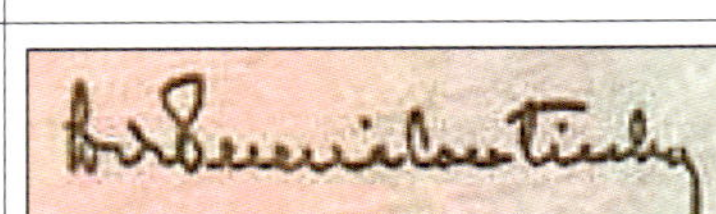

A36	António Júlio de Castro Fernandes	1951 – 1972	 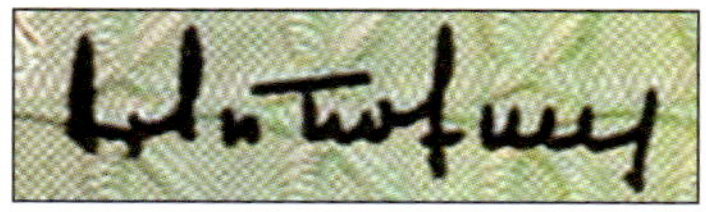
A37	Gastão Bessone Basto	1956 – 1968	
A38	Abel Beja Corte Real	1957 – 1973	
A39	Gabriel Maurício Teixeira	1959 – 1962	
A40	José Guerreiro Murta	1958 – 1966	
A41	Pedro de Mascarenhas Gaivão	1963 – 1973	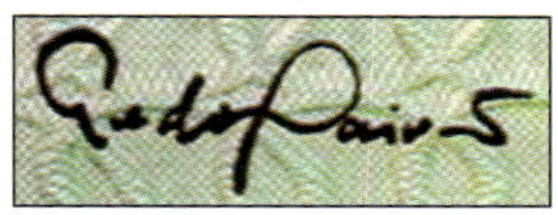
A42	Samuel Rodrigues Sanches	1964 – 1973	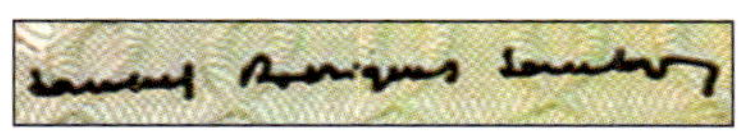
A43	Luís Esteves Fernandes	1966 – 1973	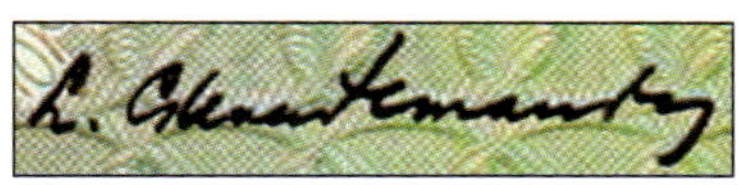
A44	Camilo Afonso Máximo Cimourdain Ferreira de Oliveira	1968 – 1974	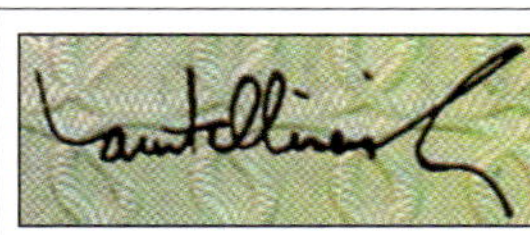
A45	José Manuel Passeiro	1963 – 1974	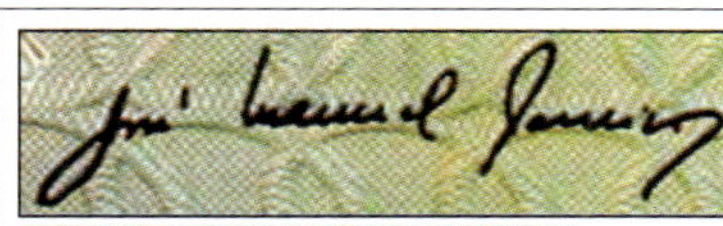